Cheated

Cheated

The UNC Scandal, the
Education of Athletes,
and the Future
of Big-Time
College Sports

JAY M. SMITH and
MARY WILLINGHAM

Potomac Books
An imprint of the University of Nebraska Press

Library of Congress Control Number: 2014042237

Set in Minion Pro by Lindsey Auten.

To the memory of Bill Friday
and to UNC *athletes of the past,*
present, and future

Contents

Figures

Tables

Acknowledgments

In the course of researching and writing this book, we accumulated many debts to generous individuals. Jonathan Weiler, David Rice, Fitz Brundage, William Ferris, Jim Woodrow, and Alyssa Smith provided invaluable feedback on early draft chapters. Richard Southall, the director of the College Sport Research Institute at the University of South Carolina, allowed us to draw on his expertise on college sport and its history on many occasions both before and after his migration from Chapel Hill to Columbia. Active members of the Athletic Reform Group at the University of North Carolina at Chapel Hill (UNC)—including especially Willis Brooks, Lewis Margolis, Silvia Tomásková, Rudi Colloredo-Mansfeld, Hassan Melehy, George Baroff, Richard Cramer, and Miles Fletcher—furnished encouragement, occasional reality checks, and an important sounding board (as did ARG member Jonathan Weiler on occasions too numerous to recall). Harry Watson, Michael Hunt, Madeline Levine, Elliot Cramer, Bob Orr, Sarah Shields, Frank Baumgartner, Joseph Lowman, Peggy Bush, Mark Witcher, Melinda Manning, Richard Kwok, Norman Allard, David Kiel, Bob Reinheimer, Patti Reinheimer, Virginia Taylor, and John Shelton Reed offered vital moral support at critical junctures in the book's evolution. Hodding Carter bucked us up whenever the going got tough, which was more often than we would have liked. Taylor Branch provided kind words and his own inspiring model of righteous indignation. Philip Jackson and the Black Star Project invited Mary Willingham to join their crusade to erase the educational achievement gap in America's schools. Allen Sack, Gerald Gurney, David Ridpath, and Kadie Otto shared the great benefits of their wisdom and long experience with athletic reform, and the Drake Group as a whole helped to keep us afloat during difficult times.

By keeping the story of the UNC scandal alive through his persistent reporting, Dan Kane of the *Raleigh News & Observer* (N&O) provided a platform for all who demanded accountability from the university. Sarah Lyall, Frank Deford, Sara Ganim, Pat Forde, Joe Nocera, and Paul Barrett saw the importance of the UNC story, and by directing their attention to it—and to us—they helped to convince us of the potential value of this book. The many people who agreed to sit down for interviews—some of them identified in these pages and some not—give the book much of its context and color, and we thank each one of them for coming forward. UNC alumni who shall remain anonymous—but you know who you are—lifted our spirits, gave living proof of the power of a UNC education, and reminded us often of the institutional imperative to tell the truth. The helpful staff at the University Archives at UNC–Chapel Hill helped us to navigate the records of the College of Arts and Sciences, and they responded to every request with smiles and efficiency.

The late William Friday went out of his way to encourage us both. And as a defender of academic integrity who enjoyed sports and supported athletes, he set an example of balanced and careful analysis that continues to inspire.

The most helpful individuals of all were our spouses, Deb Smith and Chuck Willingham, who first shared our sense of outrage and then traveled with us through the peaks and valleys of a long writing process, showing amazing patience and fortitude along the way. This book would never have seen the light of day without their support and forbearance, and we are happy to have the chance at last to send them a permanent expression of our love and gratitude.

Introduction

The Scandal beneath the Scandals

During a summer session sometime between 2003 and 2013, a senior football player for the University of North Carolina Tar Heels scrambled to get his grade point average (GPA) over the eligibility bar in time for the fall playing season. By taking a series of mismatched and notoriously easy courses, he managed to make the grade. One of the fruits of his efforts, however, was a seriously daunting fall course schedule. His schedule was daunting because, though he still clearly hoped to graduate, his advisers had put off until his senior year his basic math, science, and foreign-language requirements. These were some of the most challenging courses he would need to pass in order to collect his UNC diploma. (Indeed, he had already tried and failed the math and science courses for which he was now enrolled for a second time.) Heading into his senior year, it looked very unlikely that this player would ever play a down in the National Football League (NFL); it looked nearly as unlikely that he would ever leave Chapel Hill with a degree in hand. This particular scholarship athlete should be outraged by the way his education was managed. His experience should also trouble every sports fan in America.

This book is about the University of North Carolina and its experience with athletic and academic scandal in the years that followed Marvin Austin's tweet heard 'round the world on May 29, 2010.[1] The narrative of scandal provided here sheds much new light on the modes of corruption that came to afflict UNC in the 1990s, and it exposes to scrutiny a long record of questionable actions (and inaction) by university leaders. Through negligence, willful blindness, and some degree of conscious intent, key actors at the university first permitted the development of widespread academic fraud and then covered up the reasons behind that fraud when the wrongdoing at last came to light. As longtime employees of UNC–Chapel Hill, we take no pleasure in filling in the details of this sad history; we both have great respect for the institution, its traditions, and the many friends we made there. We have grown heartsick from seeing the extent of the moral compromises university leaders were willing to make over the years; we would both very much like to imagine that the whole thing never happened. But a full, unobscured record of what transpired at UNC–Chapel Hill between about 1990 and 2013 needs to be established for the sake of posterity—and for the sake of the future of college sports.

The UNC case is important to the national cause of athletic reform because it exposes the true scandal that lies beneath the headlines that sports fans take in with their breakfast each morning. Observers of college sports have been conditioned to feel annoyance or outrage when they confront reports about under-the-table payments to players, recruiting violations, cheating in the classroom, and an out-of-control "arms race" that has given us millionaire assistant coaches, lavish training facilities, and skyrocketing ticket prices. All of these signs of university priorities gone askew are deserving of attention, but they pale in importance to the fundamental violation of trust for which America's system of higher education has never been held accountable.

To put it simply, virtually every big-time sport university stands in breach of contract for many of the scholarship agreements they casually extend to their recruited athletes in the "profit" sports of football and men's basketball.[2] Athletes are promised that if they come to play for the coaches who avidly recruit them, they will be given the opportunity to seize a valuable college education. The fact of the matter is that for a great many players, this purported "opportunity" is a mirage. And universities are fully cognizant of the game of bait and switch they force on unsophisticated and unrepresented high school athletes year after year. This betrayal of the university's mission can be regarded as the foundational sin, the original moral outrage, committed by colleges that have been seduced by the lure of the big time. Laying bare the anatomy of that betrayal, which has never been done in microscopic detail by well-informed insiders, is the chief purpose of this book.

Much ink has been spilled over the past few years on the so-called pay-for-play debate. In the wake of Taylor Branch's scintillating 2011 *Atlantic* article "The Shame of College Sports," commentators from around the country have increasingly embraced the position that college athletes in the profit sports deserve monetary compensation for their labors. Branch, drawing on his considerable expertise as a historian of civil rights, laid out a compelling argument for sharing the profits of a six-billion-dollar enterprise with the players whose talents make the entire operation possible. Since 2012 *New York Times* columnist Joe Nocera, ESPN announcer Jay Bilas, the producers of the powerful documentary film *Schooled: The Price of College Sports*, and an array of thoughtful commentators have effectively embellished and amplified Branch's message, which continues to reverberate.[3]

We are largely agnostic on the issue of pay for play. The logistical obstacles to the payment of player salaries are considerable. A number of pending (and long-developing) lawsuits, the results of which could conceivably force a major restructuring of the college-sports business model, make short-term solutions to current injustices practically impossible. In any case, the proposal to pay players for their services, laudable and commonsensical though it is, ignores an elephant in the room. The billion-dollar business of college sports has been grafted onto a group of institutions whose raison d'être is educating students. Unless and until the athletes who play football for the Gators or Trojans or Crimson Tide are no longer students—that is, until the entertainment industry of sport is definitively severed from the intellectual arteries of the college campus—the essence of the relationship between universities and their recruited athletes will remain academic. Treating athletes purely as employees deserving of financial compensation overlooks the special character of the student-to-educator relationship. The formal and enduring character of that relationship means that some, if not all, of the compensation that athletes are likely to receive from universities will come in the form of the educations promised in their scholarship agreements. The debate about compensation for college athletes therefore must focus first on whether schools are fulfilling their primary commitment to their recruits—to provide them a meaningful education.

Coincidentally, this would seem to be the terrain over which the National Collegiate Athletic Association itself wants to fight the battle over compensation. Mark Emmert, the current NCAA president, has explained his own opposition to the pay-for-play principle by noting that universities are already "providing athletes with world class educations and world class opportunities."[4] Players already receive rich compensation, in other words, and the purity of the "collegiate model" of athletics should not be contaminated by careless association with the "professional model" that reigns over the NFL and the National Basketball Association (NBA). We contend, in defiance of NCAA claims, that the current compensation model is fraudulent at its core; too many athletes simply do not follow (or are not permitted to follow) an educationally defensible curriculum. The current model, the one that posits the exchange of education for play, requires a major overhaul if it is to stand as the alternative to professionalism in college athletics.

The underlying scandal of college sports is that universities play make-believe in order to disguise the academic experiences of a special subset of athletes—the ambivalent, academically underprepared, or underperforming students who were recruited by coaches in the profit sports of basketball and football. Universities engage in this charade to earn the slender justification they require in order to exploit the athletes' highly valuable physical talents. Through shadow curricula, eligibility tricks, deceptive rhetoric, and warped scheduling priorities, too many athletes are forced to pursue a poor facsimile of a college education. They are handed a cheap knockoff of the academic experience their typical nonathlete classmates can reliably expect to receive. They are, of course, simultaneously deprived—deliberately and cynically—of the educations they need and deserve and to which they should feel entitled. Some will leave the university still not reading at a high school level. Some transfer or drop out after a difficult year in the classroom, never to be heard from again. A tiny fraction will make it to the pros in their sport, and may enjoy some years of relative prosperity, only to realize later that they have built an inadequate foundation on which to continue their educations or to create a rewarding postathletic life. Some acquire diplomas worth little more than the paper they are printed on. Some leave "better off" for having spent time on a college campus, but the fact that they have received something of value in return for their labor does not mean that they received all, or even much, of what they were owed.

Making the situation still more offensive are the demographics behind the dishonest game being played. The athletes thus defrauded come disproportionately from socioeconomically disadvantaged positions, and they are also disproportionately African American. The beneficiaries of the business model that their labors propel, meanwhile, are disproportionately wealthy and white. Universities, in disregarding their moral obligations to all students, have become complicit in perpetuating social injustice, unfair hierarchies of power, and corrosive racial stereotypes. By systematically neglecting the true educational needs of some of their most academically challenged students, precisely so as to facilitate their own pursuit of profits and wins, universities carry out the greatest of all scandals in big-time college sports.

The UNC case is important because it demonstrates the connection between the academic camouflage that facilitates athletic success on America's college campuses and the development of the subtle forms of corruption and self-delusion that inhibit an institution's ability to self-correct. At UNC, for a period covering two decades or more, athletic and academic officials worked together to relieve hundreds of athletes of the burden of having to follow an authentic and educationally sound curriculum. What started out as a limited set of techniques to ensure the playing eligibility of weak students on the men's basketball team eventually became a fraudulent curricular system whose "benefits" were extended to hundreds of athletes. The worst courses, which came to be called "paper classes," would eventually be made available even to athletes who were fully capable students, even to teams in the financially burdensome "loss" (or Olympic) sports, and even to students who played no varsity sport at all. Only the faintest hints of this corruption had become visible in 2010, when the UNC scandal burst onto the scene as a garden-variety "impermissible benefits" story. By the summer of 2011, however, shocking details about academic wrongdoing began to leak out through the press, and over the course of the next year it became clear to all but the most ardent Tar Heel fans that athletic interests were deeply enmeshed in, if they were not fully responsible for, the academic misconduct that had been revealed.

The nexus of athletic-academic corruption could not have been more obvious. Yet between 2011 and 2013 leading figures on and around the UNC campus decided to stake their reputations on the propagation of an untenable, even preposterous, claim—that the erosion of academic integrity at UNC since the 1990s was absolutely "not an athletic scandal."[5] The promoters of this line of argument stared straight past reality to seize on and promote an alternative version of it. They developed a strategy, with help from public relations consultants, to deflect public attention from underlying problems they wanted no outsiders to see.[6]

If the landscape of college sports is going to be changed for the better, the breadth and the power of this impulse toward wagon circling and institutional duplicity need to be confronted aggressively. The addiction to athletics, and to the revenues and alleged goodwill that they generate, has rendered good people mute in the face of abuses they know they should not tolerate. Others have become blinded to the very abuses it is their job to decry. The UNC experience demonstrates with excruciating clarity the moral compromises big-time sports require from academics who have convinced themselves that the system deserves protection.

When a plane crashes investigators hoping to prevent similar tragedies in the future search frantically for the "black box" that might explain how and why the catastrophe occurred. In the UNC scandal the records of the Academic Support Program for Student Athletes were the black box of the whole tragedy. As the crossroads between athletes and the university curriculum, the ASPSA contained the blueprint for a disaster that had been long in the making. Yet when the UNC hot-air balloon known as the "Carolina Way" went down in flames in 2011, not only did the university's leaders fail to search the contents of their own black box, but they did everything in their power to ensure that others would not find it. Time and again they opted for half measures and contorted rhetoric that spared the ASPSA close scrutiny, while they implored observers to "move forward" and stop asking questions. They gradually won the assent or indulgence of many authorities outside Chapel Hill—the NCAA, Atlantic Coast Conference (ACC) officials, the UNC Board of Governors that oversees the sixteen-campus University of North Carolina system, media figures, former North Carolina governor Jim Martin, and others—who should have known better. They engineered a successful conspiracy of silence that inadvertently provided the nation a revelatory case study (while it also made this book necessary). That such a long series of outrages could unfurl at an institution as serious and self-respecting as UNC–Chapel Hill, a so-called public ivy staffed with many earnest, intelligent, and well-intentioned people of the highest academic reputation, is a sign of the magnitude of the moral challenges facing the big-time sports universities. It is well past time that they faced up to them.

At universities the principles of honest inquiry, integrity in truth seeking, and educational quality for all students are emblazoned in institutional mission statements and palpable in almost every classroom. These principles define the life of universities and confer whatever value is carried by the degrees they award. UNC's commitment to these high ideals has long been a source of pride for Carolina alumni; for decades that commitment also underlay the institution's sterling reputation. Yet honesty, integrity, and educational quality all took a pummeling in Chapel Hill between 1990 and 2013. An embarrassing set of failures happened there because the continuing performance of the athletic machine had come to matter more to university leaders than either the educational well-being of the athletes entrusted to their care or the reputation of the university itself. There are many good reasons to think that this debilitating institutional disease has metastasized throughout the "big-time" echelon of higher education. (The symptoms of the wider malady are discussed in chapter 9.) To find the only cure that will work—a cure derived from universities' embrace of their fundamental educational responsibility to all their students—the well intentioned and the reform minded must first honestly confront the nature of the affliction. Perhaps the most important contribution of *Cheated* is that it offers a bracing confrontation with reality. The lessons from that confrontation need to be absorbed not only by the UNC community but by college campuses across the land.

. . .

The book focuses both on the essence of the UNC scandal—the corrupted academic experiences of a generation of UNC athletes—and on the fascinating cover-up that followed the initial exposure of the scandalous wrongdoing. Our assessment of the fraudulent academic experiences of hundreds of UNC athletes is based on personal experiences and recollections; interviews with former students, faculty, and administrators; the seven years of intensive help and remediation provided to athletes by Mary Willingham after she joined the Academic Support Program in 2003; and a wide variety of data concerning university advising practices, curricular paths, grading patterns, graduation rates, and other expressions of athletes' academic experiences—most of it made available to Willingham as a learning specialist, assistant director of the Center for Student Success and Academic Counseling, and graduation adviser. This evidence covers the period from the late 1980s to 2013. The account of the UNC cover-up is based on copious public documentation and our many encounters—almost always painful and revealing—with some of the principal architects of the cover-up.

Readers interested mainly in the anatomy of the academic scandal might focus especially on chapters 1, 2, 7, and 8, while those interested particularly in the anatomy of the cover-up will want to follow chapters 3–6 with special care. The relationship between the wrongdoing and the cover-up is essential to the overall story, however, and readers should see the two distinct strands of the narrative forming an integrated whole. All who wish to see American universities face up to their breach of educational responsibility will need to reflect on the ways in which academic corner cutting and administrative squeamishness and denial endlessly reinforce one another. These two complementary forces have created a remarkably stable compound essentially defined by corruption. The pervasiveness of the problem is outlined in chapter 9; some solutions for dissolving the dangerous compound of corruption are offered in the conclusion.

A Word on Our Voice

Cheated is less a memoir than an analysis of one revealing case study of athletic-academic corruption told from the vantage point of two insiders who had a privileged perspective on critical events. Because we occasionally interacted with some of the players in the drama, we make appearances in the narrative. In all cases we are referred to in the third person—it can be assumed that Smith writes about Willingham and that Willingham writes about Smith—in order to preserve consistency of tone and to keep the focus on the power brokers whose influence might actually have made a difference.

Abbreviations

AFRI/AFAM	African and Afro-American studies
ASPSA	Academic Support Program for Student Athletes (eight academic counselors, assigned to teams, one or two learning specialists, and eighty tutors)
BOT	Board of Trustees (oversees the UNC–Chapel Hill campus and provides counsel to the chancellor)
BSM	Black Student Movement (formed at UNC–Chapel Hill in the 1960s)
FAC	Faculty Athletics Committee (an elected committee of the Faculty Council, consisting of a half-dozen faculty members and four ex officio members with ties to the Athletic Department)
FEC	Faculty Executive Committee (an elected committee of the Faculty Council that provides advice and guidance to the chair of the faculty)
N&O	*Raleigh News & Observer*

One

Paper-Class Central

The University of North Carolina is rightly proud of the academic achievements of its many "student-athletes" (a term studiously avoided in this book, for reasons that will become clear). The university fields dozens of athletic teams with hundreds of athletes, and most of them are capable and ambitious students who perform well in the classroom. Every year football and basketball players, along with athletes from the so-called Olympic sports, number among the success stories. Despite this record of success, however, UNC–Chapel Hill has been tarred by an academic-athletic fraud scandal the purpose of which was to enable athletes to cheat the system. The main argument of this book is that the athletes themselves were cheated in the process.

The underlying cause for the decades-long academic fraud at UNC is, we believe, straightforward. The university knowingly and eagerly admitted athletes with poor academic training or little to no interest in school and further served the needs of the athletic program by creating paths to academic eligibility that kept those athletes on the field year after year. Those eligibility paths led first to subtle compromises with academic principle and then finally to outright corruption.

This basic dynamic has been repeated on college campuses across the land for many years, and the nexus between the academic preparedness and commitment of athletes and the curricular fakery that developed at UNC—a particularly revealing example of a national problem—will be examined in greater detail in chapters 7 and 8. But the story of UNC's specific form of academic malpractice really begins at the intersection of several historical currents, some of them specific to the environment in Chapel Hill and some of them reflecting changes in the landscape of collegiate sport during the 1980s and early 1990s. Opportunity, mutual need, convenience, personality, NCAA pressures, and sheer chance converged to push UNC toward systematic hypocrisy by 1993. Chapters 1 and 2 will explain the genesis of the now notorious paper-class system of athletic eligibility and show for the first time exactly how it worked when it was at its peak between the late 1990s and the middle 2000s.

Tangled Origins

Race lies at the center of the UNC story, and few stories offer a more vivid illustration of America's conflicted relationship with race than the one involving sport and the black athlete at Carolina. The story of UNC's scandal opens not on a gridiron or a hardwood floor, however, but in the offices and conference rooms of UNC's College of Arts and Sciences, where the emerging discipline of African and Afro-American studies (AFRI/AFAM) struggled for respect, standing, and resources in the 1980s. Like many universities around the country, UNC had established a curriculum in African and Afro-American studies amid the tumult of the civil rights era. Designed to redress regrettable intellectual imbalances in the standard curriculum, to help attract more African American students to Chapel Hill, and to create a more welcoming and affirming environment for all students, the curriculum had been created in 1969. Although it attracted few majors, its courses proved popular. During one extraordinary period of growth, while it enjoyed the vigorous leadership of historian Colin Palmer, the curriculum's enrollment figures grew by an astonishing 850 percent in just seven years (from 251 students in 1979–80 to nearly 2,200 students in 1986–87).[1] The curriculum's teaching staff remained small, and it relied heavily on faculty rooted in other departments such as History, Political Science, and Anthropology, but AFRI/AFAM clearly enriched the undergraduate curriculum and was much appreciated by students.

As Dean Gillian Cell would note in a letter to Chancellor Paul Hardin in 1989, UNC's AFRI/AFAM curriculum had surged to become "the largest such program in terms of enrollment in the country."[2]

By the late 1980s, however, the faculty who called the curriculum their home had grown frustrated by what some perceived as lackluster support from the university administration. When Colin Palmer accepted an appointment as chair of the History Department in 1986, the AFRI/AFAM curriculum endured several unsettled years without a new leader. For three years running, search committees struck out in their hunt for a prominent national figure to take Palmer's place. (Palmer stayed on as a part-time chair for two years, and then a succession of acting chairs filled in for two more years.) Professor Sonja Haynes Stone called on Dean Cell to "end this state of limbo" by making an expeditious appointment in the spring of 1989, but time constraints and bitter disagreements over the quality of the leading candidate led to yet another failed search that year—despite what seems to have been a good-faith effort by Cell.[3] The installation in 1990 of a highly regarded specialist of African American literature, Trudier Harris of UNC's own English Department, brought sighs of relief and renewed hope for the future. But the good feelings would not last. Harris found no joy in administration. Before two years had passed, she decided to go back to the English Department to resume her former life as a distinguished professor.

Nor was the leadership vacuum the only problem. Despite the amazing enrollment growth since 1980, the college had done little to put additional faculty resources into the curriculum. Stone chided Dean Cell for the "snail-like pace" at which the university had invested in the AFRI/AFAM program. Only one permanent faculty member—political scientist Catherine Newbury—had been added since the early 1980s. (Stone would later refer to Cell's failure to attract more black faculty to UNC as "an abomination.")[4] Inadequate staffing stood out as a perennial problem, and chairs pushed the college insistently. "As usual," Palmer complained in 1987, "the curriculum is understaffed. It relies entirely too much on fixed term faculty to meet the necessary instructional needs." Two years later the needs had become only more urgent. The curriculum's introductory courses were "always oversubscribed," according to its annual newsletter in 1989. Acting chair Sherman James called for "2–3 new tenure track appointments" as well as a new chair with the requisite national standing to provide "balanced and creative leadership" for an emerging discipline.[5] Among the projects this new chair should tackle: the establishment of a research center for comparative African and Afro-American studies. It was hoped that such an institution, for which Palmer and others had already laid the foundations, would serve as an intellectual center of gravity that would boost the visibility of the curriculum and help to attract the brightest minds to Chapel Hill. The college supported the idea in principle, but progress had been slow.

In their annual report for the curriculum in 1990, the acting cochairs, Thadious Davis and Robert Gallman, pointed to the discrepancy between the curriculum's always impressive enrollment numbers and its modest national reputation. The national standing of the AFRI/AFAM curriculum still lagged behind those of the University of California (UC) at Berkeley, Cornell, Indiana, Ohio State, Yale, and Penn. They noted, "An academic program the vast majority of whose students are taught by graduate students and temporary faculty" would never be ranked among the best in the nation. "Our program lacks prestige and strength" because the university had failed to make AFRI/AFAM an institutional priority.[6]

The struggles endured by the curriculum found parallels in the student experience on campus. Ever since 1968, when UNC's Black Student Movement had formed out of the protests of the civil rights era, some had called for the construction of a campus building dedicated to the study and celebration of black culture. Leaders of the BSM began championing a "freestanding" center in the late 1980s, about the same time that the curriculum in AFRI/AFAM began to press its case more urgently with college deans. When Professor Stone died unexpectedly of a brain aneurysm in August 1991, the tragedy kicked off a turbulent period in campus political life. Stone had believed, as she wrote in a 1989 letter to Dean Cell, that "the entire university must bear the onus of advancing African and Afro-American studies" and "increasing and enhancing the African-American presence at Chapel Hill."[7] Stone had been revered by many students, including key figures in the BSM, and her well-known commitment to these two imperatives—boosting the fortunes of the curriculum and enhancing the experiences of all black students, faculty, and staff at the university—served as a rallying point for student activists over the next several years. After months of controversy and debate, in September 1992 student protesters led a series of marches in which they demanded that the university commit to a freestanding center. In a sign of the depth and breadth of student feeling over the issue, UNC athletes joined in these marches and offered vocal support for the cause.[8]

Chancellor Hardin resisted these efforts at first, even after one dramatic late-night rally in front of his home. He feared that creation of a separate building would waken echoes of segregation and that the center might become a "fortress" rather than a forum for open discussion. But tensions escalated. "We gave him an ultimatum," football player Tim Smith would later recall. "If you want us to be quiet," they told the chancellor during one heated confrontation, "give us a BCC [Black Cultural Center] by November 13."[9] Later in the fall semester, after a committee that he had appointed endorsed the idea of a freestanding center, Hardin finally relented. By 1993 campus opinion had swung strongly in favor of a separate building for the Black Cultural Center, and fund-raising efforts had begun. In 2001, after nine million dollars had been raised from private donors, the university at last broke ground on the Sonja Haynes Stone Black Cultural Center.

These events are relevant to the story of the UNC scandal because the frustrations of the late 1980s and early 1990s help to explain both the rise to prominence of scandal linchpin Julius Nyang'oro (as well as the wide latitude he was given by college administrators after 1992) and the attitudes of his longtime assistant, Debby Crowder, who had been the one indispensable staff person in the AFRI/AFAM curriculum since her hiring in 1979. After the decision of Trudier Harris to relinquish the position of chair of the curriculum, UNC leaders faced a quandary. The senior distinguished people to whom the college might have turned in previous years—Harris, Palmer, James—had either left the university or definitively left the curriculum's leadership role. A national search for the chair position seemed out of the question, given the protracted pain earlier such searches had caused. Uncertainty and added turmoil in the curriculum were precisely what the college wanted to avoid in 1992, but the viable candidates to succeed Harris were few. The eyes of the dean fell inevitably on Julius Nyang'oro.

Nyang'oro had recently experienced a meteoric rise through the ranks in AFRI/AFAM. He had first come to the curriculum in 1984 as a postdoctoral fellow. He stayed on as a "visiting" faculty member through 1990, teaching a variety of courses on the political and economic development of Africa, focusing particularly on his native region of East Africa. After word got around that he had received an offer for a tenure-track position at another institution in 1990, the college felt pressure from others within the curriculum to make an effort to keep Nyang'oro.[10] In 1989 acting chair Sherman James had reminded the dean that "the recruitment and retention of outstanding black academics" remained a pressing challenge in Chapel Hill.[11] Now UNC faced the troubling prospect of losing the services of the young and promising Nyang'oro. In an unusual move the college therefore approved the curriculum's offer of a tenure-track position to Nyang'oro, even though no real search had been conducted and no alternative candidates were seriously considered for the job.[12]

Nyang'oro received generous treatment over the next several years. In part this reflected his obvious merits: he won a teaching award in his first year on the permanent faculty, and he had already established himself as a publishing scholar with an active research agenda. But structural conditions and sheer chance also worked in favor of his rapid advance. He was granted tenure early, after only one year as an assistant professor, and when Trudier Harris left the curriculum in 1992, her absence created a vacuum that Nyang'oro was poised to fill. In the wake of Stone's death and Harris's departure, Nyang'oro stood as the lone remaining black faculty member based in the AFRI/AFAM curriculum. The other members of the faculty were all capable people, but none had yet earned sufficient scholarly distinction to overcome the symbolic affront that white leadership of AFRI/AFAM would have represented at this sensitive point in the curriculum's history. One student activist had reminded Dean Cell, in a 1989 editorial in the student newspaper, the *Daily Tar Heel*, that she had confirmed "our worst fears" when she appointed a white male—the economist Gallman—as interim chair that year.[13] After the loss of Stone, others in the BSM had immediately begun to push university administrators to show greater respect for the field by making the curriculum into a department.[14] Julius Nyang'oro thus quickly emerged as the obvious—perhaps the only—choice to succeed Harris, even though he was of relatively junior status and had been a member of the permanent faculty for only two years. By the summer of 1993, in less than three years' time, Nyang'oro had gone from the insecurity of "visiting" faculty status to become the tenured chair of one of the most visible and politically sensitive academic units in the college.

Nyang'oro put his leverage to good use. The college authorized two new faculty searches for the 1992–93 academic year, and Nyang'oro gained permission for four more such searches the following year. By the summer of 1995, with nine permanent faculty now on the staff after he had spent only two years at the helm, Nyang'oro could rightfully say that he had presided over the tripling of the size of the curriculum since the sad low-water mark of 1991. He had also shepherded through the college approval process a new modern language program, Kiswahili, that went into effect in 1995. And in that same year Nyang'oro began work on the proposal that would finally turn the AFRI/AFAM curriculum into a full-fledged academic department; the transition would become official on January 1, 1997.[15] His predecessors had performed important groundwork, but Nyang'oro had clearly brought great energy to the chair position. The college responded to his efforts with resources and moral support, and by the middle 1990s the AFRI/AFAM curriculum had come to be a dynamic and intellectually exciting place.

From the very beginning of Nyang'oro's reign as chair, however, the AFRI/AFAM curriculum was also marked by another characteristic: it attracted a disproportionate share of athletes—especially from the profit sports, and even more especially from the basketball team. To be sure, there would have been nothing sinister in the initial attraction. At a time when African and African American studies was at the forefront of campus discussion, and when UNC's Black

Student Movement actively promoted study of and respect for the culture of the African diaspora, it made perfect sense that athletes from the profit sports, who were disproportionately black, would take a new interest in the AFRI/AFAM curriculum. The curriculum, like several other small academic units on campus, also had a well-established track record of offering independent study courses—in part, no doubt, because the faculty wished to meet growing student demand and compensate for the limited course offerings available in a curriculum with few permanent faculty. Independent study courses were always a boon for athletes because they met irregularly and thus eased pressures on class and practice schedules. In the late 1980s and early 1990s, athletes routinely sought out independent study courses for their class schedules, especially during their playing seasons, and they had regular success finding them in the Departments of Geography, Philosophy, and Radio, Television, and Motion Pictures as well as AFRI/AFAM.

Athletes also streamed toward AFRI/AFAM, however, because the key figures in the curriculum went out of their way to be friendly and accommodating. A faculty member from another department, one who had frequent contact with Debby Crowder, remembered in 2013 that Crowder "wore her politics on her sleeve." According to his recollections, Crowder had long thought that African American students at UNC had been handed a "raw deal" and that they deserved more help, and a more welcoming environment, than they typically encountered.[16] One assumes that these sensitivities would only have been heightened by the travails of the curriculum and the controversies surrounding the Black Cultural Center from the late 1980s through 1993. Crowder's sympathies were certainly not limited to students in the Athletic Department, nor were her kindnesses parceled out by race (Crowder herself is white), but athletic teams provided a steady supply of requests and demands and Crowder seems to have done what she could to meet them. According to former AFRI/AFAM faculty member Michael West, Crowder "took in hand and assumed a motherly relationship" with more than a few athletes.[17] (When senior basketball player Mike Copeland gave his parting speech at the celebration that followed the 2009 national championship, he gave a shout-out to "Miss Debby."

"I know Miss Debby's here," he said as laughs rolled across the auditorium. Pointing into the stands, Copeland expressed heartfelt gratitude. "Thank you for everything, Miss Debby. I love you.") Crowder got to know many players on the basketball team because she was fast friends with Burgess McSwain, the longtime academic counselor for basketball. McSwain—dedicated, tireless, and well meaning—"worked the system" aggressively and sought out academic paths that would make life somewhat easier for "her boys," whom she loved with a legendary passion.[18] She seems to have parlayed her friendship with Crowder into a new kind of partnership once Julius Nyang'oro joined AFRI/AFAM as a member of the permanent faculty.[19]

Nyang'oro also threw out the welcome mat for athletes. In part this may have reflected his own enthusiasm for sports. In his first years on the UNC campus, when he served as a postdoctoral fellow, he supplemented his salary by tutoring football players in the Academic Support Program; his keen interest in UNC athletics may have derived from his hands-on contact with athletes in need of extra help in the mid-1980s. Certainly, by the time he joined the regular faculty, he made little effort to hide his enthusiasm. In the fall of 1992, at an Indianapolis seminar on pedagogy that had attracted college teachers from all around the country, Nyang'oro playfully teased two faculty colleagues who had earned their PhDs from Duke University. Sharing lunch before the keynote speech, he razzed them while passing on dramatic news. "We got Stackhouse," he told them with his characteristic chuckle. He referred to high school basketball prodigy Jerry Stackhouse, who had been heavily recruited by both UNC head coach Dean Smith and Duke basketball coach Mike Krzyzewski. Stackhouse had announced his intention to attend UNC the night before the seminar, and Nyang'oro, who followed the basketball recruiting wars closely, enjoyed celebrating this victory in the presence of Blue Devils fans. Later, in 1993, Nyang'oro exchanged pleasantries with Dean Stephen Birdsall. "As you continue to be swamped by much," he ended his letter, "remember there is light at the end of the long dark tunnel: basketball season. See you there." In 2009 Nyang'oro would also "guest coach" for the football team, and his emails show a pattern of socializing with Athletic Department staff who were ready to supply tickets and special access to a favored professor.[20]

Nyang'oro's identity as a sports enthusiast was no secret among the student body, either. Adam Seipp, a Texas A&M historian who majored in African studies and history as a UNC undergraduate in the 1990s, took several courses with Nyang'oro and still regards him fondly as a former academic mentor. (Nyang'oro supervised the research for Seipp's honors thesis, which he completed in 1998.) Seipp would sometimes joke with his parents back in Baltimore that there was one easy way for them to get a certain perspective on their son's academic experiences in Chapel Hill. "If you'd like to see who I'm working with," he would tell them, "look for the small Tanzanian man sitting behind the Carolina bench" during basketball games. Watching the games on television with his classmates, Seipp more than once spotted Nyang'oro in a choice seat near the court. "Hey, there he is—right behind Vince Carter!"[21]

Whatever his attachment to the players as athletes, Nyang'oro's relationship to them as students became unusually close from his first years on the faculty. One of the earliest independent study courses he taught at UNC, in the fall semester of 1988, was offered to two basketball players with marginal academic records.[22] How they had known to come to him to request such an independent study is not clear, but Nyang'oro's history as an athletics tutor, the students' weak academic profiles, and the existing friendship between Crowder and McSwain suggest that preplanning almost had to have been involved. Independent study courses are relatively rare offerings in the College of Arts and Sciences, and opportunities to pursue independent study are generally extended only to outstanding students whose intellectual interests or research agenda cannot be properly accommodated by the permanent courses in a given department or curriculum. Most faculty teach them irregularly if at all, and they do so only if they know the students and their abilities well.[23] The structure of independent study courses tends to be much more elastic than for other courses, and faculty want to have no doubts about the work ethic or the intellectual gifts of the student(s) in question. The main product for a typical independent study course, at least in the humanities and social science fields, is a long paper reflecting a great deal of original research. Consequently, the student's initiative, analytical acuity, and research abilities need to be well above average. In ordinary circumstances faculty do not agree to supervise an independent study for the random person who shows up at the office door.

We will never know the nature of the work performed in this independent study, but the two basketball players earned Bs in Nyang'oro's 1988 course. They did so even though neither was an AFRI major and even though both had struggled in their other course work. One of the two students, who clearly needed much help, may well have been, like Adam, present at the Creation— the creation of rule-bending forms of curricular improvisation that would later define the entire course-fraud scandal. This player quickly followed up his 1988 Nyang'oro experience with two more AFRI/AFAM courses—one of them, in the summer of 1989, an independent study course in African American studies.

One of two things appears to have happened with this course. Either Debby Crowder assigned the student to an independent study section linked to the name of a graduate student or other part-time instructor (unfamiliar names show up in other course records as "instructors of record" in the early 1990s), or Nyang'oro handled the course himself. Nyang'oro, trained as an Africanist, really would have had no business supervising African American independent study courses. But we know that his name would later be attached to many fraudulent versions of African American and Swahili courses he was not trained to teach, and the player who had taken his 1988 independent study was in great need. (Despite compiling far more credit hours than necessary for a UNC degree, this player would never graduate; his course itinerary shows a straining and perhaps inevitably unsuccessful student.) With the game of musical chairs in the curriculum's leadership position not yet having ended in 1989, it would have been easy enough for Debby Crowder to schedule Nyang'oro an AFAM independent study without raising an eyebrow. Here may be the first sign of what would become an essential component of the long-running course scandal: the manipulation of multiple subject codes in the curriculum— AFAM, AFRI, in addition to the later additions of SWAH (for Swahili),

WOLO (for Wolof), and LING (for Lingala)—to disguise the multiple benefits distributed by Nyang'oro and those he persuaded or coerced into helping him.

In 1991, after he had become a tenure-track faculty member, Nyang'oro continued to serve the basketball team. In the summer he taught two more AFRI independent study courses exclusively for three basketball players, though none of the three were AFRI majors, and one of these players was given the benefit of pursuing both an AFRI and an AFAM independent study in the same compressed summer session. (The need again seems to have been acute: the player earned a 2.82 GPA in his courses with Nyang'oro, but he had a 1.75 GPA in all his other courses.) Immediately after, in the fall of 1991, another basketball player took yet another AFRI independent study with Nyang'oro; the player was the only undergraduate enrolled in a course section that would seem to have been designed for two doctoral students. Then, in the spring 1992 term, Nyang'oro taught a section of Topics in African Studies to two people. One of the two students enrolled was a member of the basketball team. This same player would subsequently take two other courses with Nyang'oro.

The pattern repeated itself the following year. Nyang'oro's regular availability during the summers quickly became one of the hallmarks of his teaching regimen. The peculiarity of this practice deserves emphasis. Faculty cherish their research time during the summer, and because independent study courses represent uncompensated labor, few faculty consent to offer them in the summers, unless lab work or ongoing collaborative research projects make them easy to accommodate and convenient for the lead researcher. The history of AFRI/AFAM summer course offerings is telling in this respect. Before 1989, when Nyang'oro offered his first summer independent study to that exceptionally needy basketball player, no one in the history of the curriculum, going back to the early 1970s, had offered an AFRI independent study during the summer. One finds only a sprinkling of AFAM independent studies during the summers over those two decades, and none of them enrolled basketball players.[24]

Nyang'oro's activity between 1989 and 1991 thus marked a sea change, after which AFRI/AFAM course offerings would always be partially dictated by the needs of the athletic program. In the summer of 1991, as noted, he taught three independent studies solely for the benefit of four basketball players. In the summer of 1992 he taught two more independent studies featuring six basketball players and three nonathletes. One of the six athletes would take a second independent study in African studies with Nyang'oro in the fall—he was the only student enrolled—even though Nyang'oro was on leave at the time.

The anomalous character of this fall 1992 course arrangement cannot be overstated. Faculty on leave and working on research projects hope to escape all entanglements with regular teaching and service duties. Indeed, when a leave is funded by the university—as Nyang'oro's was in 1992—the university generally requires that no teaching be done; the point of the leave, after all, is to advance a scholar's research agenda. Yet this basketball player was a needy one. He was on his way to completing a total of six courses in AFRI/AFAM identified either as independent studies or as "variable topics," both of which could be repeated on the transcript multiple times. Nyang'oro had clearly come to see himself as a patron of the basketball team. In the spring of 1993 one finds two more independent study courses on the AFRI schedule. One enrolled four students, three of whom were basketball players. The other course enrolled one student only, and he too was a basketball player.

The experience of the athlete who took this second independent study in the spring of 1993 spotlights the newly busy intersection between the basketball program, which was clearly plotting this person's course itinerary with special care, and the office of the receptive and obliging Julius Nyang'oro. Academic counselor Burgess McSwain, a longtime geography buff, had once studied in UNC's Geography Department and had maintained relationships with a number of people there. For years she had sent players to that department for Special Topics and other courses she thought would benefit them academically. In the case of the 1993 athlete in need of extra nurturing, courses from geography and philosophy—another department that was home to several friendly courses—provided a safe harbor on several occasions during what turned out to be a treacherous curricular journey. Since 1989, though,

McSwain had been cutting a new path through even friendlier territory, and she could not resist the temptation to use the developing Nyang'oro course slate as a life raft for her imperiled student. In a period of two years McSwain directed her challenged athlete to ten AFRI/AFAM courses, including at least seven with Nyang'oro. Some of the Nyang'oro courses were independent studies, but all of them, including lecture-style courses, had enrollments of fifteen or fewer students. All the grades from these courses, some of which had to have been scheduled after Athletic Department prompting, proved extremely helpful to the player's GPA. McSwain certainly realized by now, if she had not recognized it before, that Nyang'oro was more than just another friendly faculty member. He was a curriculum head willing to place his own major, or a parallel major of his secret devising, in the service of athletes with checkered academic records.

Athletes outside the basketball team had also begun to hear the message. (Basketball had its own, physically separate, advising office in the Dean Smith Center until at least 2004, and this may have been one reason the favoritism tended to be basketball specific in the early years.) One football player who had annual eligibility difficulties at the end of each spring semester was still relying, in 1992, on summer courses such as Issues in P.E. to get his grade point average back over the eligibility bar in time for the fall playing season. But one year later, when he faced familiar problems after a difficult spring semester, he and his academic counselor adopted a new strategy. In the summer of 1993—the year Nyang'oro became the permanent chair—this player took three AFRI/AFAM courses, including one independent study in which he earned a B+. Although he never declared a major in AFRI/AFAM, this athlete nevertheless went on to take two more independent studies with Nyang'oro in the regular 1993–94 school year. Eligibility concerns never afflicted him again.

In that same 1993–94 school year, another telling change occurred. A wrestler, a women's basketball player, a men's soccer player, and at least one other football player also discovered the advantages of independent study with Julius Nyang'oro. By 1993–94 the AFRI/

AFAM curriculum chair was providing a vital service for athletes in need. Athletics personnel knew it, and traffic was picking up.

Independent study courses were especially prized, but athletes found a medley of choices available to them in the early and middle 1990s. As is well known, four of the five starters on the 1993 national championship basketball team ultimately majored in African or Afro-American studies, even though only one or two other players had done so throughout the entire decade of the 1980s. The flow of athletes to AFRI/AFAM had begun suddenly in 1990–91. Their new awareness of the curriculum meant, of course, that in addition to the independent studies led by Nyang'oro, basketball players and other athletes had many other courses available to them, including Nyang'oro's standard courses, Contemporary Southern Africa, Political Processes and Economic Developments in Africa, Policy Problems in African Studies, and several others. Nyang'oro frequently taught these courses, too, in small sections of anywhere between one and fifteen students. Basketball players tended to be overrepresented on the class rosters. In the fall of 1994, for example, two basketball players were given the opportunity to enroll in an advanced lecture course—AFRI 174, Key Issues in African and Afro-American Linkages—made available to no one else.

Unless the participants begin talking about their experiences someday, there will never be a way to verify whether any lecture courses from the early 1990s were the "no show" type that later proliferated in such staggering numbers. It will also be impossible to determine definitively whether Nyang'oro or his assistant, Crowder, ever purposely segregated athletes into certain lecture-course sections designed from the get-go for especially favorable treatment (though the AFRI 174 just mentioned seems a very likely candidate). But it would be misleading to fixate on these variables, which, despite their titillation value, were never essential to the developing system. Long before the paper-class eligibility scheme attained full maturity sometime around the year 2000, the Nyang'oro course menu served well one of its initial purposes: to provide athletes easy grades that kept them eligible and academically on track. The no-show aspect of the later courses constituted only an added frill, a logical extension of a devious curricular strategy founded from the start on one bedrock principle. the acceptance of an academic double standard benefiting athletes.

During the first decade of the course fraud, most if not all of Nyang'oro's lecture courses appear to have had regular meetings, and players regularly attended those class meetings. What set the courses apart, and what made them the nucleus of the profit-sport athletic curriculum once ASPSA counselors fully recognized the nature of the gift they were being handed, was that they required meaningful work only of those students who were *not* athletes. Systematic preferential treatment—a consciously applied double standard—was the key ingredient in the curricular soufflé cooked up in the early 1990s. "It was commonly understood in these classes," remembers Adam Seipp about his own course experiences between 1996 and 1998, "that the athletes were not being made to do the work the rest of us were doing." Everyone was complicit in the scheme. "There was sort of this running joke" whenever regular students happened to encounter athletes in the hallways or on the way to class. "So did you guys do that AFRI paper? And everybody would laugh. And we all knew what was going on. It was not like it was sort of under the table." Seipp remembers talking with classmates about the strange phenomenon of the foreign-language courses designed for an English-language-only clientele. "There were these Swahili courses that didn't seem to involve any Swahili. And none of us were quite sure how you got foreign-language credit for taking a class that didn't involve a foreign language. But it was understood that that was kind of an athlete thing."

Throughout the 1990s athletes went to classes (at least in courses scheduled as regular lecture courses). They showed up and sat right beside nonathlete students who used the courses as genuine learning experiences. On occasion an athlete might even contribute to a class discussion, but, says Seipp, "it was pretty clear they weren't doing the work. We all accepted that. For some reason, we all just accepted that." Seipp attributes the passive compliance of the other students to the thrill most of them felt at being so close to athletic celebrity. "Being part of the Carolina undergraduate experience is, well, basketball. We were all a little bit starstruck. . . . They would come in with these bags of food that they'd been given in Dining Services, and, you know, they were nice guys. So they would hand everything out. At the start of class [one of them] would come by and hand you a bag of Dorito's, and . . . that was just part of what we did in those classes." Having the opportunity to become familiar with talented athletes and "nice guys," some of whom would soon be making millions in the NBA, offered regular students sufficient inducement to accept the blatant double standard that left them disadvantaged and working hard for their grades. There was something for everyone in this developing scheme.

The players drew the most immediate benefits, however, even if the "benefits" consisted in part of being deprived of a real university education. Together with a bundle of a dozen or so other random courses that supplied As and Bs for the transcripts of virtually every profit-sport athlete, the courses of Julius Nyang'oro provided the GPA boost needed to offset the often dismally poor grades earned in the challenging courses the athletes could not avoid. One critical comparison tells the story. In the early years of the developing relationship between the ASPSA and Julius Nyang'oro, between 1990 and the fall semester of 1995, the eighteen athletes from various sports who were sent to Nyang'oro on multiple occasions earned marks that, on average, stood more than a full letter grade above their performance in all courses outside the AFRI/AFAM curriculum. When they ventured outside the suddenly friendly confines of AFRI/AFAM, they earned a 1.89 GPA. (This reflected grades earned not only in demanding math and science courses but also in various fluff courses.) But in their courses with Julius Nyang'oro over the same period, they averaged a solid B. Whatever the precise short-term objective for sending a player to Debby Crowder and Julius Nyang'oro—maintaining a player's eligibility, freeing up time for practice or film work, establishing the appearance of a "full-time" course schedule in compliance with NCAA rules, or just taking advantage of a perk—Nyang'oro's parallel AFRI/AFAM curriculum significantly eased the academic burdens shouldered by UNC athletes. It is hard to imagine that this was not, from the outset, the central purpose of these courses.

Table 1. First eighteen athletes with multiple Nyang'oro courses

JN GPA	AFAM GPA	OTHER GPA	JN Hours	AFAM Hours	OTHER Hours
2.85	2.51	1.94	12	18	101
3.18	3.08	2.4	30	48	75
3.03	2.74	1.52	24	36	53
3.28	3.06	1.75	21	30	106
3.36	3.2	2.23	9	24	122
3.0	2.55	2.06	12	27	101
3.3	3.0	1.71	27	39	106
2.88	2.83	2.0	24	42	85
3.4	2.87	2.1	15	33	107
3.2	2.03	1.81	9	24	98
2.74	2.36	1.69	15	27	39
3.23	2.97	1.88	24	39	113
2.9	2.21	1.64	12	18	106
2.9	2.75	2.09	9	12	52
2.9	2.61	2.0	9	21	116
3.2	2.62	1.8	15	30	129
2.92	2.71	1.73	15	21	46
1.15	2.24	1.72	6	27	112

Note: Hours and GPAs broken down into Julius Nyang'oro's (JN) classes, AFRI/AFAM classes, and other hours.

Course registration and grading patterns show that, from very early on in the Nyang'oro era, the curriculum of AFRI/AFAM led a sort of double existence. The curriculum offered good teaching and valuable scholarship on a widening array of important subjects—subjects that took on ever more urgent relevance in light of the genocide in Rwanda, the riots that followed the Rodney King verdict, the so-called culture wars that raged in American politics and higher education, and other local and national developments that highlighted both the centrality of race in the American experience and the neglected importance of Africa in world affairs. The curriculum continued to recruit talented new professors, it attracted many passionate students, and it offered courses and programs that enriched the university undergraduate experience. The faculty—emphatically including Nyang'oro himself—often provided inspiring models of intellectual activity that was both engaged with and making a difference in the real world.

Yet already by 1991 the Athletic Department had come to understand and exploit the bonanza of high-grade opportunities that awaited athletes in AFRI/AFAM. How, one might reasonably ask, did the other faculty in the curriculum adapt to the developing situation? They were teaching large and labor-intensive courses for an academic department one of whose purposes—it had become clear to at least some of the undergraduate majors—was to "crank athletes through." Did the other faculty see any warning signs? Did they offer any resistance to the developing scheme? After the course scandal went public in 2011, all current AFRI/AFAM faculty insisted that they had been blindsided, that they had had no idea that the department's courses were being misused. That may well be the case. But at least a small handful of faculty who taught in the department in the 1990s seem to have sensed what was happening, and they did not always hide their disgust. Because he aspired to a career in academia, Seipp often sought out advice and conversation with professors he respected, including several in African studies: "The message I got again and again was 'This is not the department for you.' That was tough. And looking back . . . I realize how difficult it must have been [for them]."[25]

Unfortunately, things would not be looking up any time soon. By the mid- to late-1990s, when the football teams of Mack Brown also rose to national prominence, ASPSA counselors were primed to begin sending much larger numbers of athletes to the doorsteps of Debby Crowder and Julius Nyang'oro. They welcomed them with open arms, and at that point the "gaming" of the system began to resemble a system unto itself.

Boom Times

By the spring of 1995, when six football players, seven basketball players, and dozens of nonathlete students signed up for Julius Nyang'oro's Political Processes and Economic Developments in Africa (of which several sections were offered), one would have been hard-pressed to imagine a more fertile cultural and institutional environment for the development of a course-fraud scheme favoring athletes. From the perspective of the College of Arts and Sciences, the AFRI/AFAM curriculum was thriving, its leader was energetic, and its enrollments were as healthy as ever. Given the university's increased sensitivities about the needs and wants of the curriculum, and its commendable desire to attract, welcome, and affirm African American students on the Chapel Hill campus, the administration would have been disinclined to meddle intrusively in curricular affairs. Julius Nyang'oro was left to manage things as he saw fit.

One intriguing sign of the enhanced autonomy afforded AFRI/AFAM in these years comes through the evolving format of the annual reports submitted to the dean of the college. Throughout the 1980s, and until 1992, the curriculum, like every academic unit in the college, included in its annual report details about the teaching record of each faculty member—the number of courses taught, the number of students served, specific course numbers and titles, as well as notes about the number of honors or master's theses advised and independent study courses offered. Beginning in 1992–93, however, the year that Nyang'oro took over the curriculum, AFRI/AFAM effectively abandoned this practice. In that year Nyang'oro (or Crowder or both working in tandem) provided the dean only aggregate figures about numbers of courses taught and students served, with independent study course numbers no longer individually identified as such. For any administrator who might have been interested in knowing, this switch-up would have made it impossible to see at a glance who was teaching what and to whom. (Other departments in the college—Communications, Math, Anthropology, Drama, History, Philosophy, and so on—continued with the traditional reporting pattern.) Then, between 1994 and 1998, Nyang'oro experimented with yet another style of reporting. In those years independent study classes were the only classes listed in the teaching portion of the report. Apparently seeing healthy independent study enrollments as reflecting well on productivity, the chair decided to draw attention to faculty generosity. But this practice of reporting independent study enrollments ended abruptly in 1998–99, when the department's leadership began offering supersize sections of independent study that would have been hard to explain had anyone started asking about them. Nyang'oro evidently never had to justify his ever-changing reporting techniques, and so he and his assistant, Crowder, were able to escape one small measure of accountability that might have raised bureaucratic red flags about odd teaching practices.[26]

Nyang'oro and Crowder had also worked out a governance regime that confined important decision making to a circle of two. Nyang'oro frequently traveled to Africa in the summers, and sometimes even in regular semesters; in his very first summer as acting chair of the curriculum, in 1992, he left behind a memo stating that Debby Crowder would handle "any emergencies" that might arise. The following summer he specified in a similar memo that Crowder would "handle routine business as per my instructions."[27] Their exclusion from decision making helps to explain the reluctance of the rank-and-file faculty to speak out in protest. Necessarily wondering whether Nyang'oro's frequently strange behavior had been endorsed or encouraged by the university's administrative leadership—why was he left in charge for twenty years?—the fine working faculty of AFRI/AFAM found themselves voiceless and on the margins of a shady operation they were powerless to stop, an operation whose full dimensions they probably never grasped.

Then there were the sensibilities of Nyang'oro and Crowder themselves. Crowder's connections to the basketball program only deepened over time (she eventually began a romantic relationship with a former basketball player), and everyone who knew her reports that she was always inclined to help those who needed or deserved help. Athletes recruited for the profit sports would have stood out as among the likeliest candidates for help, since many of them entered the university badly prepared for college-level work (a subject explored in chapter 7), and they often compiled grade histories that would have placed them at risk of academic disqualification absent helpful intervention from a friendly quarter. Every development in sport since the mid-1980s—the explosion of television revenue and the increased competitiveness it had created among the big-time programs, the rise of the millionaire coach, the intensifying rivalry between the remarkably successful Duke and UNC basketball teams, the rebuilding of the football program under Mack Brown, UNC's increasingly close identification with its sports brand in the wake of Michael Jordan's conquest of the globe and Mia Hamm's emergence as the face of women's soccer—pressured the university to admit more and more athletes with suspect academic credentials. In the profit sports between about 1990 and 1996, Scholastic Achievement Test (SAT) reading scores around 300, or even below, were not anomalous at UNC.

Despite, or because of, these increasing competitive pressures, the NCAA had toughened standards in the late 1980s. Proposition 48, which went into effect in 1986, set benchmarks for freshman eligibility that sidelined first-year players who did not score at least 700 combined on the SAT or whose high school GPAs were below 2.0. In 1989 Proposition 42 added a punitive, and highly controversial, feature to the Prop 48 reform. Students who failed to meet the benchmarks set in Prop 48 would be ineligible for financial aid unless and until they demonstrated adequate performance in their college classrooms. This reform, which was quickly modified after a firestorm of protest ignited by basketball coaches John Thompson of Georgetown and John Chaney of Temple, would have effectively blocked access to college for the many underprepared athletes who could not afford to pay their own way while proving their academic chops as freshmen. African American athletes would have suffered disproportionately. (In the 1989–90 school year, 65.9 percent of the so-called partial qualifiers who missed the Prop 48 benchmarks were African American.)[28] The NCAA would continue to tinker with its eligibility formula over the next decade and a half, and few talented high school players were actually denied access to college in these years. Still, the national debates of the late 1980s and early 1990s—echoes of which could be heard even in UNC's Faculty Council, a university-wide elected policy-making body—reinforced for some, with Debby Crowder and Julius Nyang'oro almost surely among them, the idea that the black college athlete faced an unfair, discriminatory, and exploitative system.[29]

Facing great demands on the field and on the court, and confronting a daunting set of graduation requirements and NCAA standards, why should the players not get some help in navigating their course of study? Athletes already had their own tutoring system. Academic counselors picked their classes for them. Was it so wrong for instructors to take the help one step further? Nyang'oro, says Seipp, "was always cautious" in his handling of the athletes in his classes. Some of the athletes were quite bright, some were clearly challenged, but all had skipped the reading. In typical discussions in Seipp's classes, he remembers, "about 60 percent of the class clearly had no idea what was going on." Nyang'oro did not want to "humiliate" those who could not keep up or who had no interest in the material.[30] So he went easy on them. Eventually, at least for a certain subset of their courses, he simply eliminated the expectation that they be present for anything at all. And Crowder, clearly of like mind, facilitated the athletes' registration for courses that never met or rarely met and, whatever the format, required little or nothing in the way of real academic work. Nyang'oro and Crowder seem to have acted, at least in part, out of genuine sympathy and a conviction that athletes "deserved" the help—not realizing, perhaps, that they only compounded the deleterious effects of an institutional racism disguised by the nonstop celebration of athletic success.

The official report of Governor Jim Martin (discussed in chapter 6) has established that there were at least a half-dozen instances of the famed no-show style of lecture course between the fall of 1994 and the fall of 1997.[31] But the best indicator of the direction of the AFRI/AFAM course fraud over the course of the 1990s is found in the numbers of students registering for independent studies—courses that, by their nature, carried no-show potential right out of the gate. From the tiny acorn of 1988, when two struggling basketball players took Nyang'oro's AFRI 190 in the fall semester, a mighty oak soon grew. At first the uptick in enrollments is noticeable but not necessarily eye-catching. From a handful of students enrolled in independent study sections in a typical semester or summer session in 1990 or 1991, the enrollment grew to fifteen in the fall term of 1993 as well as fifteen in the following spring. Tracking only the enrollments in fall and spring semesters, 34 students took either AFAM or AFRI independent studies in the 1994–95 academic year, 38 in 1996–97, and 50 in 1997–98.

Keeping in mind that most of these students were assigned to one instructor, the numbers 38 and 50 already appear to be absurdly high In what sane academic universe would any faculty member generously teach—in addition to his or her regular course load—50 students pursuing independent projects? Enrollment figures show, for example, that the entire History Department, with approximately a 50-member faculty, taught a grand total of 39 students in independent studies between 1987 and 1993—an average of 0.14 independent study students per professor per year. Over that same period, the Department of Classics had 11 students, Religious Studies 36, and Economics 20. Some departments had none at all. And AFRI/AFAM as a whole, over that same period, had had 86, almost three-quarters of the total coming in AFRI and most of them clearly attached to Nyang'oro (see figure 2).[32] Yet by the mid-1990s, a typical semester had Nyang'oro teaching dozens of students in independent studies all by himself—some of them, perhaps, pursuing legitimate projects and some of them having been funneled to the courses through a registration process largely managed by Debby Crowder, working in conjunction with her friends in athletics and other places.

But Nyang'oro and Crowder were only just getting started. In 1999–2000—again, sticking to the fall and spring semesters only—86 students signed up for independent work, thus matching the six-year total between 1987 and 1993. The next year, in 2000–2001, the same courses attracted 122 students. And in 2001–2 a whopping 175 students pursued independent study in AFRI/AFAM. The number set an impressive record, but the record would not last long. In the 2002–3 academic year, 238 students registered for either AFRI 190 or AFAM 190. Then, in 2003–4 the true record was set when 291 students completed independent studies under Nyang'oro's supervision, after which the numbers began a slow fallback in the direction of normalcy (263 in 2004–5, 149 in 2005–6, 55 in 2006–7). Summer enrollments in independent study courses, meanwhile, also broke records in these years. The summer of 1999 saw 32 students working on independent projects with Nyang'oro; 42 showed up in 2001 and 45 in 2002.

How can this phenomenon be explained? In the 1991–92 academic year, including the two summer sessions of 1992, only 19 stu-

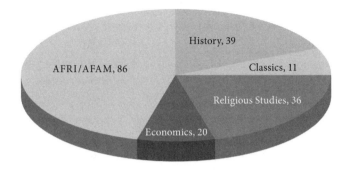

Fig 1. Departmental course offerings of identified Independent Study classes between 1987 and 1993 (from annual reports)

dents had taken independent studies in AFRI/AFAM. Even as late as 1996–97, the total number of students enrolled, including the summer sessions, was only 45. But by 2003–4, including again the two summer sessions that followed, the number had reached a stratospheric 341. What had happened?

First, there are good reasons to suppose that word had leaked out to other students on campus that certain AFRI/AFAM courses were remarkably flexible in their scheduling and surprisingly lenient in their demands.[33] Emeritus history professor Donald Mathews, who served as an assistant dean of advising in the College of Arts and Sciences between 1999 and 2004, noticed a curious pattern soon after he assumed his position. Although Mathews himself never suspected the outright abuse of independent studies, let alone the existence of fake classes, he did notice that nonathletes came to him often, early during his tenure and before his own administrative habits were well known, to seek authorization for what he calls "transfers" from one course to another. (Mathews had the authority to approve late drop/add switches in all humanities and social science fields. But he never saw prominent athletes, who had other means of accessing such transfers.) "Many students," he says, "wanted out of three specific professors' classes and into a fourth." The three AFRI/AFAM professors whose courses had suddenly begun to lose their appeal were "exceptional" scholars and teachers, but

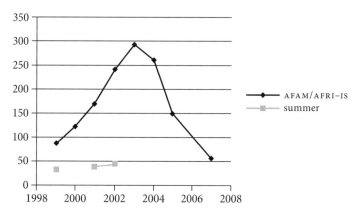

Fig 2. The number of identified Independent Study courses offered from 1999 to 2007 in African and Afro-American Studies

students were finding that the grass was greener elsewhere. "I don't know the fourth [professor personally]," says Mathews, "but his name was Julius Nyang'oro." Some students clearly thought "life was better in his classes," but "I never approved a transfer for any reason." Eventually, students learned that Mathews would not accommodate them; they stopped asking. Today he regrets that "the university hasn't done much to help anyone understand" the scandalous events of recent years or the environment that made them possible.[34]

The evolution of independent studies in AFRI/AFAM certainly helps to explain the broadening of the scandal and the curious pattern that Mathews observed. Football standout Julius Peppers, the most famous athlete on the UNC campus in the spring of 2001, signed up for a section of AFAM independent study that happened to enroll 80 students—not 8 but 80! (Across the board, at UNC and at other universities, independent study sections typically enroll 1 student, though sometimes a small handful will be involved.) The Athletic Department was well represented in the spring 2001 course, with 3 football players, 3 men's basketball players, 1 women's basketball player, and 1 student—Peppers himself—who played both basketball and football. This meant, though, that 90 percent of the people in this section of AFAM 190, 72 of the 80 students, were not athletes. Nothing like this had occurred in the early 1990s. Word had clearly gotten around that good deals were to be had at the desk of Debby Crowder and the office of Julius Nyang'oro. Because they were naturally nice and accommodating—or, perhaps, because they wanted no unhappy students grumbling to the dean of the college—they took in nearly all comers. The spring 2001 AFAM 190 was one of many such courses, numerically dominated by nonathletes but serving athlete needs as well, that would be offered over the course of the next decade. An arrangement that had been designed at first with an athletics clientele in mind had been forced to expand and adapt as a secret became more and more an open secret.

The presence in that same spring 2001 course of several football players highlights another contributing cause for the explosion in independent study numbers after the mid-1990s. Football players began showing up in greater numbers in all of Nyang'oro's courses in this period, and since athletes had to have their schedules approved—chosen, in effect—by academic counselors in the ASPSA, the rising incidence of football enrollments tells us that ASPSA personnel had become determined to share the fruits of the AFRI/AFAM cornucopia outside the men's basketball team. The football team had recently enjoyed an unaccustomed run of success that brought them greater visibility. After taking over a 1-10 team in 1989, Mack Brown had catapulted UNC football into the national top ten. Between 1995 and 2002 UNC would send at least three dozen players on to the NFL. But with success came more and more talented recruits who would also be needing the same sort of academic help routinely offered the basketball team since 1988. Peppers, who had already taken one AFAM 190 in a 1999 summer session, got a healthy B in the spring 2001 AFAM 190, even though his GPA through the fall of 2000 in all non-Nyang'oro courses had been a dreary 1.32, only slightly above a solid D.[35] From the late 1990s to 2011, football players bulked large in independent study courses. In the busy summer of 1999, Nyang'oro offered four separate independent study courses. Nineteen of the 35 students enrolled were football players. (Six more were basketball players—3 each from the men's and women's teams.) Summers would always remain the special preserve of athletes in the profit sports.

Remarkably, in discussions of the UNC scandal, the role of the independent study course has been largely overlooked. A deans' report in May 2012 (discussed in chapter 4) offered few specifics on independent studies, and in his UNC-sponsored review of AFRI/AFAM courses between 1994 and 2012, former governor Jim Martin found only what he termed "inconclusive" evidence about the vast majority of independent study courses offered in AFRI/AFAM during the scandal years. He flagged a grand total of 10 independent study courses as "anomalous" (among the 216 courses so identified). On what grounds did he label those particular courses anomalous? The instructor of record had "noted the presence of an unauthorized signature on the grade roll."[36] This meant either that Crowder had signed the grade forms or that Nyang'oro had signed forms for courses ostensibly taught by other faculty—a serious anomaly indeed.

What this technical definition of *anomalous* overlooks, however, is that the "authorized" practices in these courses were perfectly scandalous in their own right. Adam Seipp, who took an independent study in 1998 in which 4 athletes and a handful of others were enrolled, never met with his classmates and never knew who else was enrolled in the course. This was, in no sense, a coherent course with a lesson plan, required readings, or a set of defined themes. Rather, it provided a dummy course number under which a collection of students could be gathered for purposes of registration and credit-hour distribution. Seipp completed an authentic paper that semester—he remembers writing about Sierra Leone—but there is no reason to assume that the athlete-friendly double standard openly observed in regular lecture courses did not apply also to courses where independence was the name of the game. In an independent study with 80 students, an instructor teaching his regular course load would never aspire or expect to read with care the papers finally submitted by his legions of enrolled independent students.[37]

Yet, astoundingly, the 80-student AFAM 190 offered in the spring of 2001 did not even show up on Martin's list of "anomalous" courses, a list that many have taken to be definitive. Between the summer of

1990 and the spring of 2011, AFRI/AFAM scheduled scores of independent study courses that enrolled more than 2,300 students. After 1998 one finds supersize sections with 95 students, 89 students, 53 students (twice), 67 students, 57 students (three times), 60 students, and countless sections with 10 or 20 students. But all of these course sections, and the grades assigned in them, have essentially flown under the radar of those charged with reviewing the "anomalies" for which Nyang'oro and Crowder are thought to be responsible. Given all that has come to light about years of no-show lecture courses, hundreds of unauthorized grade changes, and one case of plagiarism discovered purely by accident in a course known to be anomalous, one could not be blamed for presuming that all independent study courses involving athletes between 1990 and 2011 were "anomalous" in the sense that they required little work and awarded virtually free grades to players who were valuable to their profit-sport teams.

In 2013 it was even revealed that assignments in the dummy courses run by Nyang'oro and Crowder were sometimes (if not always) created by athletics counselors who sought to ensure—at Nyang'oro's insistence?—that athletes would at least have to go through *some* form of learning exercise in exchange for the credit hours and high grades on offer in no-show courses. In one email exchange published by the *N&O*, football academic counselor Cynthia Reynolds is shown arranging a chat with Nyang'oro "to talk about the assignment for AFAM 396 [independent study] for my two students." Octavus Barnes, a counselor and former player, thanks Crowder in a separate exchange for having sent him the final assignment agreed upon for one of his students. Yet another email carried the subject line "Cynthia Reynolds' AFAM topics."[38] The free-form independent study courses piloted in the early years of the course scheme obviously provided the template for this ostensibly legitimizing system of quid pro quo. In exchange for an unread or lightly read ten- or twenty-page paper on some acceptable topic devised by academic counselors, or settled in consultation with them, Nyang'oro would hand out three credits and a good grade.

The entire UNC course scandal might be seen, in fact, as a consequence of the "independent studyization" of a portion of the AFRI/

AFAM curriculum. The lessons learned in those early courses for basketball players between 1988 and 1991—the convenience of few or no meetings, the absence of hands-on instruction, the final submission of some sort of paper that dealt with some preassigned topic, the handing out of a GPA-friendly grade to a struggling student—were applied, first, to new and larger sections of independent study after 1996 and eventually to other AFRI/AFAM courses, even including language courses, as needed. In the mid-1990s athletes were still expected to show up for normal lecture courses; the Athletic Department even continued sending "classroom checkers" to spot-check attendance in such courses. At some point, however, the expectation of attendance went by the wayside, at least in many lecture courses (in addition to all those regular independent studies in which no one had ever shown up for anything). University rules formally restricted students' access to independent studies; no student was allowed to take more than twelve credit hours (or four courses) of independent study in the course of his or her academic career. But academic counselors in athletics, fully cognizant of that rule, signed up their athletes for independent study–style courses in AFRI/AFAM semester after semester. In some cases independent study–style courses constituted a third or more of the total number of courses taken at UNC. A parallel curriculum, one with drastically lower standards than those prevailing in regular courses, had emerged to serve the needs of a select student audience.

By the late 1990s the Athletic Department was no longer classroom checking the courses in the parallel curriculum that had been constructed—it would be good, someday, to hear an account of how and when this practice was discontinued for certain courses—but athletics personnel knew well what their students were getting out of their special relationship with their favorite professor. A once-subtle form of curricular manipulation predicated on the relaxation of academic standards for certain basketball players had hardened, by 1998, into full-fledged curricular fraud. Chapter 2 explores the routinization of the system.

Two

A Fraud in Full

In the history of UNC sport, the year 1997 stands as a high-water mark. The men's basketball team made a return trip to the Final Four that spring in what turned out to be Dean Smith's final season as the Carolina coach. A revered figure whose parting was much lamented, he retired with more wins to his credit than any basketball coach before him. The women's basketball team, led by the great Marion Jones in what proved to be her final year of basketball competition, won both the regular-season and the tournament championships in the ACC. Then, in the fall semester, the women's soccer team completed yet another undefeated season and finished the year as national champions (their win-loss record for the entire decade of the 1990s was a mind-boggling 243-7-3).

The football team also garnered its share of the national spotlight. Loaded with future NFL stars such as Dré Bly, Alge Crumpler, Jeff Saturday, and Ebenezer Ekuban, the Tar Heels broke into the national top five and finished with an impressive 10-1 mark, marred only by a loss to Florida State that was featured as ESPN's Game of the Week. Fans of Tar Heel sports, in short, enjoyed an embarrassment of riches in 1997. When Dean Smith was asked that year how it felt to be the basketball coach at a "football school" (UNC football had been ranked as the preseason number one in one national magazine), he could only quip: "This is a women's soccer school. We're just trying to keep up with them."[1]

With football's arrival as a national power, and with all other UNC programs performing at an impressively high level, Nike moved to strike a deal that stood at the time as one of the richest and most comprehensive contracts ever signed with a university athletic program. The company agreed to supply $7 million worth of gear to UNC athletes, and put $4 million into the pockets of UNC coaches, in exchange for the right to outfit all twenty-eight sport teams and brand them with the Nike logo. The $11.6 million contract, and the enrichment of coaches through corporate sponsorship, caused controversy on campus—an exasperated Bill Friday, UNC's president emeritus, observed, "I don't think a great university does this kind of thing"—but the flow of sponsor and television money into university coffers would only grow in the years to come.[2] By the time the apparel agreement was renegotiated in 2001, its value had increased to $28.3 million.[3] The Nike contract of 1997 had announced a new order of things.

The academic year 1997–98 also marked the transformation of the Nyang'oro-Crowder slate of courses into a full-service curriculum for athletes in need. The dramatic jump in independent study enrollments in the late 1990s has already been noted. But the sharpest illustration of the change in direction that occurred around 1997 comes from the enrollment records in Swahili courses. The Kiswahili language program had received college approval in 1995. A handful of basketball players, in addition to a wrestler and a women's soccer player, had migrated to Swahili 001 already by 1996. Whether that course was taught as a legitimate course remains unknown, but the audit of the AFRI/AFAM Department that was conducted by Governor Jim Martin and the firm of Baker-Tilly in 2012 identified the fall 1997 version of SWAH 001 as the first of fifty-five fully bogus courses offered by the department between 1997 and 2011. ("Fully bogus" here means that the course had no meetings and did not even have an instructor assigned to it.) Among its twenty-four enrollees were two football players and a basketball player. Just one year later, in the fall of 1998, academic counselors in the ASPSA clearly realized they had a good thing going. They had one basketball player abandon his more challenging Spanish courses and put Swahili in its place. In fact, large numbers of basketball players as well as several football players signed up for the fall 1998 offering of SWAH 001. Then, in the summer of 1999 two basketball players were truly given the royal treatment. They were registered for a two-person paper-class version of SWAH 003, thus completing their foreign-language requirement with a no-show class that clearly involved no foreign language. The next summer the same thing was done for a football player. (Jim Martin recognized that one of these two independent study–style foreign-language classes was an obvious anomaly, but he somehow appears to have missed the other one.) The Swahili program had become an enormous boon to athletics. Several sports were represented on the class rosters, and the academically neediest or most privileged athletes even had access to private SWAH sections made just for them. (Later, the summer 2009 rendition of a no-show third-level SWAH course would end Michael McAdoo's UNC career; the university happily pretended that the player alone was responsible for his cheating ways.)

By 1997 AFRI/AFAM had become the go-to place for all athletes and for anyone else who presented a story of need. The forms of need presented, and the sorts of help offered, are perhaps best revealed by the academic experiences of some noted athletic success stories. Those experiences show shameless manipulation of established curricular procedures; they show a fraud in full.

Julius Peppers's Path to the Pros

A closer look at the already published transcript of Julius Peppers provides a clear introduction into the ways, and the conditions under which, athletes and their counselors used the AFRI/AFAM opportunities offered them by Nyang'oro and Crowder beginning in the late 1990s. Counselors with a conscience, who took their responsibilities seriously, used as much restraint as possible. They did not make the paper classes available to all athletes (though the circle continued always to widen), and in most cases they judiciously mixed in paper classes with real courses. They did this partly because they wanted to challenge their players, partly perhaps because they sensed that there were limits beyond which they could not push even the friendliest faculty, and partly because sheer scruples prevented them from being excessively indulgent. In his first semester the academically challenged profit-sport athlete would typically take an introductory AFAM or AFRI course in addition to other courses from across the curriculum that met certain general education requirements. The performance in those courses would be followed by a reassessment that might alter the planned course of study.

The Peppers transcript shows the process at work. In his first semester at UNC he took AFAM 41, as well as entry-level math, drama, and English courses that filled various requirements. He performed poorly in all his courses, though, including the AFAM 41 survey course—undoubtedly taught by a member of the faculty not named Nyang'oro. He earned an alarming 1.075 GPA in his first fall term. A helpful AFRI 40 grade improved things in the spring, but only barely. At the end of the spring term, the GPA stood at 1.45. Eligibility standards for the sophomore year required a GPA of at least 1.5, so Peppers would need a boost over the summer. He got it in the form of unusually high grades in two courses, one of them an AFAM independent study, where he pulled a B. The other course, French Theater in Translation, had been a notoriously athlete-friendly course at UNC for a quarter century. Since he would be taking Swahili for his foreign language (he never came close to satisfying his foreign-language requirement at UNC), one might wonder how Julius Peppers developed this sudden interest in French drama. But no wondering is required. Counselors in the ASPSA sent all at-risk athletes—every single one of the them—to this course, where they were virtually guaranteed an A or a B. (The most seriously imperiled athletes would often be sent back for a Special Topics French course with the same instructor. In that independent study–style course, and in the standard French Novel in Translation course also taught by the same man, athletes overwhelmingly received As and Bs.) Peppers got a B- in the course on French drama. Heading into the fall, his first full playing season for the Tar Heels, he carried an underwhelming but minimally acceptable GPA of 1.73.

Peppers took two more AFAM courses and a Swahili course in the fall of 1999, but life on the academic bubble was nevertheless becoming a permanent condition. The Swahili course and his AFAM 40 did not go well—a clear sign that academic counselors tried not to rely exclusively on Nyang'oro and sought to test the limits of the

Faculty/Staff Central

Alpha by Course

To protect your privacy,
close your web browser
completely when you
are finished.

		Grade Summary for Peppers, Julius Frazier Undergraduate Career Chronological by Term				
Term	Course	Title	Current Grade	Earned Hours	Quality Hours	Quality Points
SS1 1998	SPCL 090 303	SPECIAL STUDIES		00.0	00.0	0.0
SS2 1998		Withdrew 07/27/1998				
FALL 1998	AFAM 041 001	BLACK EXPERIENCE	D+	03.0	03.0	3.9
	DRAM 015 003	ELEMENTS OF DRAMA	D	03.0	03.0	3.0
	ENGL 010 005	BASIC WRITING	C	03.0	03.0	6.0
	MATH 010 004	ALGEBRA	F*	00.0	03.0	0.0
	PHYA 001P 999	REQUIRED ACTIVITIES	PL	00.0	00.0	0.0
SPRING 1999	AFAM 054 001	BLACKS IN LATIN AMER	C	03.0	03.0	6.0
	AFRI 040 002	INTRO AFRICAN CIV	B	03.0	03.0	9.0
	ENGL 011 004	ENG COMP & RHETORIC	D+	03.0	03.0	3.9
	PHIL 030 001	APPLIED ETHICS	D	03.0	03.0	3.0
SS1 1999	FREN 040 001	FR THEA IN TRANSLAT	B-	03.0	03.0	8.1
SS2 1999	AFAM 190 001	INDEPENDENT STUDIES	B	03.0	03.0	9.0
FALL 1999	AFAM 040 002	BLACK EXPERIENCE	D	03.0	03.0	3.0
	AFAM 067 001	AFAM LEADERSHIP	B-	03.0	03.0	8.1
	GEOL 018 001	EARTH AND CLIMATE	F	00.0	03.0	0.0
	SWAH 001 001	KISWAHILI I	D	03.0	03.0	3.0
SPRING 2000	AFRI 120 001	SOUTHERN AFRICA	B+	03.0	03.0	9.9
	AFRI 190 001	INDEPENDENT STUDIES	B+	03.0	03.0	9.9
	ANTH 010 002	GEN ANTHROPOLOGY	C+	03.0	03.0	6.9
	ENGL 012 020	ENG COMP & RHETORIC	C	03.0	03.0	6.0
SS1 2000	AFAM 076 001	BLACKS IN FILM	C	03.0	03.0	6.0
SS2 2000	EXSS 083 001	ELEM PHYE METHODS	A	03.0	03.0	12.0
FALL 2000	AFAM 071 001	FIELD RESEARCH	B	03.0	03.0	9.0
	AFRI 070 001	POL PROB IN AFRI ST	B	03.0	03.0	9.0
	COMM 014 001	INTRO MEDIA PROD	D	03.0	03.0	3.0
	DRAM 060 001	STAGECRAFT	D	03.0	03.0	3.0
	GEOG 020 002	WORLD REGIONAL GEOG	F	00.0	03.0	0.0
SPRING 2001	AFAM 058 001	CIVIL RIGHTS	FA	00.0	03.0	0.0
	AFAM 069 001	BLACK NATIONALISM	IN	00.0	03.0	0.0
	AFAM 190 001	INDEPENDENT STUDIES	B	03.0	03.0	9.0
	AFRI 066 001	CONTEMPORARY AFRICA	B	03.0	03.0	9.0
SS1 2001	AFAM 070 001	AFAM SEMINAR		00.0	00.0	0.0
FALL 2001	AFAM 190 001	INDEPENDENT STUDIES		00.0	00.0	0.0
	AFRI 124 001	NORTH-EAST AFRICA		00.0	00.0	0.0
	PHIL 046 001	PHIL ISSU/FEMINISM		00.0	00.0	0.0
	SOCI 022 002	RACE & ETHNIC RELATIONS		00.0	00.0	0.0
		Cumulative Total		72.0	87.0	158.70
		Cumulative GPA: 1.824				

Fig. 3. Julius Peppers's transcript

students in their care before they capitulated to unpleasant realities. Still, their response to the conditions they faced with Peppers at the end of his third semester in residence, when he carried a perilously low GPA of 1.57, shows the paper-class system hitting on all cylinders. Knowing that Peppers would need high grades that would raise his GPA to at least 1.75 by the fall of 2000, counselors began to take fewer chances. In fact, out of the next seventeen courses Peppers took at UNC, eleven came from AFRI/AFAM (at least eight of them paper classes or classic double standard lecture courses), and one was a glorified physical education course, in which Peppers earned an A. At least nine of these seventeen courses, in other words, were gift courses in which Peppers earned a 3.23 GPA. His GPA over those same semesters in courses of the normal kind was 1.16 (which happened to be nearly identical to the GPA he had earned in his troubled first semester). This uneven performance was just good enough to keep him on the field.

There would be more stumbles in the fall of 2000, with the GPA dipping below the 1.9 that would be needed before the following playing season. But since four of his next six courses would be paper classes, Peppers had little to worry about. His GPA after the spring 2001 semester was 1.93. Over the summer all he needed to do was maintain that mediocre GPA while collecting three additional credits. The academic counselors made an extra-safe choice for his 2001 summer course: AFAM 70, a Research Seminar. It goes without saying that Peppers, after completing his "research" that summer, showed up on the gridiron for the following fall season, his last at UNC, during which his grades no longer mattered.

The academic counselors in the ASPSA had done their job. Through his first three years of course work, Peppers never made it into a second-level foreign-language course (level three is required for graduation), and he never passed the basic math requirement demanded of all UNC graduates. He also skipped the "science with lab" requirement, one that weighed down the GPAs of a great many profit-sport athletes (virtually all of whom took Geology 11, but Geology 11 was no walk in the park). Most UNC students eliminate all of these requirements within their first two years on campus. But of course, Peppers was nothing like other students. Everyone with whom he ever came into contact at UNC—his coaches, his academic counselors, Julius Nyang'oro, his teammates, and the students who occasionally spotted him in class—knew that graduation had never been the point of bringing Julius Peppers to the UNC campus. The point had been winning games and clearing Peppers's path to the pros. At the end of the summer of 2001, the counselors in Kenan Field House could celebrate a mission accomplished.

Did anyone ever contact Julius Nyang'oro or Debby Crowder to lobby for grades on Peppers's behalf? He walked the eligibility tightrope summer after summer—needing consistently good grades and about six or nine credit hours between May and August to ensure his continuing fall eligibility. There was simply no margin for error. Difficult summers would have spelled disaster, and Peppers always managed to avoid them. He was also rescued by two Nyang'oro B+s in the spring of 2000, and he practically majored in Nyang'oro studies in the spring of 2001 (when Nyang'oro, following the precedent that seems to have been set in 1989, again "taught" specialized courses in African American studies as well as African studies).

Between 1999 and 2001, Peppers had two academic counselors looking out for him—Burgess McSwain for basketball and Carl Carey (who would eventually become Peppers's personal agent) for football. McSwain had direct access to the AFRI/AFAM Department through her friend Debby Crowder. Carl Carey became sufficiently familiar with the department chair that he was twice invited by Nyang'oro to teach courses in the AFRI/AFAM Department; the second invitation came even after Carey had become a registered agent. Carey had already shown his willingness to use strong-arm tactics and his full persuasive powers with UNC faculty in the fall of 1998, during Peppers's initial fall semester. As he himself later related to ESPN, Carey "banged and banged on the door of Peppers's teacher" in his Elements of Drama course after Peppers received a failing grade on a test that could have been fatal to his prospects that semester. Carey remembered that Peppers's coaches from both basketball and football were always pestering the counselor to "keep him eligible, keep him eligible," and Carey's proactive posture certainly did the trick with that drama teacher in the fall of 1998. Peppers was indeed allowed to retake his test. He got a D in the course and thus earned the minimum nine credit hours needed in his first semester in residence.[4]

Banging on doors would not have been necessary in the offices of Crowder and Nyang'oro, but did Carey or anyone else ever give them explicit instructions concerning the grades they awarded? Definitive answers to such questions will remain elusive, but it hardly seems a coincidence that more than one-quarter of all grades assigned in courses taught by Julius Nyang'oro in the four years included in a deans' review of 2012 were classified as "temporary" grades—that is, incompletes that were converted to permanent grades only weeks after the semester grade rolls had been turned over to the registrar.[5] There was one all too obvious incentive for assigning incompletes: the grade needs of the affected students could be known with certainty only after all other grades had been turned in and new cumulative GPAs had been calculated. Nyang'oro and Crowder, at least until the late 1990s, typically gave Bs, B-s and B+s in paper classes. They observed a kind of honor system, withholding As from obviously struggling students and handing out Fs to those same students if they did not at least comply with the "paper" end of the paper-class bargain. But there must have been times when the A simply had to be awarded. Whether any behind-the-scenes negotiations ever benefited Julius Peppers or other star athletes will likely never be known. The university has claimed that no records for grade changes exist from that period. The circumstantial evidence is intriguing nonetheless. When asked in the summer of 2013 whether eligibility concerns had ever helped to determine the mark permanently assigned to a temporary grade in AFRI/AFAM, one academic counselor who worked at UNC at a time when scandalous activity often occurred replied candidly, "Sure . . . Sure they did."[6]

Peppers is an unusual case only because of his level of celebrity— and the fact that his transcript, already made public, makes possible the detailed reconstruction of the course-selection process during the scandal years. But Peppers's course itinerary and the careful eligibility calculations that shaped that itinerary were perfectly typical of the academically challenged athletes in the profit sports. One football star had a sub-2.0 GPA in the spring before his final season. He needed help over the summer and got it with three As and a B in AFAM courses. He took only two courses in his final semester during the fall playing season—earning an A in AFAM 190 (independent study) and an F in a science course. AFAM 190 would push him over the 120 credit hours needed for graduation. Knowing he had those AFAM credits in the bank, the player apparently made no effort at all in his other course. (Eight of the nine As this player earned at UNC came from Nyang'oro; he picked up the other one in the French Novel in Translation.)

Another member of the football team between the late 1990s and the early 2000s had all the expected troubles with normal university courses in his first few semesters at UNC. He earned two Ds in science courses and two more Ds in social science courses. He failed not only a math course but also Acting for Non-Majors (a usually reliable course for students seeking easy fine-arts credits). Helpful boosts from the French Novel in Translation and Physical Education for the Elementary School got his head nearly above water before he effectively launched his major in Julius Nyang'oro studies. In one sequence involving two semesters and a summer, he took five courses with Nyang'oro, on his way to seven total.

Interestingly, in his final fall semester this player failed every single course he took, since by then he was free to do without the pretense that he had come to UNC to be a "student first," as the NCAA loves to proclaim. This, alas, was not an exceptional pattern. Between 1994 and 2005 at least nine football players tanked every single course, earning Fs or FAS across the board, in their final fall semesters—during which they concentrated on what really mattered to them: football. (The FA grade, meaning "unable to pass the course even with a passing grade on the final exam," indicated that they had not bothered to go to class at all.)

Academic counselors in the ASPSA were sometimes reluctant to go back to the well of the paper-class curriculum, and many of them used the additional time afforded their players through this parallel system to get in extra lessons and additional tutoring. The objective of educating their charges, in other words, was never completely abandoned in light of the unhappy curricular imperatives they faced. Still, the examples of Julius Peppers and his friends from the football team show the full functioning of Nyang'oro and Crowder's parallel curriculum and the various purposes for which academic counselors exploited it. These courses were manipulated to provide athletes all that they needed—credit hours, sufficiently high GPAs, demonstrable progress toward a degree, full-time course schedules—so that they could stay eligible and on the field for the coaches who had recruited them and invested so heavily in their athletic development.

Some of the very best examples of jaw-dropping manipulation involve the men's basketball team, which remained a prime beneficiary of AFRI/AFAM largess at least down to 2008. The period between about 1995 and the early 2000s was in many ways a golden age for the UNC profit sports, with football at last making a national splash and with the basketball team continuing a remarkable run of success. Although there were no national championships in these years, a parade of McDonald's All-Americans and future professionals, including some of the most talented players ever to don the Carolina blue, made indelible marks in the annals of UNC basketball in this era: Rasheed Wallace, Jerry Stackhouse, Jeff McInnis, Shammond Williams, Vince Carter, Antawn Jamison, Ed Cota, Joseph Forte, Ronald Curry, Julius Peppers, Serge Zwikker, Brendan Haywood. While taking Carolina to four more Final Fours between 1995 and 2000, these players and their teammates also lived through the refinement of the paper-class system of NCAA eligibility. Whatever personal benefits they may have gleaned through the generosity of that system, collectively it is clear that they enjoyed a significant edge over their competition. Julius Nyang'oro, Debby Crowder, and Burgess McSwain, as well as all who had consented silently to the elaboration and exploitation of UNC's athlete-friendly curriculum, significantly lightened the academic burdens that Carolina players had to carry. Some burdens proved to be light indeed.

As already noted, the differing subject codes within this single academic unit (AFRI, AFAM, SWAH, and so on) allowed students to pass through a miles-wide loophole in the regulations of UNC's College of Arts and Sciences. In principle, no student was to take more than 39 credit hours (the equivalent of thirteen courses) in the major of his or her choice. To ensure proper distribution of educational experiences across the university curriculum, they were to spread out their course selections among many different disciplines in their four years on campus. The proliferation of subject codes in AFRI/AFAM, however, made it theoretically possible for a student to take 90 or more credit hours from personnel in a single department. (A total of 120 credit hours are required for graduation.) Using a mix of African studies, African American studies, and language courses taught within the department, students could take scores of credit hours in AFRI/AFAM. The total number of credit hours taken there would be limited only by the availability of course offerings from semester to semester and the need to go outside the department to satisfy certain discipline-specific general education requirements; the main hurdles were in math, science, the fine arts, and—until the rise of the Swahili program—foreign languages.

One basketball player, who matriculated in the 1990s, compiled nearly 70 credits from the AFRI/AFAM Department, including courses in SWAH and ten courses each in AFRI and AFAM. (Recall that the instructor in the vast majority of all these courses was the same person—Nyang'oro.) The paper-class schedule helped him in other ways as well. His courses would have satisfied at least three different general education requirements in addition to the foreign language covered by SWAH. He used an AFRI-heavy schedule to get through a particularly tough spring semester when basketball must have occupied most of his time (he failed the only non-AFRI course he took). And a correspondence AFAM course taken during his last term of enrollment helped to push him across the graduation finish line.

Perhaps the most brazen gaming of the system came later, however, in 2004–5, when UNC won its first national championship since the retirement of legendary coach Dean Smith. A close look at that team, and the conditions under which it worked, reveals much about habits of corruption and the means people use to rationalize them.

Paper-Class Champions

Because of all that their triumph represented, the 2005 men's basketball team holds a special place in the hearts of most Carolina fans. The seniors on that team had lived through the first losing season in a half century at UNC, in 2001–2. They endured a painful 8-20 campaign as the tenure of second-year head coach Matt Doherty turned abruptly sour after its very promising beginning. The juniors on the 2004–5 team, all of them standouts, had experienced other agonies. During their freshmen year, in 2002–3, during which they were expected to help restore the luster of the Carolina basketball brand, they struggled with team chemistry and posted an uncharacteristically mediocre 19-16 record. UNC missed the NCAA Tournament once again, and the year ended bitterly after rumors of a brewing player rebellion brought an impromptu intervention from the athletic director (AD), Dick Baddour. After Baddour reevaluated the program atmosphere and held private interviews with the players on the team, including the talented but suddenly disgruntled freshman class, he forced Doherty to resign.

These were difficult days for Carolina athletics. The glories of 1997 were fading fast from memory, and the direction of the marquee profit sport programs had been uncertain for some time. Mack Brown had abandoned Chapel Hill for greener pastures at the end of 1997, and the football team had struggled to maintain his winning ways in the years since. Carolina alumnus John Bunting was brought home to lead the team in 2001, and he had a solid first season. Julius Peppers won the Chuck Bednarik Award as the nation's top defensive player, and UNC topped Auburn in the Peach Bowl. But the auspicious start proved to be misleading. All that had been gained in the Mack Brown era—the national attention, the television exposure, the top-ten rankings, the talent-rich recruiting classes—seemed to have vanished by 2003, when UNC went 2-10 and lost many games by lopsided scores. Attendance at Kenan Memorial Stadium fell sharply, and already by 2005 some were calling for Bunting's head. He would lose his job in 2006 after posting a 3-9 record; UNC's determination to throw off the blanket of mediocrity that had settled on Kenan soon led to the pursuit, and the eventual hiring, of Butch Davis.

In the basketball arena, meanwhile, an unsettled coaching situation had led to a series of embarrassments from a program the university had habitually regarded as a source of pride. Dick Baddour had made no secret of his courting of Kansas basketball coach Roy Williams after longtime Dean Smith assistant and successor Bill Guthridge announced his retirement in 2000. When Williams, after a prolonged public courtship, snubbed UNC and very ostentatiously declared his preference for Kansas, UNC basketball acquired some new tarnish to add to its middling 18-13 regular-season record from Guthridge's last year as coach. When Doherty took over the coaching job, he quickly made headlines by directing an unseemly insult toward Duke cheerleaders, and his volatile personality and up-and-down regular-season record provided many piercing reminders of the calm, collected, and supremely competent Smith, whose long shadow had begun to feel like a bit of an albatross—a legacy impossible to replicate and daunting for those charged with carrying it forward.

For the 2003 basketball team, the behind-the-scenes conflicts with Doherty, and the frequent losses, had clearly taken an emotional toll. The players consented to attend the news conference at which Baddour announced Doherty's departure only after Burgess McSwain—their ubiquitous caretaker, tutor, and guardian angel, now suffering from a debilitating illness—agreed to come sit at their side.[7] The mess surrounding Doherty and his dismissal left the fortunes of Carolina basketball at low ebb. Veterans of the program criticized Baddour for his quick sacrifice of Doherty. Even the usually reticent Michael Jordan observed, "I'm a firm believer that 18-year-old kids shouldn't be able to determine a coach's future."[8] The apparent chaos in the heart of the basketball program was as unsettling at it was uncharacteristic. Some of the players on the team had to be wondering whether they still really belonged in Chapel Hill. There had been several notable transfers out of North Carolina in 2002, and the prospect of a larger exodus seemed all too real in 2003.

Dick Baddour immediately sought to set things right by resuming his pursuit of Roy Williams. This time the recruitment of Williams, the favored protégé of Dean Smith, had an air of desperation about it. Baddour had made three highly questionable hiring decisions in the high-profile profit sports just since 1998, and the pressure to score at least one unqualified success—especially in the program that had always been the crown jewel of UNC athletics—had to be overwhelming. Baddour pulled out all the stops and lavished much public attention on Williams. He thereby thrust both UNC and Kansas into an uncomfortable contest of tug-of-war over the coach's services. The prospects for hurt feelings and bruised (or bloated) egos were high, and this only increased the stakes of the courtship. With media vultures circling, and with everyone commenting on the déjà vu character of the whole episode, university leaders had to be holding their breath in anticipation of another public humiliation. Had Baddour failed again, one suspects that it might well have cost him his job.

When Roy Williams finally stopped playing hard to get and took over the reins of UNC's fractured basketball team in April 2003, hope was at last rekindled. Basketball fans were thirsting for redemption, and in the course of the next two years the institution as a whole yearned for the taste of athletic triumph. In 2004 even the women's soccer team would experience unaccustomed adversity when it was bounced from the NCAA Tournament in the third round—the first time it had failed to make the NCAA Final Four in the twenty-two-year history of the tournament. After the recent spate of coach firings, dashed expectations, and crushing losses, Tar Heels everywhere were anxious to see Roy Williams step in and restore order.

Debby Crowder, Julius Nyang'oro, and their many friends in the ASPSA could hardly have been immune to the desperate feelings recently generated in and around the Athletic Department. Email records show McSwain and Crowder regularly exchanging messages about the Doherty situation and the coaching search in 2003. They fed each other tips, rumors, and public commentary about the drama swirling around the program, making clear their own status as rabid fans. (The tips generally came to them through the courtesy of UNC boosters and Athletic Department insiders.)[9] With Williams now back in town and ready to right the ship, McSwain and Crowder put in extraordinary efforts to keep athletes on course academically and fully supported psychologically. They had long ago worked out the kinks in the curricular system the athletes used, and they were now prepared to open the throttle and help Carolina athletes race toward glory. Men's basketball's magical run through the 2005 NCAA Tournament was assisted, in ways both direct and indirect, by the fruitful partnership between the ASPSA and the leadership of AFRI/AFAM.[10]

All the features of the system developed in the 1990s and early 2000s were still there—the inordinate number of AFRI/AFAM courses taken by most members of the team, the summer schedules with paper classes virtually dedicated to athletes, the heavy doses of independent study and "special topics" courses, the enormous discrepancy between the generous grades earned in paper classes versus those earned in all other university courses, and the almost uniform use of Swahili for foreign-language requirements. This team even began to rely with extra frequency on an accelerated SWAH 001–002 sequence that allowed the elimination of foreign-language requirements within two semesters.

Despite the familiar features, two things seemed new by 2004–5. First, Nyang'oro and Crowder abandoned all restraint in their distribution of grades. One striking contrast demonstrates the change. The 1998 team had compiled dozens of paper classes in its journey through the UNC curriculum. But a representative selection of players from that team shows that Bs and B+s predominated in the late 1990s. The players from the 1998 team who took at least a half dozen paper classes produced a solid B grade average in those courses as opposed to a mediocre C- average in courses they took outside of AFRI/AFAM. Five or so years later, however, different rules were clearly in operation.

A single statistic underlines the enormity of the fraud from which the 2005 team benefited. A handful of players from the team took a total of thirty-one paper classes over a few semesters and summer sessions. All thirty-one grades awarded, without exception, were either A or A-. Rashad McCants, a star forward on the championship team, followed a paper classes–only schedule during the spring semester of 2005, meaning that he was relieved of all academic burdens in the season in which he pursued his national championship dreams. Perversely, McCants saw his GPA rise significantly—he even made the dean's list—after a semester in which he had done no academic work. In June 2014 McCants disarmingly explained to ESPN's Steve Delsohn the logic of the arrangement. Tutors, he noted, did help some athletes with grammar and sentence structure on their paper-class assignments, but "for some of the premier players—we didn't write our papers."[11] Instead, papers were recycled from earlier semesters or cobbled together by tutors. A more daringly dishonest curricular system can scarcely be imagined. It would seem as though the basketball players on the 2005 championship team were receiving extra compensation for having stayed at UNC during difficult times. Whatever the motives behind the awarding of the generous grades, however, the effects are undeniable. Many basketball players on the 2005 championship team were able to abandon all worries about their grade point averages.

The second clear difference between the earlier and later manifestations of the paper-class system, clearly linked to the increased generosity in grading, was the naked intentionality of the favoritism displayed. The players on the 2004–5 team must have known that their every need had been anticipated and would be addressed. Their academic counselors (first Burgess McSwain, then Wayne Walden) heedlessly stockpiled courses from Julius Nyang'oro's department, with the team as a whole accounting for well over one hundred paper-class registrations. (Virtually everyone on the team also signed up for the French Novel in Translation—which by now practically functioned as an honorary paper class.) By this time the communication lines between Debby Crowder in AFRI/AFAM and athletics personnel in Kenan Field House were always humming and always friendly, with Crowder offering the equivalent of academic room service for the counselors (and sometimes for players) who would put in requests for specific courses that met certain requirements or filled specific needs.[12] New courses had been added to the curriculum over the years—African American Bioethics, the course Marvin Austin would later make famous, was rapidly becoming a favorite—and this made it even easier to accommodate the scheduling and general education requirements of favored students.

Just as important, with more than a decade of curricular experimentation under their belts, Crowder and Nyang'oro also knew that their activities had drawn nothing but positive attention from other academic officials on the campus. In addition to the tangible favors that flowed from the ASPSA, the list of casual bystanders who offered no resistance where resistance might have been expected was quite long. At least some of the regular academic advisers in Steele Building were fully aware of the games being played in AFRI/AFAM. Some advisers there put in calls to Debby Crowder's office whenever one of their own flailing students needed to be bailed out with one of the famous independent studies so often used by athletes. The dean of advising, Carolyn Cannon, met each semester with the players from the basketball team—one rank-and-file adviser has reported, "We were told that we were never to talk to the basketball players. That was Carolyn's job"—and she evidently never voiced a word of protest about their schedules or explored their strangely lopsided grade histories.[13] (Cannon also accepted many an Athletic Department gift—tickets, paraphernalia, and more tickets.) Meanwhile, the longtime graduation clearance officer in Steele Building had checked every athletic transcript since the late 1980s, at least among those athletes who presented themselves for graduation. She had to have seen the changing patterns of enrollments, grades, majors, and foreign-language classes. But like everyone else, she shrugged her shoulders. (If by chance she reported concerns to a dean, that dean remained silent.)

Other administrative offices were also conspicuous in their silence. Summer school deans had scheduled athlete-heavy AFRI/AFAM courses for years, paying attention to enrollments all the while, and they apparently never questioned the odd enrollment patterns. Officials in the registrar's office posted the grades for those courses, and no one bothered to ask why one independent study section, for example, had had ninety-five students in it. Registrar and Steele Building officials had also processed temporary grade changes by the bushel from the AFRI/AFAM Department—at far higher rates than for any other department—and no one had ever asked why this was happening. Finally, the deans of the College of Arts and Sciences rewarded Nyang'oro with reappointment to his chair position in 1997 and 2002 (and he would be reappointed again in 2007), strongly suggesting firm administrative approval of the chair's conduct. Thus, having every reason to think that others were more or less on board with their program, and quite certain that no one had shown any interest in disrupting it, by 2004 and 2005 Crowder and Nyang'oro had grown much more confident, and much less subtle, in the bestowal of their curricular bounty. The benefits of their confidence accrued to the 2005 basketball team.

One player, for example, after a disastrous semester in his first year, was rescued the next semester through a most familiar mechanism. He took the French Novel in Translation, an Exercise and Sport Science course typically packed with athletes, and two AFAM paper classes. With As earned across the board, his problems were solved forevermore. Thanks to seven additional paper classes scheduled in subsequent semesters, and an A- paper-class grade average, he kept the hounds at bay without difficulty. In fact, few players from this cohort of students ever found themselves at real risk of losing eligibility; in general, their course records were marked from the beginning with superlative AFRI/AFAM grades in high number. The perils of life on the eligibility bubble had been removed preemptively.

The 2004–5 UNC basketball team was a supremely talented group. Showing resilience and determination, they rebounded from disappointment to have a stellar season in which they won more than thirty games. Hard-fought, narrow victories over Villanova and Wisconsin landed them in the NCAA's Final Four in St. Louis, and after beating an excellent Illinois team in an exciting final game, they were celebrated as national champions. Roy Williams had led UNC back to the promised land and at a much faster clip than anyone could have rightfully expected. The victory in St. Louis elicited a powerful, collective catharsis for the team and for the entire UNC community. On his retirement in 2013, assistant basketball coach Joe Holladay, when asked to name the most memorable moment he had experienced in his two decades of coaching at Roy Williams's side, did not hesitate: "I think a real turning point in coach Williams's career, and for all of us, was in 2005 when we won it. . . . Winning that first one took all the pressure off. Besides being happy, there was a relief there for all of us who had been with him a long time."[14] Tar Heel fans everywhere felt a similar sensation of joy mixed with relief at the conclusion of that memorable 2005 tournament.

Unbeknownst to the world, Roy Williams's charges in 2005 had also earned the distinction of having become the team that best exemplified the streamlined efficiency, the purpose, and the high moral costs of UNC's long-developing paper-class system of eligibility. There were no public parades and no Franklin Street bonfires marking this particular achievement; the university, in fact, would have much preferred that it remain concealed from view. But the 2005 men's basketball team richly deserves the dubious title of all-time paper-class champion of the UNC curriculum.

. . .

From modest beginnings in the early 1990s, a slate of course offerings in the AFRI/AFAM Department grew into a large parallel curriculum whose purpose was to lighten burdens and boost GPAs for legions of students who "needed" or "deserved" help. Incubating in an academic unit where oversight was lax, governance was autocratic, and many students sought shelter from a wider institutional environment they perceived as unsympathetic if not hostile, the generous course arrangements that marked the first years of the Nyang'oro-Crowder-McSwain partnership were bound to flourish and multiply. Although many nonathletes would eventually come to feed at the trough of the paper-class system, even outnumbering athletes in many course sections, the main features of the course fraud were all piloted in independent study courses that had been offered first for the benefit of basketball players. Athletes would always benefit disproportionately from Nyang'oro-Crowder largess.

Absent personal testimony from the designers of the system, outsiders can only surmise their reasons for acting as they did. But common knowledge about their personal friendships, political proclivities, sporting enthusiasms, and sympathetic demeanors provides essential clues about the forces that disposed them to move in the direction they moved. They invented an under-the-radar mechanism that allowed challenged students to accumulate grades and credit hours they desperately needed and would have been hard-pressed to earn elsewhere in more straightforward ways. Nyang'oro and Crowder knew, Burgess McSwain certainly knew, and others also knew exactly who constituted their most obvious clientele. The administrative offices of AFRI/AFAM and ASPSA were a match made if not in heaven, then at least through an almost mystical melding of necessity, opportunity, and convenience, all wrapped up with a bow of moral compromise.

Chapters 1 and 2 have revealed the heart of the UNC course-fraud scheme; they show what the UNC scandal was technically all about. The next chapter begins to reveal how UNC leaders responded to revelations of the scandal when details began to dribble out in 2010–11. From very early on in the process, readers will see, they betrayed an instinct to conceal. At the conclusion of the deeply troubling story of UNC's efforts to cover and distract, we will see at close range exactly what the university was so determined to hide.

Three

The Making of a Cover-up

News headlines in the second week of July 2011 reignited a scandal story already thirteen months old. UNC football player Michael McAdoo, one of thirteen players suspended by the university in August 2010 as the NCAA began an investigation of alleged improprieties in the athletic program, had filed suit against both the university and the NCAA in an effort to win reinstatement to the team. A scapegoat who had already been badly victimized by UNC's blame-the-players culture and by the arbitrariness of the NCAA, McAdoo's courtroom experience would lead to his being tarred unfairly for his participation in a system of corner cutting constructed long before he had ever stepped foot in Chapel Hill. The nature of McAdoo's written work in a 2009 language course, which had been evaluated by the student Honor Court in connection with the university's internal investigation of its suspended players, was set to be the focus of a superior court session scheduled for July 14. Stories in the *Raleigh News & Observer* now refocused the public's attention on the underside of the UNC scandal—the whole academic dimension about which, until now, so little had been revealed.

McAdoo would not be the only football player in the news in the summer of 2011. In August Dan Kane of the *N&O* would also reveal that star defensive lineman Marvin Austin had received a B+ in an advanced 400-level AFAM course in the summer before his freshman year—even though his mediocre SAT scores had placed him in a remedial composition class that he had not yet taken. Together, the McAdoo and Austin stories put the UNC scandal on a new trajectory, one focused on the academic shenanigans that formed part of the athletic culture on campus. But it was the McAdoo case that offered the richest clues about the kind of academic corruption in which UNC had engaged. The McAdoo trial documents, the public exposure of which had never been anticipated by the university or its agents, offered a peephole into a strange world that was never intended for prying eyes.

For reasons symptomatic of UNC's entire handling of its scandal, the practices and assumptions revealed through the McAdoo case have never been fully confronted or explained. The university's account of events in December 2010 and its efforts to limit responsibility and blame for misdeeds committed nevertheless show just how badly misshapen UNC's priorities had become under the subtle and not-so-subtle pressures of the big-time sport enterprise. A wide institutional strategy of deception, already in development by the fall of 2010, emerged into the open only through the retrospective lens provided by the documents in the McAdoo case.

The First Signs of Trouble

There had been early signs of institutional dishonesty on the road to the summer of McAdoo, but in the first stages of the UNC scandal few had been on the lookout for suspicious words and deeds. The dancing and disguising had nevertheless begun almost immediately, soon after UNC chancellor Holden Thorp had to make the humiliating announcement that Carolina's football scandal, which had started in June 2010 as a garden-variety case of improper benefits and secretive contacts with sports agents, had spread to academics. "To anyone who loves this university," he gravely declared on August 26, "I'm sorry about what I have to tell you." What he told the UNC faithful that August day shocked a community that had been in the NCAA's good graces for a half century. A tutor employed in the home of head football coach Butch Davis, one who had formerly worked in UNC's Academic Support Program for Student Athletes, was suspected of having provided improper assistance to one or more players during the completion of some writing assignments.

The people listening to the chancellor's announcement had no idea which players were implicated in the alleged academic improprieties, they did not know the name of the tutor, they did not know that anyone had engaged in plagiarism, and they certainly did not know that the written work had been completed for a no-show class that had no real instructor. All of those (un)savory details—which were known right away by some athletic officials and should also have been known early on by various academic administrators—would be doled out only later. The details always came piecemeal, like foul air escaping from a sinking balloon.

What the world did know by September 2010, however, was that the chancellor and the athletic director, Dick Baddour, had decided to retain the football coach, Butch Davis, and that they planned to refer the new allegations of academic dishonesty to UNC's undergraduate Honor Court. The decision to stand by Davis, unconventional as it was, at least suggested restraint and fair-mindedness on the chancellor's part and brought no discernible pushback on the part of faculty. But the decision to refer the academic matters to the Honor Court offered perhaps the first hint that something was not quite right in Chapel Hill. Honor Court proceedings had the great advantage of secrecy, after all. The UNC Honor System was led by undergraduate students who had more goodwill than expertise. Hearings were conducted behind closed doors with no faculty or administrators present. (The secretive nature of Honor Court proceedings also ensured that the administration could conveniently claim it was not at liberty to disclose details.) The students in the Honor System were given training and some guidance by the staff of the dean of students, but the prospect that athletic officials might seek to exercise backdoor influence—either on the students or on the staff—was all too real. Even more troubling, the merits of the Honor Court had been hotly debated throughout the 2009–10 academic year. Several mishandled cases had sparked protest that led to a series of campus studies, a survey of faculty opinion about the Honor System, and ultimately, by 2013, a slate of sweeping reforms to a system that had been left largely untouched since the early 1970s.[1]

A Faculty Council meeting held on October 8, 2010, provided the first opportunity for skeptics to challenge the chancellor on his Honor Court strategy. Historian Jay Smith went to the meeting thinking he would likely have to wait in line to pose questions, but this council meeting—like virtually every such meeting throughout the five-year tenure of Holden Thorp—was a remarkably quiescent affair. The collective reluctance to challenge Thorp and to demand full disclosure of details was, perhaps, understandable. In general, faculty were delighted to have *this* chancellor at the ship's helm as the institution traversed a suddenly stormy sea.

An instinctive respect for and deference toward Thorp had characterized the entire UNC community since his rise to the chancellorship in 2008. A Fayetteville native, a UNC graduate, director of the beloved Morehead Planetarium, a successful chair of the Chemistry Department, and a much-liked dean of the College of Arts and Sciences for one year in 2007, Thorp rode into office on an unprecedented wave of goodwill. At his installation ceremony, novelist Allan Gurganus quite literally described the man as flawless. He was so perfect—virtuous, smart, locally nurtured, musical, unflappable, wise, the ultimate Renaissance man—that he would "never make a believable fictional character." Gurganus had known Thorp all his life, he noted, "and his faults keep NOT emerging. It's almost disappointing!" The state's "hardest job comes today to the one person blessedly ready and singularly prepared to most brilliantly fulfill it." The community now awaited the unfolding of the chancellor's greatness in a state approximating euphoria. "What might he not achieve, that one? Could I get an Amen?" Gurganus gushed. "Today, we're all Beholden."[2] There were grains of truth in what Gurganus said that day, but in retrospect the rapturous ascension of the homegrown hero was not a good thing for the chancellor or for the institution he led. The myths of perfection that both Thorp and "the people's university" struggled to sustain over the next several years proved to be incompatible with self-criticism, ugly failure, and the exposure of warts.

Still wearing a halo in October 2010, Holden Thorp enjoyed every benefit of the doubt as the manager of the developing scandal. Jay Smith, a rank-and-file faculty member who was unaccustomed to making waves and respected the chancellor as much as everyone else, still thought that good citizens of the university needed to press for a full accounting of Thorp's decision making to this point in the story. The suspect tutor's status as a personal employee of the head football coach was enough by itself to propel a certain curiosity, and so Smith asked a few direct and pointed questions. Exactly how had the football players' academic dishonesty come to light? Had a faculty member been the complaining party who alerted officials to potential misconduct? Perhaps most important, would faculty have a meaningful role to play in the investigative phase of the inquiry into the athletic wrongdoing? The chancellor responded to Smith's questions with carefully worded evasions. The Honor System, he affirmed, was "an important tradition" at UNC, and he had "complete confidence" in it. UNC undergraduates who served the Honor System took their responsibilities seriously. He and athletic director Dick Baddour had decided that the right thing was to "do what we always do in these situations" and let the Honor Court render its ruling after considering the facts. Faculty generally had no role in Honor Court deliberations "unless they are called to testify," another faculty member pointed out. (This faculty member was visibly irritated at Smith's questioning of the chancellor.) The university was willing to turn things over to the students and to let the chips fall where they may.

These bland pronouncements could have emerged straight from the UNC student handbook. They were all technically true and hardly unsettling. The more alarming answers came in response to the questions about the discovery and reporting of the incidents in question. The alleged infractions had come to light, faculty were told, when Athletic Department officials—prompted by NCAA queries—reviewed emails exchanged between players and their tutors. Some of those emails had provided indirect evidence of unauthorized academic assistance offered by one tutor, and follow-up interviews with players had apparently added to the suspicions. The chancellor was asked directly whether the faculty member teaching the course had suspected wrongdoing and whether that instructor had joined the case as a complaining party. "No," came the response. To faculty members who were skeptical about the lengths to which UNC might go to support its athletic program, this was an ominous sign. At UNC as at other universities with Honor Codes, the vast majority of academic dishonesty cases are referred to the Honor System by faculty members who suspect their students of cheating, the absence of the affected faculty member in the strange case of the misbehaving football players signaled that something was off-kilter. How was it possible that the professor teaching the course had had no role in identifying the suspected wrongdoing?

We know today why there was no faculty complainant. The course in which the most serious academic dishonesty occurred (Swahili 403) was not really a course. The summer 2009 version of Swahili 403 would later be revealed as having been instructorless; no faculty member in the department has ever admitted responsibility for the course, and no instructor has admitted assigning a grade. The SWAH 403 had been a classic paper class—this one evidently administered from beginning to end by Debby Crowder. So, no, there would be no faculty member defending the integrity of the university's courses. How could there be?

The chancellor did not say this much in October 2010. In retrospect, it seems unlikely that he knew the full details. But in the course of the Honor Court proceedings, and in the course of the university's preparation for the Honor Court hearing, many university officials had to have learned a series of strange facts that should have set off alarm bells. When an alleged academic infraction occurs in a normal university course, the "defense counsel" assigned to the case in the office of the student attorney general typically collects relevant documents from the course—including the course syllabus with its course description, the exact assignment for which the student sought improper assistance, and any documentary guidance the faculty member might have provided to students about the rules to be followed when working on writing assignments. Had a request been made for these materials, all concerned would have quickly realized that the course had had no faculty supervision whatsoever.

The course syllabus for SWAH 403, after all, was nonexistent. (What sort of syllabus would lay out the strictly non-Swahili content of a third-level Swahili language course?) The assignment guidelines, whatever their nature, came not from a professor's office but from the ASPSA. The transcript for the Honor Court hearing would later indicate that tutor Jennifer Wiley was the person who "set dead-lines for certain components" of the written work.[3] It is simply inconceivable that the university's leaders were so distracted that they failed to recognize in the fall of 2010 that the SWAH 403 from the summer of 2009 had been a scandalously unsupervised course. Julius Nyang'oro, whose name was on the paper submitted by the suspect football player, had to have been contacted by someone at some point—by the chancellor, by the athletic director, by the student attorney general, by someone. Failure to reach out to the professor would have constituted gross negligence. If no one sought him out, what could possibly have been the university's excuse for having no interest at all in the professor's perspective? If Nyang'oro was questioned, was he already denying that he had taught the SWAH course? If not, did he try to explain the absence of a syllabus? Whatever answers they did or did not get from the AFRI/AFAM chair, how did academic officials fail, at this critical early moment, to launch a thorough probe of ASPSA activities and of Nyang'oro's teaching habits? This failure is hard to fathom—unless, of course, they had actually learned nothing new when they recognized that SWAH 403 was a paper class.

Telling signs suggest that university leaders, at least some of them, did fully understand the gravity of the academic wrongdoing that had been uncovered, but that their priority was to minimize problems rather than to expose and correct them. In November 2013 a student investigative reporter for the campus online publication *Synapse Magazine* revealed that the university had already made the decision in the summer or fall of 2010 to hire an attorney, Rick Evrard, whose most important credential seems to have been that he had "worked as an NCAA investigator for seven years." A few months later, in January 2011, the university hired a second lawyer for its consulting team, William King of Birmingham, Alabama. Both Evrard and King had experience "dealing with the NCAA," and they both had the ability to anticipate "the damage the NCAA could inflict." The university would go on to spend nearly a half-million dollars on these two legal specialists, and the investment speaks volumes about the institution's priorities.[4] Over the next three and a half years, university leaders signaled repeatedly that their values had been thrown out of balance. Disclosing the truth, revealing the full extent of all problems, responding to faculty critics, and answering to the citizens of North Carolina would always take a back seat to the overriding imperative to protect the Athletic Department from the NCAA. Within months, if not weeks, of the NCAA's move to notify the university of the problems it had detected, the university adopted a siege mentality. By the end of 2010, fending off the enemy had taken precedence over all other concerns.

Uncertainty persists about exactly what academic officials knew and when they knew it. In the fall of 2010, Chancellor Thorp certainly had a full plate of other concerns and was inclined to delegate the whole matter to Dick Baddour. Other academic officials may not yet have known about the peculiar organizational features of the famous SWAH 403 course, and even if they did they may have been awaiting some signal from the chancellor.

Athletics officials, however, should not be extended any benefit of the doubt. People connected to the ASPSA would later admit that the academic counselors who worked with athletes in Kenan Field House knowingly signed them up for paper classes.[5] Those counselors knew full well that Debby Crowder, their longtime contact in the AFRI/AFAM Department, was the go-to person for students needing access to such courses. When Thorp and Baddour stood in front of the Faculty Council and announced their decision to refer the 2009 academic infractions to the Honor Court—thus shielding the entire affair from curious faculty eyes—Baddour's deputies in student services had already known for years that some courses in the African and Afro-American Studies Department were seriously suspect. They already knew that no real teaching had been going on in those courses, and they also knew that their athletes had been benefiting from ridiculously low performance standards since the 1990s. If Dick Baddour himself did not know these realities, and it is possible that he did not, one has to wonder what other sorts of things athletics staff routinely hide from their bosses.

By October 2010 university officials knew other things, too. In September, about a month after the academic improprieties had first come to light, UNC's internal investigation eventually led university representatives to Mary Willingham's door. As a learning specialist who had worked closely with the athletes most challenged in the classroom, Willingham had an intimate knowledge of athletes' course itineraries, their working relationships with tutors and other personnel in the ASPSA, and the structural limits placed on their educational options. On September 30, just a week before the chancellor and the athletic director were to face the Faculty Council, Willingham met with the investigative duo Lissa Broome (a law professor who was also UNC's faculty athletics representative) and Steve Keadey (a lawyer from the Office of University Counsel). They had been charged to find out what they could about the nature of UNC's wrongdoing and to prepare a report for the NCAA.

In this two-hour conversation, preserved for posterity on two different digital recordings, Willingham shared many troubling details about the practices of the support program. She told Broome and Keadey about the excessively cozy relationships that had developed between players and mentor-tutors. She told them about her discovery of one football player's plagiarism in 2008 and the failure of her bosses to do anything about it. (After her initial reporting of this 2008 incident, the managers of the ASPSA saw to it that Willingham saw no more football players.) She told Broome and Keadey about the firing of a study-hall monitor who had made the fatal mistake of reporting to her superior that she had seen a football player receiving improper writing help from a mentor-tutor. (Willingham's disclosure of this outrage should have caused a scandal in its own right.) Willingham also noted the chilling effect the firing of the unfortunate study-hall monitor had had on her own attitude at work—"I need this job for the benefits," she volunteered.

There was more. Willingham told Broome and Keadey about the routine flouting of NCAA rules regarding extra benefits to players (mentor-tutors were forever bringing in food to study sessions) and respect for academic-athletic boundaries (players and the mentor-tutors, all women, socialized regularly, and the players gave them their "family" game tickets in clear violation of NCAA rules). She told them about the many times she had gone to her supervisors to complain about suspected cheating and slipping standards and her superiors' determined refusal to confront evidence of corruption. She decried the woeful lack of leadership in and around the support program ("The coaches are in charge," she lamented). She also told Broome and Keadey about the low state of academic preparedness among many of the athletes, a challenging situation that practically required wholesale fraud.

Willingham spoke breathlessly during this interview. Having been frustrated for years, she was relieved finally to share her perspective, and the details poured forth. She had had to ask for this meeting through a third party—tellingly, no one from athletics had suggested that investigators talk to her—but the optimism in her voice was obvious and poignant. She expected UNC to take this new information, reflect on its failures, and get its house in order. Athletic director Dick Baddour, after all, had announced at an August news conference that "we will certainly use the opportunity [of this scandal] to take a complete look at everything that we're doing in the academic support program."[6] Broome and Keadey seemed oddly limited in their own curiosity, asking only narrow follow-up questions. They focused on Jennifer Wiley and whether Willingham could help them identify other Jennifer Wileys lurking in the support program. Not once did they ask directly, "Was the support program corrupt?" or "Was cheating pretty common?" or "Do you think your superiors were dishonest?" or "Should they be held accountable?" or "Is this system even workable?" Willingham nevertheless left her meeting with the two UNC officials feeling hopeful that meaningful reforms would ensue and fully expecting that there would be other opportunities to talk.

Yet nothing happened. UNC's grand strategy to "see no evil, hear no evil, speak no evil" first put itself on display in the handling of the encounter between Willingham, Broome, and Keadey. Officials have since claimed that the NCAA was provided all information collected by UNC in the summer and fall of 2010—including Willingham's detailed testimony—and that may well be true (though if it is, the NCAA has some explaining to do). But outside of the NCAA's Indianapolis headquarters, no one seems to have learned of Mary Willingham and her privileged perspective on UNC athletics. Her testimony disappeared into an administrative black hole. She was never contacted for a follow-up interview—even after the scandal mushroomed in 2011 and the scale of UNC's academic dishonesty began to attract national attention. Key administrators never reached out to her to learn more about what she had seen and heard. Subsequent investigators, including an ad hoc working group convened by the chancellor in the summer of 2011, were apparently never told, "You must speak to Mary Willingham." (This is especially curious given that one of the members of the working group was Steve Keadey's superior—the university general counsel, Leslie Strohm.) For more than two years after Willingham's conversation with Keadey and Broome, the UNC community and the wider world remained in the dark about all the suspect procedures in the ASPSA, until Willingham at last relented to journalistic pressure and shared some of her experiences with Dan Kane of the N&O.

Whether through cunning calculation or through a conspiracy of silence and averted gazes, UNC officials had decided to feign local ignorance of Mary Willingham's troubling allegations and to hope that she would simply go away. (In January 2010 she had accepted a new position in the university's Learning Center; maybe her memories would fade.) The news of what she had reported was not shared with anyone who might have demanded action in response to it. The reasons are not hard to guess. Willingham had clearly implicated ASPSA personnel in academic fraud. She had called out her superiors for gross negligence. She had drawn attention to a pattern of both petty and serious NCAA violations. Through simple inference anyone could see that her testimony potentially cast doubt on the eligibility status of many players enrolled at the university over a period of at least several years. Her allegations suggested systematic corruption, perhaps even a "lack of institutional control" in NCAA parlance. The university leaders who learned of Willingham's testimony would have wanted no part of that. Much better to deal with the situation by scapegoating a few football players and forcing them to face the music, alone and unprotected, before the secretive Honor Court. Suspensions and probation might be embarrassing, but the damage to the institution and to the athletic program would at least be contained.

At this early point in the history of the scandal, UNC chose to surrender its claim to the moral high ground and gave up its best chance to deal openly, honestly, and creatively with its disaster.

Whoever learned of Willingham's September 2010 revelations might have briefed the Faculty Athletics Committee (FAC) or the full Faculty Council on what they had heard. They might have pushed for a sweeping review of UNC's institutional culture. They might have initiated a housecleaning designed to change the way UNC does business. They might have tried to set a salutary national example of structural reform in college sport. Instead, they followed their instinct to conceal, to continue a focused search for scapegoats, and to deny reality.

In October 2010, though, all of this was unknown to casual observers. Outsiders could not see the opportunities already missed; the institutional instinct to cover up problems and tamp down concerns went undetected. Willingham remained an anonymous figure in the shadows. Smith, vaguely uneasy and seeking reassurance from Thorp, sent a letter to the chancellor's office that pointed out the peculiarities of the facts so far divulged. That the cheating had been discovered by happenstance, for example, certainly seemed symptomatic of a far greater problem. "Everything about it," he wrote, "the fact that the offending tutor worked in the home of the head coach, that multiple players (evidently) thought nothing of having a tutor write papers for them, that the discovery of the misconduct was inadvertent—suggests that we're seeing only the tip of an iceberg."[7] Smith asked for a deeper probe. If the chancellor had any inclination to dive beneath the surface to measure the full dimensions of the problems in UNC's path, however, he ignored the urge. Instead, he referred Smith's letter to athletic director Dick Baddour (thereby illustrating in 2010 the belief for which he gained notoriety in 2013—namely, that all athletic matters should simply be left in the hands of athletic directors).

The AD, in turn, had his senior associate athletic director, John Blanchard, call Smith at his History Department office.[8] Blanchard, who was in charge of student services in the athletics complex, jovially suggested a face-to-face chat, and Smith took him up on the offer. Blanchard is a genial and charismatic man, a former Stanford football player with many years of experience in athletic administration. He has a disarming sense of humor, and he exudes sincerity. But there was no mistaking the purpose of the meeting.

Blanchard wanted to assure Smith that he was worrying needlessly, that many people in the Athletic Department were working hard to address the problems that had come to light. Professors had been complaining about athletics since time immemorial, Blanchard noted—pointing out that the first athletics scandal had involved the Harvard-Yale boat race way back in the 1850s. He did not dismiss Smith's concerns, but he reduced those concerns to the status of perennial irritant—an outgrowth of the inevitable monkey business that just comes with the territory of big-time college sport. Sometimes, he implied more than once during the meeting, misbehaving athletes just need a swift kick in the pants.

Blanchard seemed genuinely interested in improving relations between faculty and people in the athletics office. He asked Smith to keep in touch with him, and he even suggested that he might soon be invited to join a committee Blanchard was cochairing with senior associate dean Bobbi Owen, a committee that had begun to conduct a review of the ASPSA. (That invitation never arrived.) The associate AD clearly wanted Smith to feel reassured about the Athletic Department and to have confidence in the good intentions of the officials there. The Honor Court business arose, he said, because of the actions of a sympathetic and overzealous tutor who had innocently just tried to do too much. She had crossed the line from tutoring to friendship—but her intentions had remained always good.

Blanchard had a soothing and reassuring presentation style, but he told Smith something that day that would rattle around in his brain for many months after. When asked how athletes chose their courses, and whether academic support staff ever steered them in the direction of faculty known to give free rides, Blanchard answered in no uncertain terms: "Oh, no. You should be proud of your colleagues on this campus," he said. "Many years ago there may have been a few soft professors, but I don't know of any, not a single one, on the campus today. UNC faculty are serious about standards. Our student-athletes work hard for their grades." Blanchard's assurances suggested that the recent troubles were indeed anomalous and that he and his colleagues were working hard to stay informed about what athletes were up to in UNC classrooms. His words also appealed to Smith's vanity as a professor who took pride in working at a highly regarded institution. The flattering of his faculty comrades improved his feelings about his institutional surroundings and made it easier for Smith to let down his guard.

In retrospect, in light of what the world now knows about a certain professor who passed out As and Bs like candy for decades, with many a star athlete buoyed or rescued by the gifts he gave, Smith cannot escape the feeling that his desire to believe the best about his institution was taken advantage of that day. Blanchard's alacrity in affirming that "not a single one" of UNC's instructors bent standards for athletes contrasts sharply with the associate AD's own testimony from 2012. During successive investigations that year, Blanchard conveyed to a faculty committee and to former governor Jim Martin that he had tried on two occasions— once in 2002 and then again in 2006—to alert a faculty governance committee to the possibility of suspect instruction in independent study courses. Leaving aside the veracity of that claim—hard evidence would later contradict it—Blanchard's memory in 2012 was that he had been worried about low standards and faculty generosity in 2002 and 2006. He certainly never let on to Smith in 2010 that he had ever had such concerns. On the contrary, he roundly denied the basis for any such concerns.

Blanchard's enthusiastic vouching for faculty integrity when talking with Smith also contrasted with the message frequently communicated to Mary Willingham in the ASPSA. In 2008, for example, Willingham had expressed concerns about how the university would manage to keep eligible a certain basketball player who was struggling with literacy: "Stop worrying, Mary," her supervisor told her. "Professors on this campus would never fail a basketball player. It's not going to happen. Athletics are in charge at this university." The supervisor, Robert Mercer, was the nominal director of the Academic Support Program, but he reported to Blanchard and spoke with him regularly. Blanchard was at least partly responsible for the ambience established in a building where athletic superiority over academics was taken for granted. In the precincts of the ASPSA, professorial integrity was clearly understood as a relative thing.

In the short term, Blanchard's charm offensive did the trick. For most of the next eight months, Smith focused on his work as teacher and historian and trusted the university to plot the proper course forward. Between the late fall of 2010 and the summer of 2011, he followed the occasional news release and listened to rumors, but he generally went about his business and waited patiently for news. But the game changed for everyone in July 2011.

Michael McAdoo v. UNC

The McAdoo case, in which the former Carolina player sued both UNC and the NCAA in an effort to regain his athletic eligibility, exposed sordid details from the football scandal that the university's public pronouncements had thus far concealed. First came the realization that the university had embarrassed itself by failing to notice that McAdoo had cut-and-pasted virtually the entire paper that had prompted the Honor Court inquiry in the first place. The students on the Honor Court found McAdoo guilty of some lesser offenses—most notably, having relied on a tutor to format his footnotes for him. But the much more serious infraction had been missed. The Honor Court, the professional staff members who provide guidance to the court, the chancellor and his small circle of advisers, Dick Baddour, the instructor in the affected course (whose existence the public did not yet doubt): all had failed to notice the strangely archaic language ("The religion of Africa may be unequally divided under three heads: Christianity, Mohammedanism, and Paganism") and the jarringly outdated facts ("Its population of about one hundred and sixty million seems enormous") that filled McAdoo's analysis. Only after the McAdoo documents had been posted online by the Durham County Superior Court did the world learn the full extent of the fraud committed—all thanks to the investigative enthusiasms of the North Carolina State fan base. One determined poster on the Pack Pride fan forum had spent some time with Google and, within minutes, had exposed the McAdoo paper for the complete fabrication that it was. (McAdoo would later insist that he only used the techniques for composing papers that had been modeled for him by academic support staff. Mary Willingham recalls, in fact, that academic counselors instructed mentor-tutors to retrieve the sources for players' papers at the library or on the Internet. Displaying those sources on the screen or scattering them on the desk, they would say, "Here, use these," and the copying would begin.)

Even to hardened skeptics of the Honor Court, it eventually became clear that the students on the court were among the least blameworthy of all UNC representatives in the whole ugly drama. The transcript for McAdoo's December 14, 2010, reinstatement hearing was also included in the dossier posted online, and it supplied a whole new set of outrages. The transcript reveals most of the building blocks for an institutional cover-up and a mentality of denial that would manifest themselves over and over again in the years to come.

Much about the UNC scandal still lay beyond the public's grasp, but already in 2011 the arguments offered by the UNC team in favor of McAdoo's reinstatement seemed to come from the land of make-believe. (In October 2010 the NCAA had announced McAdoo's permanent ban from collegiate football based on what it considered to be his "knowing involvement" in academic fraud.) Dick Baddour, John Blanchard, Steve Keadey, and compliance officer Amy Herman—no faculty were in the room—argued strenuously that McAdoo was being punished unfairly because, after all, he had committed only minor and inadvertent academic infractions. Baddour insisted that "we do not take appeals lightly" and that the desire to safeguard "the integrity of the institution" had been a foremost concern as UNC contemplated whether to contest the NCAA's ruling. The university had challenged the decision because the NCAA had acted on a misunderstanding. McAdoo, Baddour and the others argued, was academically responsible and exceptionally virtuous. He had committed inadvertent errors because one well-meaning but misguided mentor had stepped over the line and offered inappropriate assistance. And even the mentor's errors had seemed to be basically consistent with the university's academic practices.

The description of UNC's academic culture was telling. No one said, "They offer freebie paper classes at our university! The students never even meet the professor! Can you believe it?!" On the contrary, the officials gathered around the telephone pursued a very different strategy. They sought to portray McAdoo's course experiences, and his encounters with tutoring services, as perfectly ordinary and fully in keeping with unobjectionable institutional practices. Keadey explained that "the academic culture here is one that encourages students to seek help with writing assignments, and that's athlete and nonathlete alike. Our Writing Center encourages students to proofread their paper by 'giving the paper to a friend,' that's the way people proceed here." This assertion about "the way people proceed here"—offered in defense of an athlete who had produced uncharacteristically sophisticated prose in the papers he submitted—would have been enough to raise the hackles of most any university professor. Nonathletes do not routinely submit their papers to third parties for editing, grammatical corrections, and additions before they turn in assignments to their professors, nor would professors condone the practice. Even the Writing Center (virtually never used by profit-sport athletes), though it indeed encourages the solicitation of feedback on drafts, warns against having others make modifications to one's paper. The handbook for Writing Center counselors specifies: "It is the student's role, not ours, to make decisions about a text. Accordingly, we do not write on students' papers."[9]

Ignorance about the functioning of the Writing Center would have been excusable on its own, but Keadey's demonstration of the strangely insular understanding of academic practice in the Academic Support Program was just getting under way. With a tone of righteous assurance that would long echo around the campus of NC State, he went on to assert about McAdoo's suspect paper from Swahili 403 that "this work reflects his ideas exclusively. It is not a rip off. This really is his work." The humiliation that the university might have been spared had Keadey asked any humanities or social sciences professor on UNC's campus to review McAdoo's paper is still painful to reflect on—as it was when this testimony first went public in July 2011. Anyone could have instantly told Keadey, "Oh, this is a rip-off, counselor, most definitely not his work."

In fairness it must be said that Keadey was developing a legalistic argument, and since McAdoo had never been formally charged with plagiarizing his paper, the university lawyer's challenge to the NCAA's arbitrary punishment was understandable and justifiable. In fact, to the extent that Keadey and the others wanted to save

McAdoo from having to pay the price for the breakdowns they knew had occurred in the academic support structure, their motives were good and even admirable. But the strategy they developed, whether it came principally from Baddour and Blanchard or from Keadey himself, was nonetheless fundamentally dishonest. They proceeded to describe the culture within the ASPSA as perfectly healthy and geared always toward the academic achievements of the players entrusted to the program.

John Blanchard explained to the NCAA officials that a mentor is assigned to a first-year athlete whenever that athlete "is going to be challenged academically." Blanchard described the mentor as "an academic coach," one who "helps the student organize time, . . . has all the assignments, collects the course syllabi, helps the student plan out the semester in lieu [*sic*] of practice and competition, . . . then monitors progress." McAdoo had trusted Wiley, Keadey added, "because she was the person the university told him to work with from the first day he was on campus." Blanchard explained that the Athletic Department believed such relationships to be "working properly" if "the student feels safe and is able to fully express what he doesn't know, what his questions are." It is "very important to us," Blanchard added, that a "trusting relationship is built."

McAdoo certainly came to trust Wiley. They developed "a good working relationship," according to Keadey, and McAdoo "had every reason to believe that Jennifer Wiley was doing things correctly." One of the chief motives for emphasizing the "trusting" relationship between Wiley and McAdoo, of course, was to lay the blame for academic violations at Wiley's door. Her heart was good—Keadey thought it relevant to mention that "her father is a pastor"—but she "crossed the line," and McAdoo could not have been aware that, in following his tutor, he had skated onto thin ice. "He was a freshman. He had no reason to think that Jennifer would do something different than what was appropriate. He was essentially accepting the help that Jennifer was offering." The pattern of close, hands-on assistance had developed over three courses spanning McAdoo's entire freshman year. "I think we can all understand that students are vulnerable when they are doing academic work like this," and the "help provided" had become "a sort of intimate kind of relationship." McAdoo was only "keeping faith with the academic mission" of the university when he sought guidance.

McAdoo, who was of course desperate to win reinstatement, aided and abetted the university's rhetorical strategy. As he put it in the prepared statement that he read to the NCAA, athletes had to trust the staff to "guide us through our experiences." Leaning on "the information provided to me during my recruiting process," McAdoo had simply trusted "the help I was given." The degree of help needed is suggested in the wording used by McAdoo as he described the assistance provided by Wiley. "For me it was a struggle because I needed somebody to really explain and break down the information to me." This is why he continued to call on Wiley even after he had been assigned to a new tutor and even after Wiley had left the ASPSA to work in the home of Butch Davis. "She had a way of breaking it down so I understood and could come up with my own ideas. . . . She was willing to look over my work and make sure I was straight and I thought that's what most students do." Blanchard said the same. McAdoo needed to "have the information broken down for him," which was why his tutor was "an academic mentor his freshman year."

The university executed a brilliantly coordinated plan. Their basic argument was that McAdoo, conscientious and focused on his studies, "did the work." He could not really be blamed for the trivial misconduct he had committed, since he had only trusted the good-hearted mentor who had worked by his side from his first days on campus. That mentor, they were careful to point out, had received training from a conscientious staff.[10] But in the end the mentor, Wiley, fell into temptation and offered forms of assistance that—though relatively innocent in the grand scheme of things— should never have been offered. This event was an anomaly, basically harmless, and caused by one unfortunately careless former employee. Here was the classic "rogue" defense—a defense typically used by institutions facing discipline from the NCAA.[11]

No one pointed out, of course, that the rogue Jennifer Wiley had been singled out for her exemplary work in 2008 when she was awarded the ASPSA's "Outstanding Tutor" honor; that detail would have sent the team off message. But the detail is significant nonetheless. Wiley's conduct as a tutor, far from having been anomalous, was symptomatic of the governing culture that had been constructed in the ASPSA. That culture and its purposes are revealed in the subtexts lurking just beneath the UNC testimony to the NCAA and in the longer history of the Athletic Department's handling of Michael McAdoo.

A defensive end from Antioch, Tennessee, McAdoo had been a prize recruit for football coach Butch Davis. A lanky and agile player, McAdoo would later be drafted by the NFL's Baltimore Ravens. (His dreams of an NFL career ground to a halt in 2013 after he suffered a series of season-ending injuries that led to his release from the team.) Back in 2008, when he was being recruited to UNC, McAdoo had needed a special clearance to win admission to the university. His academic preparation in high school had been at least somewhat deficient, and he appears to have been one of the so-called committee-case recruits that required review and approval by a small faculty subcommittee that listened to the requests of coaching staffs and granted permissions to admit on a case-by-case basis. McAdoo was identified at the outset, as Blanchard himself acknowledged, as a student in need of extra help.

Like most players with his academic profile, McAdoo quickly found that his major would be more or less chosen for him. He would later explain to Joe Nocera of the *New York Times* that counselors in the ASPSA placed him in African American studies because, he was told, that major worked best with his football practice schedule. (Coincidentally, basketball star Sean May would also later cite the superior convenience of AFRI/AFAM when he explained his choice of major in an interview with the *Indianapolis Star*.)[12] Academic counselors also put McAdoo in Swahili language courses, since athletes had been passing Swahili with flying colors ever since the program had entered the college curriculum in 1995. McAdoo's academic counselor in the ASPSA knew full well that McAdoo would learn no Swahili in Swahili 403. ("There wasn't any class," McAdoo reported to Nocera. "You sign up. You write the paper. You get credit. . . . I had never seen anything like it.") He or she further knew that the paper for which McAdoo would earn his Swahili 403 credits would be written in English. This oddity bears special emphasis. Here the ASPSA was helping McAdoo to circumvent a general education requirement that had been tackled by other UNC graduates, often against their will, for decades. By seeing to it that McAdoo would satisfy his final foreign-language requirement through the composition of an English-language paper submitted for a fake class that never met, the ASPSA and its friends in the AFRI/AFAM Department made an open mockery of the university's graduation requirements. The UNC team, in its appeal to the NCAA on McAdoo's behalf, never felt compelled to explain this peculiarity. The NCAA, with its characteristic fecklessness, failed to notice it.

But enrollment in fake language courses was all just part of the system. Recognizing on day one that McAdoo was going to need some help to stay on the field, the ASPSA had immediately set in motion the gears of the eligibility machine. McAdoo was earmarked for the paper-class curriculum and was guided to three paper classes within his first ten months on campus. (No one mentioned it at the time, of course, but all three of the courses that were the focus of the NCAA's attention in the appeal hearing of 2010—SWAH 403, AFRI 266, AFAM 428—were paper classes.) His course schedule for the 2009–10 academic year has not been made public, but the trial documents from 2010 show that in the fall semester of that year—the very semester in which his Honor Court and NCAA hearings were held—McAdoo was taking at least one additional independent study course.[13] These four courses, probably in addition to others—was McAdoo one of the fourteen athletes in the spring 2010 section of AFRI 370 since identified as fraudulent?—had been chosen for him by academic counselors who exploited independent studies and paper classes for the express purpose of cutting corners.

Exactly what kind of work was McAdoo expected to perform in these classes? What sort of work did counselors and tutors demand from the athletes they were helping? Only in light of such questions do the true contours of McAdoo's relationship with Jennifer Wiley come into view. Steve Keadey had provided a wholesome description of this particular tutoring relationship: "In AFRI 266 [Michael] worked with Jennifer Wiley three days a week. In AFAM 428 he worked with her every day. They developed a good working relationship and Michael had every reason to believe that Jennifer was doing things correctly." But if Keadey's camouflage is peeled away from the relationship that actually developed between Wiley and McAdoo, one finds an underprepared (or possibly indifferent) student and an Athletic Department employee who was laboring to help him meet shockingly minimalist expectations.

McAdoo's Honor Court hearing had focused on email exchanges between the player and the tutor-mentor that had to do with the formatting of footnotes for papers written in two courses—SWAH 403 and AFRI 266. One might reasonably ask how it was even possible that McAdoo still did not know how to cite a book or a website in a footnote in the summer after his freshman year. But the more revealing question is this: Why did Wiley and McAdoo, in all their email exchanges, have so little to say about the actual body of the paper? Why would a student unsure about how to format a footnote not ask for guidance and feedback on the actual content of his composition?

Football academic counselor Beth Bridger, in a 2010 email she wrote to one discouraged tutor, provided a clue to anyone seeking an answer to this essential question. "Just remember, guys are in this class for a reason—at-risk, probation, struggling students—you are making headway . . . keep it positive and encouraging!" Another academic counselor, Jaimie Lee, sounded the same refrain when she sought to reassure another tutor who had expressed concerns to her about an athlete's technique of copying and pasting from the Internet: "[These students] have not necessarily developed the skill of critical analysis." Tutors should therefore "try to get some in there." If the analysis came from elsewhere in the form of "a ton of historical information," that was only "to be expected."[14] Plagiarism, Lee erroneously but revealingly claimed, could be avoided if the source from which material was taken was simply cited in the notes. (McAdoo's academic counselor has never been identified, but Lee, who worked with many football players, provided a statement on McAdoo's behalf to the Honor Court; it seems likely that she was his primary counselor.)

Academic counselors and the tutors who worked with profit-sport athletes understood, in other words, that the papers produced for paper classes were not always, or even often, expected to be original compositions. (In the spring semester of 2005 a women's basketball player revealed to Mary Willingham her own understanding of the expectations in this system. Of the papers she simply noted, "Nobody even reads them." Many athletes would echo the sentiment in the years to come.) The papers could be cobbled together from any available sources on the Internet or from a library, so long as they ostensibly spoke to the assigned topic. (Much of McAdoo's material came from a textbook published in 1911.) Jennifer Wiley, in short, was helping McAdoo perform the one task in the SWAH 403 assignment that required substantially more than pointing and clicking—the writing out of the citations. The nature of McAdoo's own involvement in this task is suggested by his unguarded answer to an impromptu NCAA query about his working relationship with Wiley: "She, uh, told to me you know to go home and try to you know do the citations or whatever, so when I went home that night I just, you know, got some help from [another] tutor and then came back the next day and it was there. We had our um, the citations and everything ready, ready to go." Keadey would earnestly insist to the NCAA: "Michael did the work, all of the work, except for the end." But "the work" had involved lifting things from the Internet, and the "end"—citing the sources for the plagiarized passages—had been accomplished thanks only to Wiley and the unidentified second tutor. Not one but two tutors had collaborated in getting Michael McAdoo what he needed, and what he seems to have assumed was permissible—an acceptable disguise for a plagiarized paper.

This brings us back to the broad dishonesty on display in the UNC teleconference with the NCAA. Keadey had said of the tutoring process, "In AFRI 266 [Michael] worked with Jennifer Wiley three days a week. In AFAM 428 he worked with her every day." McAdoo had reinforced the message: "With everything I have to juggle on my daily basis I really appreciated [Wiley] . . . and the more she got to know me the more she could help me learn what my professor was trying to teach me. Everything she did for me . . . was meant to help me learn." The schedule sounds arduous, the work demanding, the relationships caring and wholesome. What no one mentioned was that AFRI 266, offered in the fall semester of 2008, never met. The course had no content, and the entire semester's demands boiled down to one paper—all of ten pages in length— due on the last day of classes. If Wiley and McAdoo were meeting three times a week, it was not to discuss the nonexistent material from AFRI 266. And as for AFAM 428—the spring 2009 course that required daily meetings with the tutor in Keadey's rendering—it, too, never met. McAdoo had had little if any contact with the professor, who performed literally no teaching. No professor was "trying to teach," and it seems doubtful that any student was trying to learn in AFAM 428. The picture of academic labor that the UNC team conjured that day was an image constructed through smoke and mirrors.

The testimony of McAdoo and his defenders would seem to describe a struggling student who was slowly but surely growing intellectually thanks to a nurturing staff and a demanding curriculum that posed stiff challenges. The player had inadvertently taken an impermissible shortcut, but he was barreling down a path toward academic achievement. Amid all the sweat and toil, he had simply failed to notice that there were a few land mines laced along the path. "This has been a huge learning experience for me," McAdoo said in his prepared statement. "All I want to be is a successful student." He wanted to "continue on the path to earn a degree from this great university." Now that the rogue mentor was at last out of the way, McAdoo simply asked for a chance to resume the pursuit of his degree.

McAdoo's own formal statements, with their uncharacteristically calibrated language and their calculated appeal for sympathy, were obvious products of the Athletic Department rhetorical factory. McAdoo himself cannot be blamed for the false picture presented to the NCAA in December 2010. Instead, the systematic disguising was the work of those who tried to pin all the "misconduct" on the rogue mentor, Jennifer Wiley. Key players involved in the teleconference that day understood that McAdoo had been shepherded through a course schedule designed not for his education but for GPA maintenance and the appearance of academic progress. With all their talk about institutional integrity and hard work and "keeping faith with the academic mission" of the university, the UNC team put on a carefully choreographed performance for the NCAA on the day of the appeal. McAdoo played the part of an athlete who had had experiences fundamentally similar to other students—because that is the pretense the NCAA expects its member institutions to perpetuate. In emphasizing the player's studiousness and his naïveté, the UNC people simply carried out the masquerade they were obliged to perform.

Reality hides just beneath the surface of the UNC team's testimony, however. From the moment of his recruitment, Blanchard and others made clear, Michael McAdoo was taken into the protective custody of the ASPSA. Because he was "going to be challenged," counselors in the ASPSA gave him his major, selected his courses, assigned him a mentor, kept track of his syllabi, and mapped out his schedule of assignments while ensuring that nothing conflicted with practices and games. With McAdoo as with so many other athletes, they also took systematic advantage of fluff courses and used the services of an exceptionally friendly faculty member who helped clear an easy path through the curriculum for a student whose athletic prowess outstripped his abilities as a student.

To understand why athletics officials and lawyers would presume to characterize UNC's academic culture without bothering to invite a faculty member to the discussion, we need only recognize the three things they did not want faculty to know and that they could not afford to acknowledge in the presence of the NCAA: UNC routinely admits athletes who are not up to the challenge of meeting UNC's academic demands; a large "support" infrastructure has been put in place to disguise, defer, and mitigate the many academic problems that ensue from the admission of these athletes; and the university understands that the athletes themselves cannot really be blamed for the academic corner cutting to which they are inevitably reduced. To save the athlete now on trial, they had to continue with their stagecraft—but only in the presence of reliable cast members with much practice in rehearsing the script.

The Michael McAdoo reinstatement hearing had it all: an underprepared or manipulated student, an excluded faculty, a "support" system predicated on hypocrisy, an arbitrary rulebook designed to keep up appearances, a technical discourse dominated by lawyers and athletic officials practiced in the lingo of "compliance," and the surreal sense that all the participants in the hearing saw and understood the need to ignore the subtext of the entire discussion. But that subtext—the imperative to disguise a system built for the purpose of academic malpractice—repeatedly threatened to rise to the surface in Chapel Hill in the eighteen months that followed the pivotal summer of 2011. Soon it would become clear that McAdoo's experiences were symptomatic of much broader problems. The UNC cover-up would need to become even more careful, more calculated, and more deliberate.

Four

Lost Opportunities

The late summer and fall of 2011 saw a continuous stream of bad news for UNC–Chapel Hill, as the stain of scandal continued to widen. Like the blind men feeling the elephant, interested parties on campus had to sort through disconnected scraps of information that continued to dribble out in media reports. Every tiny fragment suggested the existence of a large and menacing creature. A sports agent had taught a course in AFRI/AFAM? The chair of that department had stepped down? Football star Marvin Austin had taken a 400-level course in bioethics in the summer *before* his freshman year? The NCAA was in town again? Those on the outside looking in could be certain of little other than the fact that the full picture of corruption and wrongdoing had not yet come into focus. The only other certitude was that the university had little interest in filling out the picture.

Despite the uncertainties, the 2011–12 academic year saw many glimmers of hopefulness even as frustrations mounted. A small grassroots faculty reform effort began to pick up steam, and the new AD, Bubba Cunningham, who took over for Dick Baddour at mid-year, signaled a willingness to think and speak with an open mind about the future of UNC athletics. In October Taylor Branch's explosive *Atlantic* article, "The Shame of College Sports," had exposed the need for root-and-branch reforms in the college sports-business model.[1] Soon after, the news of the horrors at Penn State raised real hope, at least for a short while, that the accumulated outrages of recent years might force structural changes in the national culture of college sports.

Carolina, in the unaccustomed position of having to be embarrassed about one of its sports programs, seemed well positioned to assert leadership in an emerging national discussion about the role of athletics in university life. In February 2012 the Friends of the Library sponsored an electrifying panel discussion featuring an impassioned and eloquent Taylor Branch (a UNC alum) as well as UNC's own Bill Friday, the revered former president of the UNC system and a longtime critic of commercialized college sports. The standing-room-only crowd listened in rapt attention and reacted warmly to the panelists' various denunciations of the college sports status quo. When NCAA scold Joe Nocera visited the campus a few weeks later, he remarked that Chapel Hill seemed suddenly to have become a "hotbed of reform." It was not hard to imagine, for those looking toward the horizon in the fall of 2011, that real change was coming and that UNC could help set the course for the future.

Yet the obstacles to reform remained formidable. The big-time conferences were too busy carving up their shares of TV revenue to pay any attention either to the welfare of athletes or to the erosion (or absence) of academic standards in the classrooms of their member schools. The NCAA was refining its defense of what it likes to call "the collegiate model of sport." Locally, UNC's leaders were busy worrying about the ongoing NCAA investigation of the football program and the possible consequences of the wrongdoing exposed since 2010. To initiate a movement for real reform, someone at a big-time institution would need to display attention-getting courage and candor, but despite 2011's cascading embarrassments at Ohio State, Miami, Penn State, and UNC, no fearless crusader had stepped forward to take the mantle.

Over a period of about six weeks, beginning in mid-September 2011, Jay Smith had a series of meetings with UNC leaders that left him deeply pessimistic about the prospects for bold action in Chapel Hill. Back in the middle of July, after the McAdoo plagiarism case had hit the newspapers and just days before Holden Thorp made the decision to oust football coach Butch Davis, Smith had contacted the chancellor to express his concerns about the latest news. He urged the chancellor to convene a faculty committee to conduct a thorough review of the many places where athletics and academics intersected on the UNC campus. Thorp expressed interest in the idea, but he noted the importance of getting all the critical "stakeholders" on board before moving forward. He suggested a meeting for later, after the beginning of the fall semester, when it might be possible to settle on a plan of action. Smith was encouraged by the chancellor's willingness to listen.

The firing of Butch Davis was a pivotal event in the UNC saga. Thorp absorbed a tidal wave of criticism in the weeks that followed, both for the decision itself (he had repeatedly expressed support for Davis in 2010–11) and for its timing, coming just days before the beginning of preseason football practice. But the chancellor clearly believed that jettisoning Davis was the one dramatic move that could bring UNC out of its public relations tailspin. Plenty of people on campus agreed with him, and he weathered the immediate storm without incident. Later events would suggest, though, that the chancellor had crossed a psychological threshold the day he fired Butch Davis; for Thorp, the time for active problem solving in the UNC scandal had come to a definitive end.

When Smith showed up in South Building for his much-anticipated meeting with the chancellor on September 16, he noticed that Thorp moved with an extra spring in his step and a look of relief on his face. "Things have certainly changed since we last talked," the chancellor cheerfully but ominously noted. When Smith reminded Thorp of their earlier conversation about having a faculty group lead a top-to-bottom review of athletics, the chancellor answered—evasively, impatiently—that any such review would need to be carried out in conjunction with the Faculty Athletics Committee, a standing committee of Faculty Council. He suggested that Smith arrange a meeting with the chair of that committee. Only if the chair agreed that further probing was needed, he said, would it be possible to move ahead with a new faculty initiative.

Feeling surprised and rebuffed, but not yet defeated, Smith moved on to schedule his next meeting. But the conversation with the FAC chair, psychology professor Steve Reznick, proved even more deflating. Reznick told Smith that he was sure the Carolina athletic program could not be cleaner or better run. The problems that had surfaced had all been the fault of a few bad apples, now thankfully removed. A number of college initiatives were already under way, and NCAA enforcement staff had also entered the picture. Reznick thought it highly unlikely that new problems would reveal themselves. Besides, the FAC collected admissions and "student-athlete" academic performance data for its presentation to the Faculty Council each year. What more could anyone want? New questions could always be directed to the Athletic Department if the Faculty Council deemed such questions necessary. Should UNC professors not trust their own governance committees?

Smith learned, in short, that the chair of the Faculty Athletics Committee—the committee that served as the faculty's designated watchdog for athletics—was an unabashed sports fan inclined to take athletics personnel at their word.

Eager to talk to someone willing to cast a skeptical eye on the UNC sports complex, Smith went next to the dean of the College of Arts and Sciences, Karen Gil. Having already sent Gil a pained, imploring two-thousand-word letter about the athletic scandal in late September, Smith scheduled a meeting with the dean in early October. Gil, who had known Smith for years, welcomed him into her office cordially—but warily. She indulged Smith as he shared his frustrations over his recent meetings with the chancellor and the FAC chair. But when he suggested that Gil, as dean of the college, might initiate her own thorough review of the academic experiences of athletes (the college teaches 90 percent of the credit hours taken by athletes at UNC), her response conformed to a pattern that was coming clearly into view. She assured Smith that she was already doing everything that needed to be done. She had launched a review of the African and Afro-American studies curriculum, she had instructed one of her senior associate deans to review procedures for establishing independent study courses at the university, and she had appointed a committee (cochaired by associate athletic director John Blanchard) to look at the academic support system for athletes. When Smith pointed out to her that it seemed unlikely that these distinct and simultaneous reviews would actually expose the nuts and bolts of the entire athletics enterprise, she answered by promising careful attention and a commitment to thoroughness. She invited Smith to come back anytime as she showed him the door.

Gil's impatience can be partly explained by context. In the fall of 2011 the university system had just absorbed its fourth consecutive annual budget cut from the state legislature. Those cuts, all of them significant, were now touching bone. In 2011 alone UNC–Chapel Hill had its state appropriations sliced by 17.9 percent, amounting to more than one hundred million dollars. Because earlier waves of cuts had been aimed at administrative offices where a certain amount of "fat" could be found, the new cuts would take their toll on the university's teaching mission. The College of Arts and Sciences, which accounts for more than three-quarters of the undergraduate teaching hours performed by the university, would therefore be hardest hit by the new slash in funding. In 2011–12 Gil and the senior associate deans struggled desperately to preserve educational quality in the college, even as class sizes exploded in some departments and the student-instructor ratio rose steadily. (Even the First Year Seminars program, one of the jewels in the college crown, had to raise enrollment caps from nineteen to twenty-four.) Facing such a crisis, no dean should have had to deal with the distraction of an athletic scandal. The lack of vigorous action at the top made every midlevel administrator's life more difficult during the scandal years.

In any case, the words and actions of administrative leaders in the fall of 2011 made one thing abundantly clear. They wanted no internal turbulence as they hunkered down for the NCAA storm. They would be focusing their energies on mitigating the forthcoming sanctions and returning to athletics business as usual as soon as possible. Further criticism was unwelcome, and it would be tolerated—barely—only if critics respectfully channeled their suggestions toward some vague postscandal future.

There is nothing unethical, of course, about hoping for the best when the NCAA has come to town. The first purpose of having an athletic program is to engage in competition, and any university anticipating sanctions from the NCAA will inevitably hold its collective breath while wishing for minimal penalties that spare the athletes who have done nothing wrong. At UNC, however, the desire to mitigate punishment led leaders to avoid confrontation with the truth. And someone at some point in 2011 made the fateful decision to hide the full truth—either from the NCAA or from the public at large (or both). The maelstrom that awaited—the independent review led by Governor Martin, the Board of Governors' inquiry, the shameful exposure of the transcript of football star Julius Peppers, the bitter divisions that split the campus, the fall of a popular chancellor, the recriminations that fell on the chair of the faculty—was made possible by that pivotal and unfortunate decision to deceive.

An entire year had passed since Mary Willingham's interview with Lissa Broome and Steve Keadey, the one in which she had talked about chronic cheating, leadership failures, and procedural breakdowns in the ASPSA. Yet over this twelve-month period, not a single administrative officer in South and Steele Buildings—where chancellors, provosts, and deans reside—had picked up the telephone to ask Willingham to share more of what she knew. Even in the wake of the McAdoo and Austin revelations, which had moved academics to the forefront of the scandal still unfolding, no one on UNC's leadership team bothered to find out more about the practices and assumptions driving the ASPSA. Perhaps university leaders avoided contact with Willingham because she simply had too many embarrassing and potentially disruptive things to say. When NCAA investigators returned to campus in late summer of 2011 to follow up on the Austin and McAdoo stories, they too ignored (or were diverted from) Mary Willingham. (The pattern would continue even after Willingham went to the press in 2012; no administrator at UNC *ever* contacted her to learn more about how the athletic advising system actually worked.)[2] Given all that the world now knows about what still needed to be investigated and divulged, this apparent lack of curiosity stands as an embarrassing indictment of both the leaders and the governing processes of UNC–Chapel Hill. The university consistently averted its eyes from the one person from the athletics arena who had shown a willingness to speak with candor.

What the university did instead, in the late summer of 2011, was convene a small "working group" of highly placed insiders to conduct an inquiry into the apparent academic irregularities associated with the courses taken by McAdoo and Austin. Consisting of chief university counsel Leslie Strohm, senior associate dean Jonathan Hartlyn (the dean to whom AFRI/AFAM chair Julius Nyang'oro reported), and emeritus business school professor Jack Evans, this working group also handled communications with the NCAA investigators dispatched to campus sometime in August or September. The presence on this working group of yet another lawyer—Strohm was now joining Broome and Keadey in an active scandal-management role—reveals something about the institution's priorities: damage control would always trump truth finding throughout the long history of the scandal. But the fact that the working group had to carry out its own investigation while simultaneously mediating with the NCAA also points to the critical role of Jack Evans, who, until his retirement in 2010, had spent fifteen years as UNC's faculty athletics representative to the ACC and the NCAA. Evans spoke the lingo of compliance fluently, and he had good and long-term relationships with UNC athletics personnel as well as the people in Indianapolis. If anyone could thread this needle—identifying and defining problems while still defending Carolina's virtue in the eyes of the NCAA policemen—it was Evans. Chancellor Thorp wasted no time before calling him out of retirement.

The working group did indeed find some curious anomalies in the AFRI/AFAM Department, and this discovery led dean of the College of Arts and Sciences Karen Gil to ask Jonathan Hartlyn and another senior associate dean, William Andrews, to carry out a more thorough review of that department's curriculum in the course of the 2011–12 academic year. The working group thus deserves some credit for bringing problems to light. But the university cloaked the working group in secrecy—to this day UNC refuses to turn over any documents or emails collected, generated, or exchanged by the members of the group—and it is not hard to guess why.[3] One can glean the nature of the working group's balancing act in two fragments of powerful evidence that would appear only in 2012. First, when the NCAA finally announced its sanctions against UNC in March

2012, after an agonizing nine-month wait following the 2011 "notice of allegations," UNC escaped draconian penalties and had its hand slapped mainly for failing to uphold the amateurism principles so dear to the NCAA.[4] The football program was placed on three years' probation, it sacrificed some scholarships, and it had to sit out the bowl season for one year. But the NCAA's committee on infractions simply overlooked the many academic problems that had come to light since 2011; the discussion of academic wrongdoing in its report focused squarely on the "rogue" actions of long-departed tutor Jennifer Wiley, who was charged with having offered illicit academic help to exactly three UNC athletes. The infractions committee did not even hint at the possibility of a wider course scam. The working group, in managing the NCAA investigators while it simultaneously looked into the strange Austin and McAdoo courses, had succeeded in fending off more damaging sanctions.

The contours of the working group's strategy for this task came into public view only in the report from Deans Hartlyn and Andrews that appeared in May 2012. The working group had been a stealth committee. Its activities were largely unknown to the wider campus community, and it never produced a formal report of any kind. But Hartlyn (who had migrated from the working group to the new smaller committee) and Andrews explained in their own official nine-page report that the working group had carried out an important preliminary investigation during which it had reviewed "relevant documents" and spoken to a "sample of students and [AFRI/AFAM] department faculty."

On the first page of their own report, which would be devoted to exposing widespread course anomalies in the suspect department, Hartlyn and Andrews highlighted the working group's critical preliminary conclusions: "No instance was found of a student receiving a grade who had not submitted written work. No evidence indicated that student-athletes received more favorable treatment than students who were not athletes. In addition, no information was found to indicate that the department personnel involved in these courses received a tangible benefit of any kind" for having offered the suspect courses.[5] In other words, the working group's principal conclusions all suggested that the NCAA had nothing more to worry about at UNC. Critically, Evans and company had determined that no athletes received "favorable treatment" from the AFRI/AFAM Department, and no grades had been awarded without the submission of "written work." If the reverse had been true—if course grades had been awarded in exchange for no meaningful work, and if ASPSA counselors and athletes had understood all along that AFRI/AFAM happily awarded such gifts to athletes—UNC would likely have been in violation of NCAA Bylaw 10.1-(b) and subject to penalties for the gravest of all academic offenses in the eyes of the NCAA: "arranging fraudulent academic credit" and thereby making "erroneous declarations of eligibility."

Why had Hartlyn and Andrews gone to the trouble of prefacing their own findings with the working group's exculpatory conclusions, which had obviously already been communicated to the NCAA? The answer would seem to be a simple one. The NCAA, in its "Public Infractions Report" released in March, just six weeks before the publication of the Hartlyn-Andrews report, had issued a warning to UNC. The committee on infractions announced that it would continue to monitor the situation in Chapel Hill. "[Any] additional violations shall be considered grounds for extending the institution's probationary period or imposing more severe sanctions or may result in additional allegations and findings of violations."[6] The institution was not yet out of the woods. Further disclosures of academic irregularities, if those irregularities implicated athletics personnel or seemed rooted in the eligibility needs of the athletic program, would have the potential to bring harsher sanctions against the university. Hence the deans' emphatic assertion that their own findings had in no way altered the working group's preliminary conclusions.

The rhetoric in the remainder of the deans' report suggests the authors' acquiescence in the grand strategy being deployed for the NCAA's benefit. After announcing the working group's findings on page 1, Hartlyn and Andrews never again used the terms *athlete* or *student-athlete* in their review. The deans refused even to mention the number of athletes enrolled in the strange courses they had found—despite the fact that their entire inquiry had been prompted by the discovery of suspect course itineraries among star athletes.

As though fitted with blinders, the deans proceeded as if they had discovered an egregious but isolated lapse of academic standards attributable to the utterly mysterious moral failings of two academic officers. All blame was laid at the door of the academic department and its leadership. (Conveniently, the deans were able to announce that Nyang'oro would be retiring from the university in the summer of 2012. Debby Crowder had already retired in 2009.)

The deans had certainly exposed an inexcusable pattern of academic abuse. And their findings provided some illuminating context for the puzzlingly unorthodox academic experiences of McAdoo and Austin. Hartlyn and Andrews showed that the Department of African and Afro-American Studies had in fact been host to more than fifty "anomalous" courses in the period between 2007 and 2011 (the years Gil had asked them to review). Although Hartlyn and Andrews did not label these course anomalies "paper classes"— that felicitous term would make its appearance only after other startling revelations in the fall of 2012—the deans indicated that the courses required only some form of "written work." Scheduled either by the department chair, Julius Nyang'oro, or by his administrative assistant, Debby Crowder, the courses fell into one of two categories. *Aberrant* courses featured no faculty involvement at all. Although the deans claimed to have found "evidence that students completed written work" in these courses, there was "no evidence" that a faculty member had graded the work or provided any form of supervision to the students enrolled. In *irregularly taught* courses, by contrast, paper assignments were apparently handed out by an actual faculty member (Nyang'oro) who "*evidently* graded the resultant paper" (emphasis added). Yet these courses, too, required little or no class time and seemed to involve no real instruction. All the classes, whether of the aberrant or the irregular variety, were university courses in name only. For the period under review, these fraudulent courses had accounted for 686 student enrollments.

To their credit, Hartlyn and Andrews expressed their exasperation at what they had found. They were clearly embarrassed to have to acknowledge the existence of little-work and no-show courses at UNC–Chapel Hill, and they even confessed to having struggled to maintain their impartiality as they uncovered abuses that had compromised the educations of hundreds of Carolina undergraduates. To a campus community that had waited for a year to hear someone—anyone—in a UNC leadership position express outrage or remorse over the embarrassing breakdowns exposed in the summer of 2011, the deans' emphasis on their "acute dismay" at UNC's academic failures came as a sip of cool water in the middle of the Sahara.

Yet the Hartlyn-Andrews report, like the working-group findings that preceded it, had been engineered to reveal only so much. Anticipating techniques that would be applied masterfully in the Martin report, the deans worked to present the appearance of disclosure and transparency while nevertheless obscuring or ignoring damaging facts and figures. Amazingly, nowhere in their report did they bother to mention that nearly two-thirds of the students who took the paper classes they had identified were athletes (only about 4 percent of UNC undergraduates were athletes). Nowhere did the deans address the possibility that some athletes might have used fake courses to boost grade point averages and thus maintain athletic eligibility. Nowhere did they speculate about what might have motivated a department chair and his longtime assistant to water down and degrade their own curriculum. Although the deans mentioned the name Marvin Austin—they acknowledged that he had taken an *aberrant* course—they offered no explanation for how he had registered for the course in question. (Nancy Davis, a university spokesperson, lamely offered an explanation for this strange course registration during a mid-May meeting in the chancellor's office. Responding to questioning from Jay Smith, she said, "Football players arrive on campus later than other students in the summers. He probably just took the only class that was still open. There's nothing suspicious about it." Davis perhaps did not know that every course registration for athletes was approved by an ASPSA counselor. In any case, the aberrant AFAM 428 that Austin took was placed on the schedule by Debby Crowder, with no participation by a faculty member. The only explanation for this event is that Crowder was colluding with the Athletic Department to make available a slide course for favored students like Austin.)

The most inexcusable omission from the Hartlyn-Andrews report involved a course that had been offered in the second summer session of 2011, AFAM 280 (Blacks in North Carolina). Julius Nyang'oro had added this course to the summer schedule at the last minute as a favor to the football team, which took all the nineteen available registration slots. Like most of Nyang'oro's many summer courses over the years, AFAM 280—a course that he, as an Africanist, would have had no business teaching—was offered as a no-show course in which grades were handed out in exchange for a paper. In a letter to the Board of Trustees (BOT) that he would write on June 7, a month after the release of the Hartlyn-Andrews report, Chancellor Thorp admitted that this AFAM 280 course "was among the reasons that we notified the NCAA of new issues last summer"; the discovery of that course, he continued, was "why we created an internal working group" to look into anomalies in AFRI/AFAM.[7] Yet Andrews and Hartlyn, the latter an original member of the working group, said not a word about AFAM 280 in their report. With the evasion of NCAA discipline evidently regarded as their priority, they thought it best (or had been told that it would be best) if the NCAA heard no further specifics about the peculiar course that had helped call forth a year's worth of campus investigating. With their strategic silence on this and related issues, Hartlyn and Andrews effectively announced, long before Jim Martin would coin the phrase, "This is not an athletics scandal."

Dean Gil released the nine-page Hartlyn-Andrews report on a sleepy Friday afternoon in the middle of final exams and just about a week before graduation day. Perhaps Gil hoped that the document would draw little notice and that the text's release, coming a few weeks after the NCAA declaration, would provide a solemn conclusion for the two-year scandal. The importance placed on the Hartlyn-Andrews report by UNC leaders would be shown repeatedly throughout the summer and fall. They absorbed its rhetoric about "no evidence" and no "favorable treatment" in multiple public statements and presentations, and the findings of Hartlyn-Andrews formed the bedrock of subsequent key documents, including not only the Martin report but also the serial university responses to the academic accrediting agency the Southern Association for Colleges and Schools (SACS). Karen Gil confidently told the Board of Trustees at its May 2012 meeting that "new policies and practices that have been put in place will make us stronger moving forward."[8] UNC system president Tom Ross boldly told the press there was "no need to look further" at academic wrongdoing in the wake of the Hartlyn-Andrews report, which had uncovered only "an isolated situation"; he would add later that the Carolina fraud was a "confined circumstance."[9] After May 4 Holden Thorp, Tom Ross, a broad range of Chapel Hill administrators, and all supporters of the UNC athletic program desperately wanted the deans' report to be the final redemptive word on Carolina's recent record of wrongdoing. As they would say repeatedly in the months to come, they were ready to "move on."

UNC's leaders would be disappointed. The public circulation of the Hartlyn-Andrews report ignited a new firestorm. First, local media wasted no time in using freedom-of-information requests to force the disclosure of details that Hartlyn and Andrews had omitted from their report. On May 7 Dan Kane of the N&O revealed a startling fact that Hartlyn and Andrews had somehow considered irrelevant to their investigative efforts: nearly 40 percent of the students enrolled in the fraudulent courses came from the football and men's basketball teams. They had crowded into these courses in such numbers even though they made up a little more than one-half of 1 percent of UNC's undergraduate student body.[10]

Later in the same week Kane exposed the faulty reasoning and incomplete research that lay behind one of the working group's key conclusions. That group had claimed, according to Hartlyn and Andrews, that "no information" indicated that Nyang'oro or Crowder had received any form of "tangible benefit" in exchange for the fraud they had committed. But where had the group searched for its information? In an explosive N&O story that would lead to a State Bureau of Investigation inquiry and an eventual indictment, Kane showed that, on the contrary, Nyang'oro had been paid a generous summer-school stipend of $12,000 for at least one course—the infamous AFAM 280—he clearly had not taught in any meaningful sense of the term. Rank-and-file faculty who followed the UNC scandal story found it equally outrageous that Nyang'oro had evidently collected $120,000 in extra teaching and administrative stipends in the four summers covered by the Hartlyn and Andrews review. His name, meanwhile, had been attached to no fewer than seventy-five courses in the same four-year period. Professors at research universities typically teach sixteen courses over a four-year period, perhaps with a few extra summer courses added in; the challenge of teaching seventy-five courses in four years would represent a degree of difficulty "beyond category" for any mere mortal. Yet no one at Carolina had noticed this bizarre pattern? Could administrative neglect and petty self-dealing on the part of faculty leaders at UNC be any more obvious? Had Nyang'oro simply been exempted from annual reviews by his superiors (who included both Hartlyn and Gil)? Had Hartlyn and Andrews really never bothered to ask these questions themselves?

In discussions on campus, other issues also came to the fore. In using passive voice to communicate the working group's conclusions—"no instance was found," "no evidence was found"—the deans inadvertently raised questions about the working group's research methods. To whom had the working group spoken? In which offices had they gathered evidence? Had they interviewed football and basketball players? Had they spoken to the counselors in ASPSA? Given the first audience for the Hartlyn-Andrews report, which consisted of academic professionals whose institution was now being subjected to humiliation, was it even appropriate to draw firm conclusions about the AFRI/AFAM curriculum on the basis of "sample" interviews with students and faculty? How had they chosen their sample? Who had been excluded and why? What steps had been taken to ensure the candor and truthfulness of the people interviewed?

There appeared to be other instances of sleight of hand. The working group had determined, according to Hartlyn and Andrews, that no student received a grade "who had not submitted written work." But given the broader picture provided in their own report, with dozens of courses in which no meaningful instruction was ever provided, what could it even mean to claim that students had "submitted written work"? Who evaluated the written work? For what pedagogical purpose would written work be performed in a course that lacked content? What would have been the criteria for evaluation? In some of the courses, no university-certified instructor had even made an appearance. And even in those courses that boasted an identifiable instructor of record, and where reading and grading of papers had "evidently" taken place, the deans noted that the "written work" was "typically submitted to departmental administrative staff [that is, Crowder] either in person or via email." The deans said nothing about how they had verified that a professor ever read this work.

In light of these conditions, to claim that "no instance was found" of a student receiving course credit without having "submitted written work" was tantamount to saying, "We are happy to confirm that words appear to have been placed on pieces of paper by someone—most likely the students or others close to them—in each course where grades were assigned." In no logical universe would such a minimalist claim to course legitimacy be accepted. This was legalistic gibberish that had to have been aimed at one rhetorical bull's-eye: the NCAA rulebook. (The NCAA, of course, received its own copy of the Hartlyn-Andrews report.)

The Hartlyn-Andrews report and the critical newspaper coverage it generated brought the first concerted faculty action in response to the university's stumbling exercise in scandal management. And to the surprise of many, faculty anger made a real impact on the course of events. In the days following the release of Hartlyn-Andrews on May 4, members of a loose coalition of reform-minded faculty began to exchange opinions about the sobering conclusions and surprising shortcomings of the deans' report. This informal group had been meeting off and on since the previous fall, and in February it had caught the momentary attention of the campus community when it released a "Statement of Principles for Athletics at UNC." The statement, endorsed by more than a hundred faculty and embraced by both Chancellor Thorp and AD Bubba Cunningham, had pointedly called for institutional transparency at UNC as well as a renewed commitment to providing "a rigorous and meaningful education to every student." The statement expressed what most faculty anywhere would regard as common sense, but it also carried a sharp edge. It provided a rationale to resist the university if and when it proved to be less than forthright when discussing athletic matters and the academic lives of its athletes.

Some members of the group, which would acquire the title "Athletic Reform Group" in the course of the summer of 2012, quickly concluded that Carolina was now clearly in violation of the ARG's recently enunciated principles. The chancellor's remarkably weak response to the Hartlyn-Andrews report and the uproar it created—he told the press he was "sad that these things could happen here"—only added to the sense of faculty indignation.[11] Beginning on graduation day, Sunday, May 13, about a dozen faculty of the ARG inundated the Faculty Executive Committee (FEC) with impassioned requests for an open-ended inquiry that would finally address the many questions still left on the table. Why had there been no review of the ASPSA's role in athletes' course choices? Why had no one reported problems sooner? If the university really believed that the whole scam was due to the unpardonable recklessness of a single faculty member, why had he been allowed to walk off into retirement without having first answered for his actions? Why had the administration and its handpicked investigative teams made absolutely no effort to explain the origins of this entire disaster?

The faculty would get their wish for further probing, but the administration's response to the fierce faculty pushback throws into relief the delicate high-wire act that Holden Thorp was forced to perform through the duration of the UNC scandal. A man of conscience whose heart was with the faculty, Thorp of course wanted to oblige a faculty request for a deeper inquiry—especially now that scattered complaints had turned into a loud chorus. And sure enough, when chair of the faculty Jan Boxill, the ex officio chair of the FEC, responded to faculty pressure by offering to take the lead in appointing an FEC subcommittee to conduct a campus-wide inquiry that could identify unaddressed issues, Thorp gave her the green light. That FEC subcommittee, consisting of three widely respected members of the faculty from three very different fields, would go on to write a thoughtful and far-reaching report that would be released in late July. In describing a campus with "two cultures," and in calling for an outside inquiry into the nature of the UNC scandal, the FEC subcommittee set in motion the wheels of the later Martin report and much else that would follow.

But Thorp and the other powers that be in the UNC system understandably regarded this faculty inquiry with a certain degree of trepidation. The FEC group might fault previous actions (or inaction) by campus leaders. Its findings could complicate the university's defense of the integrity of the UNC curriculum in the event that the accrediting agency SACS paid the university a visit (which it soon did). Most worrisome of all, the FEC faculty might somehow implicate athletics personnel in academic malfeasance. This would offend vital constituencies on and off campus. More important, it would potentially arouse the attention of that NCAA infractions committee that the working group and Hartlyn-Andrews had successfully mollified. The NCAA might react irritably if suddenly confronted with evidence that it had been deliberately misled.

Thorp knew he walked a treacherous path, which is probably one reason he had so little to say in the spring and summer of 2012, even as a torrent of new media revelations suggested long-standing problems in and around the ASPSA. In opening the next chapter in the history of the UNC scandal, the FEC subcommittee proceeded to do what conscientious faculty committees do. The chair, Laurie Maffly-Kipp of religious studies, and her two subcommittee colleagues, Steven Bachenheimer from the medical school and Michael Gerhardt from the law school, interviewed a wide range of people, they listened to concerns with an open mind and the appropriate critical filters, and in the end they produced an honest assessment of the state of academic-athletic relations on the UNC campus. The report evoked images of the Cold War, with the two sectors of campus largely sealed off from each other, mutually suspicious if not outright hostile, and with the warring jurisdictions often leaving athletes suspended in a no-man's-land where effective academic guidance could not be found. The subcommittee's specific recommendations—in addition to the call for an "outside entity or commission" to conduct a thorough evaluation of UNC's culture—aimed to bring down the iron curtain, to make transparency the operative principle on both "sides" of campus, and to foster better and more frequent communication between faculty and all athletics personnel. The FEC subcommittee report was widely hailed both for its insight and for its honesty.

Yet even here, especially here, in a report compiled within an atmosphere of institutional crisis where the need for candor had grown acute, one finds the markings of the Carolina cover-up.

Even the findings of the FEC subcommittee were rigged. Not by the authors, who struggled mightily to be honest umpires, calling things as they saw them. No, the rigging was done by athletics personnel and those who had a vested interest in protecting them. The tenacity of their protective efforts shows how compromised UNC's leadership circle had become. The next chapter puts under the microscope the subtle strategies of deception that the university's leaders employed.

Five

The University Doubles Down

In any retelling of the history of the UNC scandal, the highly positive impact of the Faculty Executive Committee subcommittee report of the summer of 2012 deserves its due. The recommendations ultimately conveyed in that report, had they been followed in spirit as well as by the letter, had the potential to launch a thoughtful, thorough, and self-critical examination of the intersection between athletics and academics at UNC and in the wider world of collegiate sport. The authors of the report could not have known that they were being led to produce a report with a tone, and with findings, that would effectively quarantine the ASPSA. The powers that be, already in the summer of 2012, were hoping to tailor the report's results so as to protect the athletics enterprise and to ensure that the report would be harnessed to a "prospective" agenda rather than a "retrospective" consideration of what UNC had done wrong. The university's failure to act forcefully and effectively on the committee's recommendations in no way detracts from the quality of the report the committee produced, but there is no getting around the evidence, now made public, that the report was made to be consistent with the yearlong university strategy of fending off a deeper investigation into athletic admission policies and ASPSA practices.

A broad range of people conspired to mitigate and contaminate the findings of the hardworking FEC subcommittee. Standing squarely at the intersection of the athletic and academic worlds,

these people performed their work first by supplying misinformation to the committee and then by pressing insistently for wording changes that helped deflect responsibility for the scandal away
from the Athletic Department. The identity of the saboteurs, as
well as their basic motives, are best exposed by working backward
through two delicate but important acts of sabotage.

"To make it as accurate as possible"

Professors Laurie Maffly-Kipp, Michael Gerhardt, and Steven Bachenheimer spent several weeks in May and June 2012 talking with interested parties, listening to the concerns of both insiders and outsiders,
and surveying the institutional dynamics that shaped the athletic-
academic relationship at UNC. Through interviews with people who
had known key personnel in both the AFRI/AFAM and the Athletic
Departments, the Maffly-Kipp team had determined that Debby
Crowder had had "extremely close" ties to people in athletics (her
relationship with a former UNC basketball player and her friendship with longtime basketball adviser Burgess McSwain were well
known). These ties, they reasonably surmised, made her a likely "athletics supporter," one who had used the ambiguities and loopholes
in the course registration system to "help players" by directing them
toward the bogus courses she helped to set up in the African and
Afro-American Studies Department.[1] When joined to another key
finding—"We were told that athletes claimed they had been sent to
Julius Nyang'oro by the ASPSA"—the committee's identification of
Crowder as a fan with "extremely close" ties to athletics provided
a picture of a fertile two-way communication chain between the
caretakers of athletes in the ASPSA and the leadership of the AFRI/
AFAM Department. In the course of their interviews, the FEC subcommittee had unwittingly uncovered the motor of the scandal,
and they were prepared to convey this basic reality in measured
tones and in a context where the priority was to develop future safe-
guards, not to cast blame or dole out punishments.

But this was not to be. Jan Boxill, the chair of the faculty and the
head of the committee that would ultimately submit the report to
the campus and the wider world, was one of several who saw the

trouble that these statements could potentially create for the athletic program. She and her allies intervened to head off the difficulties.

The critical role of Jan Boxill in the university's management of the athletic scandal has not received the attention it deserves. Upon her election as faculty chair in the spring of 2011, she was the first "fixed-term" (meaning nontenured) faculty member elected to this important leadership position in the history of the university. She had won the election over anthropology professor Vincas Steponaitis, both of whom had been nominated to stand for election by the chancellor's advisory committee. (UNC faculty elections proceed through a partly co-optive process whereby suitable nominees for various positions are chosen by insiders on standing committees.) Why had the chancellor's advisory committee chosen this moment in UNC history to nominate a fixed-term faculty member as one of the two people to stand for election as faculty chair? Undoubtedly, Boxill's role as a prominent supporter of the athletic program worked in her favor. A University of California at Los Angeles (UCLA) basketball player in the 1960s, she had earned her PhD in philosophy before joining the faculty at the University of Tampa and serving as that school's women's basketball coach in the mid-1980s. When her husband, Bernard Boxill, was hired as a professor of philosophy at UNC in 1986, Jan followed him to Chapel Hill. She worked as a visiting assistant professor, first at UNC and then at Elon University, before being hired full-time at UNC as a philosophy lecturer and academic counselor for athletes. As counselor she worked especially with the women's basketball team, and she eventually also became the voice of the Lady Tar Heels on radio broadcasts. (She continues her announcing to this day.) For an advisory committee searching in the fall of 2010 for faculty-chair nominees to be placed on the spring ballot, someone with Boxill's extensive experience in the Athletic Department would have had great appeal. Given that her own specialty within the philosophical discipline was "sports ethics," she might have seemed the optimal choice for a university suddenly embroiled in scandal. Steponaitis was also a fan of UNC athletics, but Boxill knew both athletics and academics from the inside out.

Indeed, one of the great unacknowledged obstacles that the proponents of disclosure and transparency faced between 2011 and 2013 was the embarrassing reality that Boxill—whatever the exact nature of the AFRI/AFAM fraud and its connection to the Athletic Department—had to have been caught up in the whole mess. As someone who had worked in athletic advising since 1988, and who had been around to watch the evolution of UNC's eligibility system, Boxill understood better than most that the ASPSA was the location for the "black box" of the course-fraud scandal. Her own women's basketball advisees had taken plenty of independent study and paper classes in AFRI/AFAM; the weaker students among them had survived academically only because of the availability of paper classes (in addition to the independent study courses they took in philosophy). Like many others at the university, Boxill wanted no attention placed on the ASPSA or on the process of academic counseling for athletes. In 2012 and 2013 she resisted repeated calls for public discussion of the entirety of the UNC experience with scandal; she scheduled, instead, focused discussions of athletics-related issues in which she always controlled the agenda.

As chair of the faculty and as a longtime academic counselor in athletics, Boxill was a walking conflict of interest during a summer in which she charged one of her own committees to review the athletic program. In July 2012, when she read the initial version of the Maffly-Kipp report, Boxill reacted by working to counteract or neutralize anything in the subcommittee's text that pointed a finger in the direction of athletic advising. What the subcommittee took to be the final version of its report was completed on July 5, but it would be released to the public only on July 27. This delay gave Boxill ample opportunity to apply pressure to soften the report's suggestions of wrongdoing within athletics. Her tactics were those of a conflicted but determined person whose devotion to athletics ultimately led to compromised judgment.

Boxill, like Chancellor Thorp, walked a tightrope in the summer of 2012. She, too, had a conscience. She, too, had a hard-earned reputation for ethics that she wanted to uphold. But she also had a protective instinct toward anything athletics related, one that she had developed over many years of coaching and advising. Jay Smith had seen this instinct up close when he had collaborated with Boxill to host *New York Times* columnist Joe Nocera for a public colloquy in March. Smith had planned the campus event, had invited Boxill to serve as moderator during the public dialogue (at Steponaitis's urging), had arranged for her presence at the dinner that followed Nocera's presentation, and had also given her instructions, on the day before the event, about the script for UNC's night with Nocera. Smith would introduce the speaker and moderator, say a few words about Nocera's recent interest in NCAA issues, and relate the evening's discussion to the ongoing work of UNC's Athletic Reform Group. A brief Nocera presentation would then precede the main event, a lengthy Q&A with the audience.

Smith was standing at the podium, testing the sound system and preparing to make the introductions, when Boxill approached: "I've prepared some remarks I'd like to begin with." After an awkward speechless moment, Smith reminded Boxill that he had planned a set of introductory remarks of his own. Boxill persisted. "This will only take a few minutes. Maybe I'll speak, and then you make the introductions." When Smith said he was uncomfortable making changes at the last minute and that he thought it important to stick with the original plan, Boxill stood motionless, still hoping for victory. "Maybe we could both address the audience?" she said. Only after being reminded that she would be free to get her message across in her role as moderator did she reluctantly take her assigned seat in the middle of the stage. Smith was convinced at the time that this surprise attempt to hijack the evening preliminaries reflected Boxill's fears about how the discussion was to be framed for the audience. She apparently found it hard to tolerate the idea that an Athletic Department critic would be commanding the microphone.

Boxill thus approached her role as FEC leader and faculty chair with cross-purposes in mind. She had to be, and wanted to be, respectful of faculty governance processes. She wanted and needed to show respect for the time investments, conscientiousness, and intellectual honesty of her faculty colleagues who had sacrificed much of their summer to prepare the long-awaited report. She also had to balance the concerns of a wide range of interested parties—

including not only Thorp and the members of the FEC but also AD Bubba Cunningham, UNC-system president Tom Ross, and an increasingly anxious Board of Trustees. But in the end, Boxill also felt an overriding need to remold the subcommittee's message into a shape more favorable to the athletic program. She tried to do this through the FEC. When that failed, she simply did it on her own.

The full FEC was scheduled to meet on July 16, and the whole committee would then have the opportunity to respond to the contents of the subcommittee report before it was released to the world. On Monday, July 14, Boxill sent an email to Maffly-Kipp, Gerhardt, and Bachenheimer: "I would like for us to discuss this report [at the FEC] to make any revisions we might deem necessary to make it as accurate as possible and represent the full Council." Emails subsequently exchanged between the authors of the report show that Boxill's message caught them by surprise. They were a little offended that their report might be deemed a mere "draft" subject to revision by others. This seemed a clear violation of protocol. A group commissioned to write a university report generally does not expect that its report will be doctored to meet audience expectations or to represent the views of people who had no hand in determining its results. Gerhardt insisted that "we need to object" to any effort to revise what the subcommittee had written, and the others agreed with him. They discussed whether they should make their expectations clear to Boxill before the FEC convened. Maffly-Kipp noted that in a recent phone chat with Boxill, she had also "raised a few other potential 'concerns' about our wording in the report—but stopped short of objecting or asking that anything be changed. I certainly feel as strongly as both of you that a report is just that—it is not a compromise bill that can be negotiated." Bachenheimer weighed in: "I agree completely with you that the report stands as it is."

With his two colleagues out of town and having to phone in their comments, Bachenheimer was the only author able to attend the FEC meeting on Wednesday, July 16. At first, the subcommittee's fears that Boxill might try to usurp their authority seemed to be confirmed, as Bachenheimer later reported to his coauthors. "Before you were both connected and the meeting hadn't officially started . . . Jan said she thought there were 'serious errors' in the report, which she referred to as a 'draft.' I assured her that we didn't see it as a draft." In the course of the committee discussion, however, Boxill backed away from her objections as the rest of the committee showered the subcommittee with praise. Bachenheimer shared that the "mood in the room was very positive," and apart from a few suggestions that required some minor tinkering, there would be no need for substantive changes to the text and no need to address "serious errors."

The next morning, however, with witnesses no longer around, Boxill again changed her tune. She emailed the subcommittee about next steps: "There are a few comments that I have that I would like to bring up with you in doing the revision and so I was wondering if I could meet with you when you next meet to work on the revision." She added that she would be meeting with the chancellor the next day, July 18. Why was Boxill saying these things beyond the earshot of the whole FEC, which had met to discuss this very report less than twenty-four hours before? And what did she mean by "work on the revision"? There were only cosmetic changes left to make, and the subcommittee had planned to carry out those final touch-ups through email communication. Clearly suspicious of Boxill's intentions, the authors exchanged a flurry of emails on the morning of July 17 in which they strategized about how to respond to Boxill and how to head off any changes she hoped to make to their report. "I'm concerned procedurally," Maffly-Kipp wrote to the others, "about making changes to the report if they weren't vetted by the entire FEC(?)" Gerhardt concurred. "It seems to me that we might need to tell Jan that there is a line we hope she does not cross." In the end their "game plan" (Gerhardt's words) to counter Boxill would involve four steps. They would make the final revisions they had intended to make, call Boxill to ask her what modifications she had had in mind, make any subsequent alterations they were willing to make, and then send a PDF version of the report to Boxill—a version that "can't be edited" and "water[ed] down," as Maffly-Kipp and Gerhardt put it.

The record of email correspondence shows that Boxill did manage a meeting with Gerhardt and Bachenheimer on the afternoon of July 18. (She had joked, when first requesting a face-to-face meeting, that "I didn't want my comments winding up in the *N&O*.") She apparently informed them of certain changes that "[UNC president] Tom Ross and others" wanted, which led to another round of refinements. Despite Maffly-Kipp's anger on learning of this event—"I don't feel right about easing the impact of whatever we plan to say" for the benefit of administrators, she protested—Gerhardt assured her that Boxill, in person, had once again come across as quite reasonable. "She was nodding when we pushed back," he noted in an email on the morning of July 19. "As a result neither Steve nor I felt compelled to change the tone or substance of what we say in the report." They had had to "push back" against the chair of the faculty, but another bullet had been dodged, and good feelings of collegiality had prevailed.

But Boxill had more ammunition, and later events would suggest that she had chosen once again to be accommodating in person so as to hold her fire for later, when another opportunity might present itself. That opportunity appeared a week later, on July 26, when Boxill learned that the Board of Trustees was now expecting, and had even announced, the imminent release of the report. "[The] report is to be released today!!!" she wrote to the subcommittee in an urgent morning email. "So I need your help."

The email record shows that Boxill had already been communicating with others at the highest levels about the content of the FEC report and that a strategy for heading off problems and making possible fixes had already been agreed upon. In an email to UNC's public relations office at 10:01 a.m. on July 26, Boxill informed three members of the staff that she was about to contact the FEC subcommittee "to ask if they would agree to change the one paragraph." Except for that one paragraph, she said, the report was "ready to go." Boxill was alluding knowingly to "the one paragraph" that some feared could detonate a bomb in NCAA headquarters. Who exactly had been party to the conversations in which concerns about that paragraph had been expressed? President Ross? He had apparently already pressured Boxill to effect some changes in wording. Was Thorp driving the discussion? He had met with Boxill privately on July 18. Had the Board of Trustees also become involved? Had AD

Bubba Cunningham reacted? All of these parties had received copies of the report. And what about members of the working group? Had Jack Evans been consulted? Whatever behind-the-scenes wrangling took place in July 2012, it has remained behind the scenes.

The content of "the one paragraph" that had drawn attention suggests that any or all of these people might have had an interest in colluding with Boxill to make changes. In her email to the Maffly-Kipp team, sent at 10:24 a.m., she claimed to have heard new objections to the report voiced by unidentified FEC members not present at the July 16 meeting. Boxill then asked the subcommittee if they would be willing simply to "remove Deborah Crowder and the 'extremely close' [relationship to athletics]. The worry is that this could raise further NCAA issues and that is not the intention." (Who had now specified for Boxill the nature of the "intention" behind the FEC subcommittee report?) Besides, Boxill added, the FEC critics, who would never be identified, had considered this information to be "gossipy and unfacultylike," even though "it may be true." (When later pushed by an irritated Gerhardt about the insulting "unfacultylike" comment, Boxill claimed she could not recall who said it.) Boxill also specified, oddly, that the tardy critics "feel this [the "extremely close" observation] is not relevant" to the report anyway. (If the observation carried such little import, why was she struggling so tenaciously to have it removed?) Boxill then moved to the next sensitive passage—the one about ASPSA personnel having directed athletes to see Nyang'oro. "The other concern is the last part of that bullet point: 'We were told that athletes claimed' . . . since you did not interview any athletes, would this be appropriate to put in?" To their considerable credit, the subcommittee steadfastly refused to make this change; their source must have been an unimpeachable one.

Boxill used not only the urgency of the moment ("the report is to be released today!!!") but also the prospect of messy contradictions and the need for FEC unity to put pressure on the subcommittee. Suggesting the possibility that release of a version without the appropriate corrections could lead to embarrassment later, she observed, "I don't want to release this [report] and then craft another one." Then, implying that an unmodified version would fail to reflect the will of the FEC (none of whose other members had raised any of these objections when they had the chance, and some of whom might even have objected to the changes she was now proposing), she added, "I would like this to be it from the FEC." She closed the email with a softener: "I know sending emails is always difficult because they are sometimes read in a way not intended. So these are friendly comments and requests." But leaving little to chance, she added one final bit of pressure: "Because it has been talked about by the Trustees for the past 2 days, I need to release the report today if possible to the faculty council before it gets to the media."

Laurie Maffly-Kipp immediately communicated to her coauthors in a tone of disbelief. "Why is it a good thing to remove Deborah Crowder's name from the report? The fact is, she was close to people in athletics." She said she would go along with this revision only if outvoted and then only "reluctantly." Gerhardt, having been distracted for a few hours by his anger over the "unfacultylike" accusation, would only later signal his accord with Maffly-Kipp—"I agree with your skepticism about the [Crowder] suggestion"—but by then the subcommittee, working under pressure-cooker conditions and communicating only intermittently through email, had confusedly voted to accede to Boxill's request on the removal of Crowder's name. Bachenheimer would first say, "I'm not happy with the way Jan is handling this at all," but his terse one-word email delivered twenty minutes later, at high noon on July 26—"Yes"—led Maffly-Kipp to send in the final PDF report after acceding to Boxill's change. Boxill had managed to secure a subtle but important revision to the text, one that eliminated the report's sole suggestion that a specific motive to help athletes may have been behind UNC's long and curious experience with academic fraud.

The subcommittee members, relieved to be finished and ready to exhibit the kind of comity characteristic of committee relationships on university faculties, congratulated Boxill on completion of the task and expressed great confidence in the final document. Bachenheimer, with an observation that seems to explain his own final willingness to go along with the deletion of Crowder and her "extremely close" ties, even reassured Boxill that "we have tried to be forward looking and not dwell on the minutia of the N'yangoro-Crowder [sic] abuses," even if the "press coverage" would fail to appreciate that distinction. A year later, when asked by the press whether they still stood by the report even in spite of the revelations about Boxill and the pressure that had been applied to them, Bachenheimer told the N&O's Dan Kane that he and his colleagues were "completely comfortable" with the final report.

Given the overall quality of the report, the FEC subcommittee had every right to be proud of its work, and the desire of all parties to preserve collegiality and demonstrate the efficacy of faculty governance ensured that there would be no lingering acrimony. But Boxill had secured an important substantive change to a report prepared by a special subcommittee, and she had done so by pushing insistently at the boundaries of academic professionalism. Instead of simply allowing the report to reflect the collective wisdom of its authors, she made repeated personal interventions in an attempt to modify their honest accounting of their findings. She worked behind the backs of her own Faculty Executive Committee. She attributed views to faculty members that no existing evidence suggests they actually had. She applied subtle but unmistakable pressure to a subcommittee that had to render a decision under severe time constraints. From her superior position in the committee hierarchy, she took advantage of her colleagues' desire to be collegial and accommodating.

Boxill would eventually apologize to the subcommittee "for the tone" of the email exhorting them to delete Crowder's name from their report, and later—after her emails went public—she went to great lengths to muddy the waters and to confuse N&O readers and the UNC campus community about the chronology and nature of the FEC report's evolution.[2] But Boxill's efforts to overcome her own scruples show the strength of the imperative at work at Carolina in the spring and summer of 2012. The ASPSA had to be protected, the NCAA had to be kept at bay, and Jan Boxill was prepared, within limits, to do all she could to assist in this project. She knew well, of course, that she was not alone.

Slandering the Faculty Athletics Committee

The ASPSA clearly had many protectors other than Jan Boxill. Celebrated concussion researcher Kevin Guskiewicz, who had a cordial working relationship with the Athletic Department but who also attended early meetings of the Athletic Reform Group, expressed exasperation at the university's failure to zero in on the practices of the ASPSA. In a July 2012 email he wrote to Jay Smith just weeks before the release of the FEC report, he noted that he "remain[ed] puzzled (as you know because I continue to press this point)—as to how Blanchard, Mercer, and others in academic advising for athletes fly under the radar" of the university's various inquiries. He indicated his intent to convey to the chancellor his concerns about this apparent blind spot.[3]

The FEC report would provide further clues "as to how" the ASPSA repeatedly managed to elude scrutiny in the wake of the scandal. On the very same page of the FEC report where Debby Crowder metamorphosed into an unidentified "department staff member," the Maffly-Kipp team briefly discussed the operating procedures of the ASPSA. The authors professed uncertainty on the subject of how athletes learned about and migrated to the bogus classes offered in AFRI/AFAM. It was less than clear, they wrote, whether "staff at the Loudermilk center [ASPSA headquarters after 2010] actually contacted departments to *ask* about the availability of classes." The FEC subcommittee asserted that counselors in the ASPSA had been actively "discouraged from contacting faculty or questioning decisions about pedagogy." They reported, in fact, that the directors of the program, John Blanchard and Robert Mercer, had actually gone to the Faculty Athletics Committee in 2002 "to discuss the teaching of IS [independent study] courses." At the FAC they "were told that faculty members have great latitude to teach courses as they see fit. Counselors, then, concluded that it is not their responsibility" to question what academic units do with their courses.

Here was the second subcommittee "finding" that delicately deflected critical attention away from the ASPSA, and it bears the fingerprints of people working in the bowels of the Academic Support Program. The report's authors chose to emphasize the "considerable uncertainty in the relationship between academic departments and athletics counselors." They lamented the "difficult position" of athletics counselors who had "less than complete knowledge or authority" over courses and their requirements. The unfortunate result of this uncertainty, according to the report, was that individual student-athletes "carried too much of the burden for the selection of classes." Ambiguity, then, was the big problem, and its main consequence was that athletes received too little guidance in their course selections.

These conclusions were grossly misleading, and they had been engineered through a misinformation campaign that affected the subcommittee's deliberations without its knowledge. When the authors wrote that it was less clear to them "whether staff at the Loudermilk Center actually contacted departments to *ask* about the availability of classes," they did not know that sand had been thrown in their eyes for the purpose of preventing clarity. Later, after more *N&O* investigative work, published emails would show academic counselors repeatedly initiating contact with Julius Nyang'oro to ask about the availability of classes. Counselors also arranged meetings with him and gave him special access to sports events, evidently for the purpose of shaping course offerings and even creating assignments for said courses. "Too much of the burden" for crafting athletes' course schedules was in fact being carried by the counselors themselves, who used their knowledge about the Carolina curriculum to forge easy curricular paths for their many indifferent or at-risk students. Some of those paths had been absurdly undemanding; others had become nakedly fraudulent. All helped to preserve eligibility. Athletes had not been receiving too little guidance in their course selections; they had been receiving too much—far too much.

Robert Mercer, director of the ASPSA, knew about the practices of his counselors, and John Blanchard, his supervisor, would have had no excuse for not knowing all the essentials by 2012. This perhaps explains their creation and repeated embellishment of a diversionary story: the account of their 2002 encounter with the Faculty Athletics Committee. Their claim about the FAC's response to their sincere inquiries about independent study courses—the faculty on the committee allegedly told them that it was "not their responsibility" to worry about pedagogy at UNC—would sound echoes throughout the next year. From the perspective of the FEC subcommittee, this allegation understandably served to inoculate the ASPSA from charges that it bore responsibility for the course fraud. The same allegation, later swallowed whole by Jim Martin and invoked for explanatory purposes in at least seven different instances in his report, would help lay the foundation for the governor's claim that the UNC fraud case was "not an athletics scandal."[4] The allegation thus proved to be one of the most salient findings conveyed to and by the FEC subcommittee. The allegation also appears to have been a complete fiction.

Not a shred of surviving documentary evidence supports the contention that Mercer and Blanchard went to the FAC to express concerns about questionable pedagogy or suspect courses. The faculty who actually sat on the FAC in 2002 (and in 2006, when Blanchard and Mercer have claimed that they repeated their concerns) have denied that the committee ever expressed any opinions on these matters. The chair of the committee from 2002 has flatly declared that "there was no discussion" of questionable courses. (Another member of the FAC caustically recollected that members of the committee spent most of their time "congratulating themselves about what a squeaky clean program they had.")[5] Even Jim Martin would later have to publicly retract his assertion that the FAC had been warned.[6] How, then, did this suspect story ever make its way into the deliberations of the FEC subcommittee? How did it become a foundation stone for the pillar of deceit erected in the course of 2012–13?

This story about FAC negligence and the virtue of the ASPSA's leaders contaminated the FEC subcommittee report because Holden Thorp placed it there. Key players at the university had clearly determined that this story would be a central plank in the institutional strategy of covering for athletics, and the chancellor therefore took pains to repeat it at several critical moments. Unlike much in the UNC scandal, the anecdote about the FAC, which was so helpful to the cause of warding off tough NCAA sanctions, had origins that are easily traced.

Thorp and the FEC actually recycled a bit of lore that had first been trotted out in the late summer of 2011. With the NCAA coming back to town, and under pressure to prepare an explanation for the strange case of AFAM 280 (the summer 2011 paper class with the football-players-only enrollment), Blanchard and Mercer fastened on their story and they stuck with it. They boldly maintained that ASPSA counselors directed athletes toward courses without regard for the courses' content or "format." (The claim would be baldly contradicted in the summer of 2013, when emails showed counselor Jaimie Lee contacting Julius Nyang'oro to request a "research paper class" format for a Swahili course.)[7] Blanchard and Mercer even conveyed to the NCAA that the Faculty Athletics Committee had told them explicitly not to meddle in such things. In other words, the counselors had had no idea that the Nyang'oro course was a bogus facsimile of a college course, one in which no teaching and little work would be done. They had no idea that their athletes would be earning helpfully high grades for minimal work. They merely directed players to a course that fitted their schedules (a course the counselors apparently just happened to notice when it appeared out of thin air two days before the summer session began). Athletes and the Athletic Department had not been complicit in fraud. On the contrary, the athletes had been innocent victims of poor teaching, and the counselors had suffered under the burden of "less than complete knowledge or authority" over courses. What more could they have done to battle Nyang'oro's nefarious scheme?

To whom did Blanchard and Mercer relate their story? Perhaps they talked directly to NCAA officials, but they most certainly talked to their old friend and NCAA go-between Jack Evans—who seems to have assisted them by corroborating their story. It would later be revealed, during the long dissection of the Martin report in early 2013, that only one member of the Faculty Athletics Committee had actually been interviewed by Martin in the course of his inquiry: Evans, the faculty athletics representative who was also the FAC's designated recorder of the minutes. Interestingly, his own minutes failed to confirm the reality of the discussion Blanchard and Mercer alleged had occurred there in 2002. Given the weight that Jim Martin would assign to this alleged event, however, one can only conclude that Evans vouched for his colleagues from athletics when he spoke with Martin. (When Dan Kane of the N&O approached Evans for an answer to this very question, he "declined to talk about what happened on the committee, or what he told Martin.")[8]

Evans also must have vouched for Blanchard and Mercer in August 2011, when the working group was navigating its way through the AFRI/AFAM morass and determining that there was "no evidence" that athletes had received preferential treatment from anyone. And it was almost certainly by way of Evans that the chancellor absorbed this key detail about ASPSA procedures. Thorp had been relying on Evans for much. The chancellor had gone to Evans as the resident athletics wise man when he formed the working group. At some point the longtime faculty athletics representative must have passed on to Thorp the very same story he would later confirm for Martin, since it was Thorp—not Blanchard, not Mercer, and not Evans—who took the trouble to inform the FEC subcommittee about this highly important fictional event in Carolina history.

At virtually the same moment, in early June 2012, Thorp also informed the Board of Trustees that counselors could not be blamed for the AFAM 280 fraud, since they had had "no reason to question the faculty member's choice of course format." A clear narrative strategy had been decided upon, and key players were bringing their stories into alignment. The ASPSA's preplanning and collusion with AFRI/AFAM were to be covered up. Only academic officials were to be assigned blame in this scandal.

Why would Thorp tell Maffly-Kipp and her team a story that he had never even bothered to check against the memories of the faculty whose performance he was calling into question? Why, during an inquiry into a scandal that clearly involved both misbehavior by academics and a grossly disproportionate number of athletes enrolled in fraudulent courses, would he privilege the testimony of those parties with an interest in protecting the Athletic Department? Why did it never occur to him to question whether the Faculty Athletics Committee was even the appropriate authority to rule on course "formats" and faculty teaching practices? (It was not. The FAC had no such authority, which resided instead in the office of the senior associate dean for undergraduate education; Blanchard and Mercer, who talked with that dean often, would have known where to take their concerns about course formats if they had really wanted those concerns addressed.) Does simple naïveté account for these missteps? Thorp would later say that he had "trusted" too much, and he would also later say about his ill-starred chancellorship that he had simply faced too steep a learning curve in dealing with the athletics portion of his portfolio.

Naïveté, alas, does not tell the full story. Thorp clearly shares responsibility for the institutional strategy of protecting athletics from further harm, even if it meant that honesty and integrity had to go by the wayside. Clues about his intentions in the summer of 2012 are found in the record of communications he had with the FEC subcommittee. On July 5, after the committee had completed its report and shared an advance copy with him—and before the subtle but persistent efforts in the coming three weeks to get "the one paragraph" modified—Maffly-Kipp had talked with the chancellor on the phone. During the conversation, as she reported to her subcommittee colleagues, she explained "our request to have an independent inquiry" that could yield sound recommendations to prevent a recurrence of "the mistakes that have been made regarding athletics." Thorp's reaction, which Maffly-Kipp paraphrased for her colleagues, was revealing indeed.

> [He] is concerned that the phrase "independent investigation" connotes something else: i. e., a look at the past, at who did what, with the goal of punishing people for past mistakes. . . . He asked whether we could consider substituting the phrase "outside entity" or something like it for "independent investigation." He is worried the latter will set off alarm bells and push an inquiry in the wrong direction. He is considering more of an audit than an investigation. . . . I think what he has in mind is a corporate entity, not a commission of beloved and wise educators.

Maffly-Kipp was bothered by the chancellor's preference for a corporate-style audit over an investigation with academics at the head of the table, but she and the others acquiesced in Thorp's request. The words *independent investigation* do not appear in their report.

Thorp's reasons for wanting the wording change—another subtle but important modification made to the subcommittee's text—repay careful parsing. He worried that the term *investigation* implied a look at the past to determine *who did what* and who should be held responsible for *past mistakes*. The word *investigation*, he had said, could easily lead in *the wrong direction*. Better to call for an "audit" that could be done by consultants rather than professors. Professors had already caused enough trouble. (The subcommittee eschewed the word *audit*, but they did cut *investigation* from their report, and they emphasized subtly and consistently that their eyes were on the future.) Maffly-Kipp reassured the chancellor when he expressed his concerns over the phone. She had told him that their goals, in calling for an independent inquiry, were "constructive and forward looking."

The *wrong direction* of any inquiry, from the chancellor's perspective, would be the direction that led toward the Loudermilk Center, especially if those snooping around started asking *who did what* and sought to uncover *past mistakes*. Thorp also made this clear in the letter he wrote to the Maffly-Kipp committee after they had finished their work. He thanked them specifically for the time they had invested into a report that was about the "academic issues in the department of African and Afro-American studies and what they mean for Carolina." Thorp said he was on board with the "thrust of where you think we need to go," and he mentioned in passing that the Board of Governors had also decided to "review the investigative work we have done related to the issues in African and Afro-American studies." The word *athletics* did not appear in the chancellor's letter. He must have assumed that the word might "set off alarm bells" and lead people in the "wrong direction." The blinkered tone of Thorp's letter caught the attention of Bachenheimer: "Were either of you struck by the emphasis in Holden's 'memo,'" he wrote to his subcommittee colleagues, "on academic issues in Af-Am rather than on our look at advising, admissions and culture, and steps going forward?"

Despite whatever misgivings they may have had about hidden agendas and the uses to which their report might be put, the members of the FEC subcommittee submitted to some of the pressures applied to them and massaged their text accordingly. This was only to be expected, since they worked with imperfect knowledge about the motives of their superiors, acted on their professorial instinct to be collegial, had faith in the core of their report and its recommendations, and also fully expected a subsequent inquiry that would engage in much broader fact gathering. The FEC subcommittee performed its task admirably and produced the only scandal-related document that raised honest and pertinent questions about the functioning of the athletic program. Subsequent events would also prove, however, that the FEC report had also handed a victory to Thorp, Boxill, Evans, and all Carolina personnel whose first priority was to squelch any further NCAA probing.

The summer academic recess of 2012 saw never a dull moment. The month of May had been dominated by the Hartlyn-Andrews report and its many reverberations. It was only in June that the *N&O* revealed that the AFAM 280 course had been custom-made for football players. Anticipation of the release of the FEC report marked the month of July. Then the mid-August exposure of Julius Peppers's transcript added a huge log to an already raging bonfire. The main cause of this inadvertent disclosure was UNC's dilatory, head-in-sand response to queries from Dan Kane about an alleged "test transcript" from 2001 that had been left on a public UNC server. After public relations officers spent weeks denying the possibility that the test transcript could be real—even though it was larded with AFRI/AFAM courses and looked suspiciously like the transcript of an athlete who had relied on AFRI/AFAM to stay eligible—Kane published a story about it and provided a link to the relevant web page, which, amazingly, university personnel had not bothered to take down. (Perhaps they had gone "all in" in an effort to bluff Kane.) Within hours one of the more resourceful posters on the Pack Pride fan forum identified the test transcript as the junior-year transcript of football star Peppers. By the following day the *N&O* had used this new evidence to connect the dots and suggest that the AFRI/AFAM scam had long predated the years covered in the Hartlyn-Andrews report. Not for the first time and not for the last, the university's stonewalling had backfired spectacularly. Carolina was making national news, and alumni had begun to voice their embarrassment. In a furious effort to put out the raging fire, the chancellor announced on August 17 that Governor Martin and Baker-Tilly would be leading a new review and that a panel of distinguished outsiders would also be invited to campus to act on the FEC subcommittee's recommendation to conduct a thorough review of the academic-athletic relationship at UNC.

Before the flames from the Peppers fiasco had fully receded, however, university leaders received the news they had eagerly anticipated for months. In a brief announcement posted on the university's website on the last day of August, Athletic Department spokesperson Steve Kirschner informed the community that NCAA staff had recently met with university counsel Leslie Strohm and senior associate dean Jonathan Hartlyn. At that time these members of the foundational working group had provided an "update to the enforcement staff" on the subject of the ongoing probes into suspect courses in AFRI/AFAM. (The working group, of course, had earlier determined that there were no "student-athlete eligibility issues" connected to the suspect courses.) Happily, the Athletic Department could now announce, at the time of the late-August update, that "the NCAA staff reaffirmed to university officials that no NCAA rules appeared to have been broken."[9] Even in the wake of the Hartlyn-Andrews and FEC reports, even after the steady stream of embarrassing academic revelations that flowed from May through August, UNC had been given a clean bill of health by NCAA enforcers. There was no reason to expect a new probe.

The university's announcement of this event was understated, and many questioned the curious timing of the news release—coming just days after the chancellor had announced the launch of a new inquiry. But if seen through the lens of the university's assiduous efforts at damage control in the preceding twelve months, the milestone character of the event is clear. University leadership had been angling toward this outcome ever since they absorbed the lessons of the McAdoo and Austin revelations. From the moment the university had alerted the NCAA to the existence of additional academic questions in August 2011, the goal of UNC personnel had been to convince NCAA investigators that no systemic academic problems could be traced to the athletic program or to a pattern of misconduct by athletics personnel. The FEC subcommittee report had posed the last significant obstacle to that objective, but the leadership of the university had successfully finessed the few problem spots in that document and the NCAA read the cues as they had been intended to read them. The painful dog days of August had therefore ended with vindication for the university's finely crafted strategy of producing showy half-measures while carefully hiding the disturbing realities centered in the ASPSA.

With his attention focused squarely on the NCAA and his many other management duties as chancellor, Holden Thorp probably never saw the falling boulder that would finally deliver the coup de grâce to his chancellorship—a fund-raising scandal involving the mother of UNC basketball superstar Tyler Hansbrough. That scandal, erupting only ten days after university leaders had quietly celebrated the NCAA grant of absolution, inaugurated a tumultuous fall semester that conveyed one unmistakable lesson. The UNC athletic scandal, despite the best efforts of the architects of the Carolina cover-up, refused to be smothered in its crib.

Six

On a Collision Course

A sense of nervous but excited anticipation had coursed through the UNC campus at the beginning of the 2011 academic year. The fall of 2012, by contrast, was marked from the outset by rancor and regret. The first Faculty Council meeting of the year, held on September 7, was tension filled. Although Chancellor Thorp confronted hostile comments from a faculty member for the first time since the scandal had begun, an oppressive atmosphere of collective embarrassment, disbelief, and muted anger—combined with residual apathy—served to stifle public discussion. About the Hartlyn-Andrews report, the FEC findings, the repeated exposure of university stonewalling, and the Julius Peppers episode—all the stunning developments that had unfolded since the end of the previous school year, that is—the faculty had virtually nothing to say. The elected members of the Faculty Council once again passed on the opportunity to demand answers from the university's leaders, and a faculty rift began to open between the "let's move on" crowd and a small but determined group that constituted what might be called the truth-and-reconciliation caucus.

Three days later came the news that Matt Kupec, the university's vice chancellor for advancement, and Tami Hansbrough, a gifts officer for the Office of Student Affairs and the mother of former superstar basketball player Tyler Hansbrough, had resigned their positions because of the impending public exposure of their misuse

of university funds. Hansbrough had had an intriguing employ-
ment history at UNC. Hired in December 2008 by the fund-raising
arm of UNC's Dental School Foundation, she had moved out of that
position after an audit revealed that she had traveled with foundation funds to see her son play basketball during his senior year,
during which the Tar Heels won their most recent national championship. Rules apparently had not been violated on those occasions because Hansbrough had solicited donors during the trips,
and she could thereby justify the expenses incurred, but her boss
nevertheless lost his job in the wake of the audit—evidently for having failed to manage this clear conflict of interest on Hansbrough's
part. After entering into a relationship with Kupec, Hansbrough
then landed a job as a gifts officer in the Office of the Vice Chancellor for Student Affairs. (The position was created expressly for
Hansbrough—at the prodding of Kupec and with the approval of
Thorp.)[1] Hansbrough and Kupec then went on to spend approximately seventeen thousand dollars on trips to see Tyler's brother
Ben Hansbrough play basketball for Notre Dame. For at least some
of those trips, transportation was provided by university-affiliated
medical planes. All expenses were covered by foundation money
that Kupec managed, money that had been given to the university
by private donors. Chancellor Thorp, it was soon to be revealed,
had accompanied the couple on more than one trip.

The revelations about what Thorp had known—he had approved
the use of university funds to place Tami Hansbrough in a custom-
made job in an office that had never had a fund-raising officer before,
and he had condoned expense-free trips that enabled her and her
boyfriend to follow her sons' basketball careers—caused the next
shoe to drop. On September 17, a week after the *Raleigh News &
Observer* had forced the disclosure of the Hansbrough-Kupec story,
Holden Thorp announced that he would resign his position at the
end of the 2012–13 school year. The exposure of favors handed to
yet another Carolina athlete (Kupec had quarterbacked the football
team in the late 1970s), in addition to the largesse showered on the
mother of the most celebrated UNC athlete of the twenty-first century, so compromised the already weakened chancellor that he felt
compelled to abandon his "dream job." A chancellorship that had

started amid the highest of expectations had come crashing down because of a series of athletics-related scandals.

An air of melancholy settled over UNC in the fall 2012 semester. Regrets about promise squandered and opportunities lost, coupled with the sensation of being caught in a downward spiral without end, left the campus embittered and unsure about next steps. Faculty chair Jan Boxill dissolved in tears when she heard about the chancellor's decision to leave his office in June. The Faculty Executive Committee organized a rally on the steps of South Building. Members of the university's Board of Trustees implored Thorp to reconsider his decision. Even those who thought a change at the top might be a good thing felt sympathy for the outgoing leader, who had clearly been dealt a bad hand. All were reluctant to begin a search for a new leader when so many important campus issues remained unresolved and when the state's political climate had suddenly made North Carolina a less inviting home for lifelong academics. Over the course of late September, as Thorp made clear that there would be no changing his mind about stepping down, the UNC community began to gaze into a very uncertain future.

While the campus was distracted and in mourning over the fall of a favored son, two countervailing and scandal-related forces set off on a collision course. The toxic cloud created by the impact of their encounter would color much of the 2012–13 academic year. First, Governor Jim Martin began his review of academic anomalies in the AFRI/AFAM Department; the review, which Chancellor Thorp had announced with fanfare only a few weeks earlier, would last four full months. Second, the *Raleigh News & Observer* continued its hard-hitting investigative reporting on problems in and around the Academic Support Program for Student Athletes. Dan Kane would produce stories that included embarrassing emails from academic counselors, indirect evidence of more ASPSA covering for plagiarism, and the bracingly candid testimony of former ASPSA employee Mary Willingham. By late December the irreconcilable claims put forward by Governor Martin and the reporters of the *N&O* led critical thinkers toward one uncomfortable but inescapable conclusion: someone was not telling the truth. For the balance of the academic year, university leaders would provide multiple, often painful, demonstrations of their own collective attitude toward truth telling.

Exposing the Need for an "Independent" Review

As the UNC scandal unfolded, the N&O proved its value to the Research Triangle area of North Carolina by serving as the most consistent and reliable source of information about the strange and troubling behavior that had occurred at UNC–Chapel Hill. Marvin Austin's curious B+ in that 400-level AFAM class taken before his freshman year, the football-players-only AFAM 280, Julius Nyang'oro's financial windfall in the summer of 2011, the astonishingly high athletic enrollments in all those suspect AFAM courses, Julius Peppers's strange academic itinerary, the Matt and Tami saga: none of these details about university malfeasance, negligence, and corruption would ever have seen the light of day had it not been for the work of the N&O's tireless investigative reporter Dan Kane. Some of Kane's best and most illuminating work appeared in the fall of 2012. His stories, by continuing to reveal facts so far undisclosed or deliberately hidden by the university, underlined the need for a no-holds-barred investigation of the athletic-academic relationship at UNC–Chapel Hill.

At the end of September Kane, in a story cowritten with J. Andrew Curliss, at last touched on one of the systemic problems—the university's admission of academically underprepared athletes—that had helped to drive the UNC scandal from the outset. In an explosive article, "UNC Players Needed Academic Help, Records Show," they published email exchanges between academic counselors (permanent staff who closely followed the academic itineraries of all the members of a given team or teams) and tutors (temporary employees, usually undergraduates, who helped athletes study and complete assignments for particular subjects) that showed the unmistakably low expectations that often guided the academic performance of athletes in the profit sports. It was this article that first introduced the concept of the paper class into the public domain, with Kane and Curliss reporting academic counselors' use of the shorthand to talk about Julius Nyang'oro's special no-show course offerings.[2]

More important, this was also the article that first hinted at the low reading and writing levels of some UNC athletes. One tutor was shown lamenting that "the process of reading and writing is slow and laborious" for one prominent football player; her superior responded to the tutor's frustrations by suggesting that she find "video lectures or demonstrations" to help the athlete absorb the course material. Such learning aids, the supervisor clearly implied, would helpfully obviate the need for actual reading.

This same concern to overcome the obstacles created by the athletes' learning deficiencies led learning specialist Amy Kleissler to promote Julius Nyang'oro's courses in an email she sent to the tutoring staff. Nyang'oro, she noted, had been "very generous" in offering independent study–style courses to students in the past, and "his expectations are very reasonable and very achievable for our students." She thus suggested that the AFRI 370 course offered in the spring of 2010—Policy Problems in African Studies—would be a good bet for "our students" (meaning those who often struggled in other classes). The course seemed a good bet mainly because it was a paper class, one that required only a term paper submitted at the end of the semester. (AFRI 370 did indeed fill up with athletes, who made up two-thirds of the twenty-one-person class.) When another tutor complained that one athlete seemed content to copy and paste his paper from Internet sources, her irritation generated no alarm in the ASPSA. Other staff emails, Kane and Curliss went on to note, showed tutors "working with athletes to turn plagiarized passages into acceptable material by paraphrasing." The techniques that had gone into the production of the notorious Michael McAdoo paper of 2009, in other words, reflected standard operating procedure in the ASPSA. (Kane and Curliss did their own review of one nineteen-page draft paper, on the subject of the oil industry in Nigeria. They found large passages "lifted word-for-word from a magazine article, a summary of a Nigerian conference proceeding, internet encyclopedias," and other sources available online. The sources were not cited.) When other players struggled to keep up in a regular Swahili class in the same semester in which AFRI 370 was offered, the instructor of the course, Alphonse Mutima, pressed the ASPSA staff to try to put them into an "independent study paper class" version of the course, where, as Kleissler had noted, the "expectations are very reasonable" for students who could not manage regular university course work.

The desire of the ASPSA staff to be "helpful," and their habitual efforts to compensate for the learning deficits of many at-risk athletes, may explain their decisive role in the plagiarism case of football player Erik Highsmith, which Dan Kane brought to light in October 2012.[3] In a communications course that he took in the spring of 2011, Highsmith had committed egregious acts of plagiarism in a blog assignment. (In one instance he stole text from an elementary school web page.) The instructor in the communications course, Janel Beckham, having spotted the theft and having suddenly realized that the lessons of UNC's athlete-and-tutor scandal had perhaps not been fully absorbed in the Athletic Department, reported the incident to staff members in the ASPSA. "I expressed my disappointment considering everything that had been going on for the last year," she told Kane. She received assurances that "it would be handled." Instead, the Highsmith plagiarism case went to the ASPSA to die a quiet death. ("I never heard anything," Beckham remembered.) Either the incident was never reported to the UNC Honor System as the UNC code of honor requires, or—much more implausibly—Honor System personnel determined that there was insufficient evidence to charge Highsmith with academic dishonesty.[4]

Why would the ASPSA staff surreptitiously snuff out the allegations against Highsmith? The reasons are many. The counselor or tutor to whom Beckham's concerns were first relayed almost surely felt sympathy for the football player. Counselors, tutors, and learning specialists know better than anyone how difficult it is for the top recruits in football and basketball to perform at a reasonable level academically while they put full-time efforts into their sports. Highsmith himself may or may not have been one of the more challenged athletes on the football team, but ASPSA staff would have seen the injustice in making Highsmith pay a steep price for engaging in a common practice that many athletes used as a life preserver in a difficult classroom environment. Plagiarism and deceptive "paraphrasing" had always been central to the paper-class experience, and at least some counselors and tutors regarded these techniques as both unavoidable and acceptable. They were morally acceptable, the reasoning went, because they kept athletes at the university and in classrooms where they at least learned something; kicking such players off teams or off campus would only place them beyond "help." Sympathy for the overburdened and often underprepared athlete would have predisposed the ASPSA staff to want to protect Highsmith from the consequences of his dishonesty.

But there were also other reasons to protect Highsmith. The high probability that the student-run Honor Court would return a guilty verdict would have meant a minimum one-semester suspension for him. (Michael McAdoo, Devon Ramsay, and others had even been suspended preemptively by the university in the fall of 2010 when their suspected dishonesty had first surfaced; Ramsay missed his junior season, even though he was convicted of nothing.) Given the likelihood that the court's ruling would not come down until early in the fall 2011 semester, this could have imperiled Highsmith's junior football season and, perhaps, his future NFL prospects. He had emerged as a star wide receiver during his sophomore year in 2010, and he would go on to have a standout junior season. Making the situation all the more delicate was the ongoing NCAA investigation of the UNC football program, which at that point was happily and narrowly focused on the tutor Jennifer Wiley and the "unauthorized assistance" she had given to three football players. (The details of the McAdoo case remained under cover, and the public as yet had no reason to suspect broad plagiarism issues in athletics.) In 2011 the suspension of yet another UNC football player for alleged academic dishonesty could have alerted the NCAA to the possibility of deeper problems in the UNC Athletic Department. This would have undermined the UNC scandal-management strategy that had been carefully developed since 2010, a strategy designed to persuade the NCAA that there were no underlying problems at UNC and that only a few rogues had to be removed.

The protection of Highsmith's eligibility in 2011 thus benefited not only Highsmith himself but also the besieged UNC Athletic Department. Whoever received Beckham's complaint in the spring of 2011 undoubtedly conferred with key players in the ASPSA (and perhaps beyond), and they made the collective decision simply to ignore the evidence of Highsmith's academic wrongdoing. After all, Beckham alone knew what had happened, and the communications instructor, who was pursuing a graduate degree in 2011, had already shown her inexperience by reporting the incident to the ASPSA rather than to the Honor System itself. Like the university lawyers and staff who went to the mat for Michael McAdoo during that NCAA teleconference in December 2010, the ASPSA personnel in the spring of 2011 assumed they could keep a tight lid on the details; they assumed they would never have to defend their decision making. They covered up Highsmith's plagiarism and moved on.

In the fall of 2012, when the story finally went public thanks to the N&O, Chancellor Holden Thorp made the perverse decision to endorse the ASPSA's earlier inaction. He, too, declined to enter an allegation against senior wide receiver Highsmith, even though he was pressed to do so by history faculty Willis Brooks and Jay Smith, who were appalled by this new lapse in university standards—one that had drawn derisive laughs from the national commentariat.[5] The instrument of student judicial governance, which regulates the operations of the Honor System at UNC, specifies that any "member of the University community" who becomes aware of an instance of academic dishonesty should "promptly submit" a report about the suspected offense to the student attorney general. Given the news headlines and the loud laughter that October, Thorp could have been expected to instruct judicial programs officer Erik Hunter to file a charge against Highsmith. Instead, he cited the principle of "faculty autonomy" to defend his own continuing inaction. To enter an allegation at this point, he said, would be to "have university administration step in and override an individual faculty member's decision," which "is not a good precedent."[6] This was a red herring of an argument if ever there was one, since Beckham herself, who was no longer even an employee of the university, had publicly expressed her own frustration at the ASPSA's earlier squelching of the case. There were no defensible reasons to allow Highsmith's blatant dishonesty to go unreported. But Thorp, Hunter, and faculty chair Jan Boxill—the three individuals to whom Brooks and Smith made personal appeals—all found reasons not to act.

In light of ongoing probes into UNC academic corruption during the fall 2012 semester—both Governor Martin and the accrediting body, the Southern Association of Colleges and Schools, were looking into UNC practices at that very moment—Thorp, one can only assume, must have seen advantages in discreetly countenancing one student's embarrassing dishonesty. The NCAA was still lurking, after all, and it was going to take careful management to ensure that the conclusions of Martin and SACS would not attract NCAA attention once again. (In the fall of 2013 the UNC compliance officer for the Athletic Department was *still* checking to make sure that no further sanctions were forthcoming from college sports' governing body.)[7] Thorp and other university leaders simply decided to run out the clock on the case of Erik Highsmith, who was soon headed to the pros. Their decision in that single case reflected the broader rope-a-dope strategy they consistently deployed against the NCAA, the press, and the public throughout the scandal years of 2010–13. Once again, the desire to protect the Athletic Department had easily overcome the imperative to defend broader university interests and values.

In November 2012 the university faced what was, until that time, the greatest challenge to its broad strategy of dithering and denial. Only a few days before the Thanksgiving break, Dan Kane published the first insider account of the activities within the ASPSA. Kane had been trying to talk to virtually every employee in the ASPSA ever since the UNC story had metastasized into a major academic scandal in the summer of 2011. He had had zero success in getting anyone to go on the record; most refused to speak with him at all. For months, though, he had had fruitful and eye-opening conversations with Mary Willingham, who had made her long-anticipated escape from the ASPSA only a few months before Marvin Austin's tweet set off the UNC earthquake. Because she still had friends in the ASPSA and worried about the fallout from public exposure of their practices, and because she kept waiting for "the adults" to step forward to own up to the massive failures of which the scandal was only a symptom, Willingham withheld from Kane the permission to use her words in print. She preferred to wait; she wanted to give others the opportunity to address the many problems that had long bothered her. (The wait had been long indeed—dating back to her days in the ASPSA and, more recently, to her September 2010 conversation with Lissa Broome and Steve Keadey.)

This attitude changed in October 2012. The death of UNC's revered paterfamilias, emeritus president Bill Friday, unexpectedly galvanized Willingham. She found a new determination to do the right thing. Moved by Hodding Carter's testimonial at Friday's memorial service, in which he especially recalled his old friend's passionate leadership in the cause of college athletics reform, Willingham began to rethink her public reticence. As she looked around her at the sea of faces at Friday's memorial service, she saw many key administrators and Athletic Department officials (including some of her friends) who had remained tightlipped about all that they knew. Watching them quietly celebrate a man who had always championed integrity, and who had warned the university repeatedly of the need to rein in its athletic enthusiasms, left Willingham saddened and angry.

Earlier, in the fall of 2010, not long after her meeting with Keadey and Broome, Willingham had made some tentative steps toward addressing some of the structural problems that had been gnawing at her conscience since 2003. She sent copies of her master's thesis, on the broad subject of NCAA academic corruption, to dozens of people connected to the university. She wanted to make them aware of her presence in the community, and also to alert them to the deeper problems that the scandal headlines left always in obscurity. She contacted a great crowd of luminaries in those months, including Holden Thorp, Faculty Athletics Committee chair Steve Reznick, longtime faculty athletics representative Jack Evans, admissions director Steven Farmer, and associate athletic director John Blanchard. Only one person reached out to her in response: Bill Friday. The president's assistant arranged a meeting in Friday's Johnston Center office, and a humbled Willingham was soon making the trek across campus with gift chocolates in hand. The avuncular Friday, clearly distressed by all the scandal news, thanked Willingham for coming and for sharing her experiences with him. But he soon cut to the chase. Why, he asked, had she not yet spoken out about the problems she had witnessed at UNC? The faculty, he said, should have been marching on Polk Place by now. Where was the demand for accountability? Such apathy would never have been seen in the old days, he lamented. He hoped that he would be able to arrange a meeting between Willingham and UNC system president Tom Ross, who—he was certain—would listen to her stories with a sympathetic ear.

Not long after that meeting, the ninety-one-year-old Friday faced a series of health problems that led to surgery, a long period of convalescence, a second prolonged hospital stay, and, eventually, his final battle with heart disease. Willingham never had another opportunity to meet with UNC's legendary leader, but the conversation they shared stayed with her in the months to come. While taking in the picture of hypocrisy presented by the attendees at Friday's memorial service in October 2012, she turned over in her mind one piece of advice that the great man had given her on the day of their meeting—"Always tell the truth." She started her own blog, calling it *Athletics vs. Academics*. A few days later she gave Dan Kane a call.

In a pivotal Kane article of November 17, 2012, Willingham finally went on the record to detail her long-building frustrations with the ASPSA's casual acceptance of dishonesty and double standards.[8] The connection between the learning deficiencies of many athletes and the pressure to cheat academically was at last laid bare in a public forum. "If you cannot do the course work here, how do you stay eligible?" Willingham answered her own question: "You stay eligible by some department, some professor, somebody [giving] you a break. . . . Here it happened with paper classes." Willingham strongly implied in the article what she would later confirm in an interview with Joe Nocera: "All the academic counselors knew about the paper classes, and they all steered athletes to them."[9]

The behavior of the ASPSA's leaders had indicated that, at least for the most part, they were only too happy to take advantage of the break that the Nyang'oro-Crowder curricular system provided for their eligibility-challenged charges. Willingham told Kane, for example, that she had alerted the director of the ASPSA in 2008 to the excessively cozy relationship between Jennifer Wiley and various football players. She had become concerned about the tutor when she looked over a football player's draft history paper, and she recognized instantly that the player could not have produced the paper's prose. (This individual struggled with literacy.) The ASPSA director, Robert Mercer, referred the matter to the football academic counselor, Beth Bridger, who promptly quashed the matter. There were no adverse consequences for the overzealous tutoring. On the contrary, Wiley won the ASPSA's "Outstanding Tutor" award later in the very same year. (Was Bridger also the person to whom Janel Beckham would later report her complaints about Highsmith? The university has not disclosed any information about the handling of the Highsmith case, but Bridger was still the principal football counselor in 2011.) Although this was not the first time that Willingham's coworkers and bosses had advised her not to worry about the evidence of cheating that she saw, this incident convinced her that she had to leave what had clearly become a toxic environment; she spent the next year looking for a new position at the university.

Among the most important revelations of the Kane article on Willingham was the disclosure that other university officials had clearly seen suspect activities long before the scandal broke and that they had taken steps either to correct some of the problems or to insulate themselves from blame for those problems. By 2006 someone in the dean's office had finally noticed that the AFRI/AFAM Department had been offering inordinate numbers of independent study courses. (Kane noted that the department was averaging "nearly 200 a year" by that time; apparently, even he did not know that the department, between 2001 and 2005, had actually offered an average of well over 200 independent study courses each year, including 341 in 2003–4 and the two summer sessions that followed.) In 2005–6 the university had been collecting teaching data in preparation for its ten-year SACS reaccreditation review, and anomalous enrollment figures may have surfaced in the course of routine data collection. Whatever the cause, Willingham recalled that senior associate dean for undergraduate education Bobbi Owen let it be known in the halls of the ASPSA that the overreliance on independent study courses in AFRI/AFAM had to stop. Owen also evidently let Julius Nyang'oro or Debby Crowder know that the college was watching them, because the annual numbers of independent study courses in their department fell precipitously after 2006. No one from the university has ever explained why that change occurred. Nor has anyone explained why the college, though suddenly alert to the abuse of independent study offerings in AFRI/AFAM, stopped short of carrying out a thorough review of the department's curricular practices.

Within the ASPSA basketball academic counselor Jennifer Townsend had also taken note of course registration patterns and had evidently become alarmed by what she saw. Arriving at UNC from the University of Minnesota only in 2009, Townsend quickly recognized that the basketball team was benefiting from a questionable arrangement with AFRI/AFAM, and she immediately moved to put a stop to it. (Townsend's sensitivity to wrongdoing may have reflected Minnesota's own experience with academic fraud. The team had vacated its 1997 Final Four appearance after it was discovered that counselors—none of them named Townsend—had been writing papers for basketball players during most of the Clem Haskins era.) Enrollment data show unmistakably that from the fall of 2009, men's basketball players stayed away from AFRI/AFAM.

To members of the UNC community who had struggled to maintain their trust in UNC's athletic program, and to keep the faith that South Building knew what it was doing, Dan Kane's article on Willingham felt like a dousing in ice-cold water. For the first time, a university employee had said publicly what many had long suspected but did not want to believe. Well before 2011 officials at the university had reasons to suspect the Nyang'oro-Crowder malfeasance. Academic counselors and learning specialists had zestfully exploited the curricular loopholes opened up by the chair of AFRI/AFAM. Those who understood how wrong these practices were had done far too little to stop them. Perhaps worst of all, since 2010 no one had had the courage and candor to step forward to confess their earlier suspicions or to announce their own conscious or inadvertent complicity in a curricular scam that had now defamed the university. By being the first to step into the firing line—reasonable people could wonder why she had not acted sooner, after all—Mary Willingham had simultaneously highlighted the self-interest, fearfulness, and moral indifference that had thus far defined the university's reaction to its scandal. Willingham's final quote from the Kane article read like an indictment. While excusing the largely blameless athletes for the mess now created, she noted, "It's the adults who are not doing what they are supposed to do."

The behavior of UNC's adults in the wake of the Willingham piece was far from inspiring. The high-priced public relations consultants that the university had hired put their heads together with athletic and administrative officials. Within a few days the brain trust had decided on a strategy to discredit the whistle-blower and her highly embarrassing testimony. (Willingham, it must be remembered, had spent more than two years working behind the scenes to get the attention of anyone who would listen to her. She only repeated for the N&O complaints she had communicated earlier to various leaders.) In a letter to the editor of the N&O, published four days after the Kane article on Willingham, associate athletic director Steve Kirschner effectively called Willingham a liar; he defended the integrity of the ASPSA, and he disputed that Townsend had ever voiced concerns about AFRI/AFAM courses. He also used the NCAA's fecklessness as a cover for Athletic Department practices. "Your readers should know," he said, "that Mary Willingham was interviewed in the fall of 2010 as part of the joint NCAA/university review of the football program, so the NCAA is well aware of the statements she made at that time." With the NCAA having given the university a clean bill of health as recently as August, what were people now to make of Willingham's claims? They were clearly rooted in fantasy, Kirschner implied.

Kirschner's letter had the awkward legalisms of a text assembled by committee—administrators and consultants had "reviewed and offered edits" to the text, Dan Kane would later reveal—but the central message came through loud and clear.[10] The readers of the N&O were told to pay no attention to the woman behind the curtain; her stories had revealed nothing newsworthy, nothing to change impressions of the magical repair work being performed in the Emerald City. Leaders had "taken steps to identify and correct any problems that have been identified." As a consequence, "dozens of reforms and new policies have been implemented across the university in both academics and athletics." The nature of "any problems" in athletics had never been specified in public—Thorp and company had blamed only academics and academic personnel in their public discourse—but the public could nevertheless rest assured that those unspecified "problems" had been caught and fixed, Mary Willingham's confused ramblings notwithstanding.

The Kirschner letter constituted the sum total of the university's public reaction to Willingham's testimony. With one notable exception, no one in a position of authority called Willingham to arrange a meeting, to hear more about her experiences, to listen to her concerns, to see the proof of her claims, or to arrange a public discussion of the important issues her disclosures had raised.[11] She met a wall of silence on the UNC campus. (One old friend from academic counseling at least had the courtesy to approach her; Jan Boxill told Willingham how disappointed and "hurt" she was to see Willingham speaking out "when everything seemed to be going so well." The FEC report had been doctored, and the NCAA had given the all clear. Boxill was evidently disturbed that her friend would not leave well enough alone.) The university had never wanted to hear all that Willingham had to say, and her public revelations only guaranteed that the pattern of avoidance, the determination to "hear no evil," would continue. After all, Willingham had told many superiors about many problems in the past, and those superiors now had their own exposed complicity to worry about. By pointing out the university's failure to honor athletes' scholarship agreements, and by complicating the message that the university had been laboring to sell the world since the previous May, Willingham made herself radioactive in the fall of 2012. Her own boss, Harold Woodard, who was one of many who had been given a very early preview of Willingham's claims, studiously avoided contact with her for the remainder of the year.

Dan Kane's reporting in the fall of 2012 had left UNC's leaders defensive and generally speechless. Their deafening silence in the wake of the Willingham story had removed whatever doubts remained about their ability to address honestly the full range of problems that lay behind the scandal. The only surviving hope was that the forthcoming Martin report would drag those problems out into the sunlight, where the university would be forced to confront them. The release of the Martin report, alas, was only the catalyst for a new series of shocks to the conscience. A critical public had to watch in disbelief as the state's flagship university placed ribbons and a bow on its tightly packaged cover-up.

The Martin Report and Beyond

On December 20, 2012, former North Carolina governor Jim Martin addressed UNC–Chapel Hill's Board of Trustees. In August he had been asked by Chancellor Holden Thorp to review the "academic anomalies" associated with AFRI/AFAM, to determine if possible when that department's problems had begun, and to find whether similar irregularities had occurred in other academic departments in the university over the same period. These anomalies, of course, had figured prominently in the curricular records of UNC athletes, and they had come to light only because of the inadvertent discovery of academic misconduct by football players. Because of the university's secret priority to fend off the NCAA, however, earlier reports had failed to answer many of the questions surrounding the academic misbehavior that had been exposed. At the chancellor's request (which had been forced by faculty grumbling), Martin and the academic accounting firm Baker-Tilly, which had been hired to assist him in his task, had therefore carried out a semester-long inquiry for the ostensible purpose of getting to the bottom of a scandal that had roiled the UNC campus for more than two years. By late December the air was thick with anticipation. When word leaked out a few days before the BOT meeting that Martin's results would at last be announced to the public at the upcoming gathering of the board, the N&O and other area newspapers ran stories recapping the history of the scandal and building excitement around its seemingly imminent conclusion.

With a politician's flair for the dramatic, Governor Martin opened his address to the BOT with words he knew many longed to hear. "This was not an athletic scandal. It was an academic scandal, which is worse; but an isolated one." The hundreds of people who had packed the room at the historic Carolina Inn, and the many others who watched the proceedings live online, were knocked breathless by the unqualified nature of Martin's announcement. How was this possible? It had long been known that athletes enrolled disproportionately in the problematic courses offered by Julius Nyang'oro and Debby Crowder. The university had already ousted ASPSA director Robert Mercer (the announcement that John Blanchard was also headed out the door would come in February). Longtime athletic director Dick Baddour had announced his early retirement when UNC first revealed that its simmering football scandal had developed an academic dimension. And Jennifer Wiley, the now infamous tutor, had been employed in the home of the fired head football coach, Butch Davis, during the period when some of the worst infractions had occurred. In short, with the exception of Nyang'oro and Crowder, all of the key actors accused of negligence or wrongdoing had been associated with the Athletic Department.

Yet Governor Martin now stood before his assembled audience and proclaimed "with confidence" that the Athletic Department bore no responsibility for the academic scandal that had rocked the UNC campus. He dismissed as mere "speculation" the idea that the needs of athletics had been behind the corruption of academic procedure at UNC. Among the dozens of people he had interviewed in the course of his inquiry was one Mary Willingham, who met with Martin in October. She told the governor in direct terms that pressure to keep underprepared athletes academically eligible had created a culture of corruption in the athletic complex. When Martin and his assistant Matt Dankner sought to minimize her concerns by citing statistics on grades and academic majors, Willingham questioned the legitimacy of the aggregate grade point averages they were using as the raw material for their comparisons and calculations. In retrospect, it became quite clear that Martin and Dankner had already settled on their interpretation of UNC's troubles, and they therefore absorbed little of what Willingham had to say. In the end, they simply placed Willingham's whistle-blower testimony in a category of "additional opinions and observations" that could not be corroborated.[12]

Careful dissection of the Martin report and the work that went into it reveals why Willingham's perspective simply could not be accommodated by the governor and his team. As with the Faculty

Executive Committee subcommittee report from the previous July, athletics-friendly personnel contaminated Martin's product—much more egregiously so than in the previous summer—by going to its very source. They subtly controlled the flow of information, opinions, and expertise to which Martin had ready access.

By carefully managing the conclusions and interpretations of the earlier reports from the spring and summer—reports that had conspicuously yielded no new NCAA concerns, "no evidence" of special treatment for athletes, no culpability for wrongdoing outside of AFRI/AFAM, and no suggestion of a need to "look at the past, at who did what"—the chancellor limited at the outset the analytical parameters for Martin's inquiry. This preliminary manipulation, the product of university-wide strategizing, helped to determine who showed up on Martin's interview list, which questions were asked, which perspectives were credited, and which records were audited. Martin effectively set out with the assumption that the problems at UNC were essentially academic in character, and he considered it his job to make sure that those academic problems had indeed been confined to a single administrative unit; such would be the nature of the inquiry carried out by Martin and the Baker-Tilly firm. (Laurie Maffly-Kipp had said about Thorp's intentions in July, "He is considering more of an audit than an investigation," one that would be carried out by a "corporate entity.") When Martin commenced his work, one administrative unit on campus particularly benefited from the presumption of innocence: the Athletic Department.

This presumption of innocence can be seen in Martin's methods of data collection, in the various filters he used to interpret his evidence, and in the unskeptical trust he placed in university officials who had athletic interests to defend. A curious and genuinely impartial investigator would have immediately ordered the collection of student records in order to map out the long-term academic itineraries of UNC athletes, both by individual and in the aggregate. Amazingly, however, Governor Martin never looked at a single student transcript. This meant, among other things, that he had never bothered to determine whether athletes in the profit sports, or in any other sports, had their eligibility restored or retained through the vehicle of paper classes. He never even compared GPAs earned in paper classes with GPAs earned in legitimate university courses, a comparison that would have alerted him to the actual function of the paper classes on the profit-sport teams.

Martin also never tried to discern course-enrollment patterns by team—though at least several of his interviewees had urged him to do so. He evidently never inquired about drop/add practices that allowed athletes to pick up paper classes midway through a semester or to retroactively withdraw from courses that threatened to leave black marks on their transcripts. He accepted at face value academic counselors' self-interested portrayal of their routine activities, and he also credited without question the Mercer and Blanchard story about the Faculty Athletics Committee and its alleged green-lighting of exotic pedagogy.[13]

Martin's scales were clearly tipped in favor of athletics, and he embraced whatever exculpatory claims that athletics-friendly personnel could muster. Equally striking, however, are the documents he disregarded and the list of people he ignored. Martin never interviewed former or current men's basketball players, nor did he chat with anyone from the basketball coaching staff. He talked to no current football players and only to two former players (one of them a walk-on whose experience was by definition atypical). He never sought interviews with students who had taken classes in which profit-sport athletes also enrolled. He never spoke with Carolyn Cannon, the former advising dean who had made advising for the men's basketball team her exclusive bailiwick. After an initial meeting in August, he never spoke again with Jay Smith, even though curricular changes that Smith had supervised in 2005–6 would come to figure decisively in some of Martin's interpretations of AFRI/AFAM malfeasance.[14] He ignored the faculty who served on the special-talents admission committee, who could have given him a clearer picture of the academic profiles of committee-case admissions. He even declined to speak with the faculty who had served on the Faculty Athletics Committee in 2002 and 2006. Although he was happy to use their alleged freewheeling negligence to excuse the ASPSA for responsibility in the AFRI/AFAM course scheme, it never occurred to him that it might be a good idea to verify the truth of the ASPSA story before going on to cite its crucial importance seven times in his report.

Perhaps most astoundingly, Martin never sought out email correspondence between ASPSA personnel, AFRI/AFAM personnel, and the regular academic advising staff in Steele Building. At least some of that correspondence clearly incriminated ASPSA counselors in the perpetuation of the fraud, and it showed Nyang'oro's familiar relationships with several counselors.[15] The world would have to wait for the university's processing of Dan Kane's public records requests before any of these emails came to light, however, as they finally began to do in the summer of 2013. Since Martin repeatedly praised the university for giving him unfettered access to all records, his failure to review email correspondence can only be regarded as the product of deliberate choice.[16]

Jim Martin thus never encountered, and in many cases never looked for, the abundant evidence detailing Athletic Department complicity in UNC's academic fraud. His performance gave perfect expression to the "see no evil, hear no evil, speak no evil" strategy that the university had used as a protective cloak over the Athletic Department since 2010. Untroubled by knowledge that would have complicated or contradicted the conclusions of his limited analysis, he went on to use emphatic rhetoric in his pronouncements to the BOT and in the wording of his report. The Martin report, in fact, as well as the public commentary with which the governor adorned its findings, often approached what George Orwell famously defined as "doublespeak"—a rhetoric that purports to capture reality but in fact brazenly contradicts it (for example, "Ignorance is strength").

Martin told the BOT, for example, that there was "absolutely no evidence" that anyone in athletics pushed athletes toward AFRI/AFAM courses.[17] This claim was breathtaking. Mary Willingham had said of the ASPSA counselors, in her meeting with Martin, that they used paper classes for eligibility purposes. Had he not been listening? Even if he had focused solely on what was widely known about the "certification of eligibility" process within the athletic program—a process that required counselors' careful selection of courses for their athletes—and facts already revealed to the public, there would have been no way for Martin to arrive at this bizarre conclusion. How would he explain, for example, the notorious AFAM 280 course from the summer of 2011? As everyone now knew, the course had appeared on the department's roster of courses just two days before the summer session began. Yet on the first day of classes, nineteen students showed up in enrollment records—every one of them a football player. It was inconceivable that this had happened without the active collusion of one or more ASPSA counselors. Indeed, this no-show course was undoubtedly placed on the schedule at a counselor's behest. Martin, like Deans Hartlyn and Andrews before him, simply ignored AFAM 280 and told the story he wanted to tell. "Absolutely no evidence"? *Ignorance is strength.*

Martin made many other statements that he ought to have known would eventually be proved wrong. To tamp down suspicions that high numbers of athletes in the problem courses might suggest a gaming of the system by the Athletic Department, he asserted, "The percentage of student-athletes enrolled in anomalous course sections was consistent with the percentage of student-athletes enrolled in all courses offered by the department."[18] This statement was patently false, as the figures belatedly released in an addendum to the Martin report would soon make clear. Between 2001 and 2012, the years for which Martin claimed to have the most thorough statistical evidence, 45 percent of the students in the fraudulent courses were athletes, even though athletes made up no more than about 12 percent of enrollments in legitimate AFRI/AFAM courses. (They make up only about 4 percent of UNC's undergraduate population.)[19]

When Martin further declared in his report that he was "unable to discern a clear motive for establishing and offering these perverse and anomalous courses," one could almost assume that he had neglected to consult his own statistics.[20] Martin, like all UNC administrators since Hartlyn and Andrews, made much of the fact that many of the anomalous courses enrolled a lot of nonathletes as well as athletes. And indeed, a few sections of the courses had no athletes enrolled at all. But if one sifts patiently through the aggregate figures that Martin and Baker-Tilly presented in their own documents, one finds telling clues to the real purpose behind the "perverse" courses. A review of the figures for the smaller, more intimate courses that enrolled between five and fifteen students—

the course sections most likely to be offered in response to a request for a favor or to address an immediate need—shows that athletes always dominated. Among the lecture courses that Baker-Tilly categorized as "Type II" anomalies, and in which concerns about the Family Educational Rights and Privacy Act (FERPA) did not restrict Martin's ability to disclose athlete-to-nonathlete ratios, athletes accounted for 67 percent of students in the small courses. In summers, when athletes' needs tended to be more acute, the rate of their participation rose to 77.5 percent. An even more impressive 66 out of 76, or 87 percent, of the beneficiaries of Martin's "Type I" course anomalies were athletes.[21] In summers they accounted for an astonishing 96 percent of the seats taken. To say that no motive was clearly discernible in such figures was to reject the blunt force of reality. Paper classes frequently preserved eligibility for star players or weak students.

Martin thus consistently put an athletics-friendly spin on the evidence, and when he had no evidence available, he made things up. Having failed, like everyone before him, to squeeze a single word out of either Julius Nyang'oro or Debby Crowder, Martin was reduced to sheer speculation in his attempt to account even tentatively for the motives of the two AFRI/AFAM leaders. A wholly uninformed observer familiar only with the broad outlines of the case might have offered several hypotheses. Maybe the two had enjoyed the familiarity, the intimacy, with athletes that their favoritism afforded them? Maybe they looked for ways to be "helpful" to all "needy" students, among whom athletes always figured disproportionately? Or perhaps they had been given various inducements from people in or around the UNC athletic program (or other campus programs, since this apparently was not an athletics story at all)?

Martin ignored or discounted all of these possible explanations. He even consigned to a chart near the end of the report the news that Debby Crowder had received a bequest of one hundred thousand dollars from the family of the late basketball counselor Burgess McSwain in 2008, a detail that suggested "nothing inappropriate" to Martin's team—though it clearly did suggest an unusually close relationship between two of the three key originators of the academic double-standard system.[22] (Martin had clearly gotten the mes-

Table 2. Semester eligibility patterns (football and basketball sample)

Football

Semester pattern of eligibility	Number of PC	Cumulative GPA without PC	Cumulative GPA
SEM 1 (fall)	1	2.1	2.53
SEM 2	0	1.9	2.13
SS 1&2	1	1.7	2.18
SEM 3 (fall)	0	1.6	1.75
SEM 4	1	1.7	2
SS 1&2	1	1.85	2
SEM 5 (fall)	0	1.9	2.33
SEM 6	0	1.3	1.89
SS 1&2	3	1.6	2.1
SEM 7 (fall)[a]	0	1.73	2.1

Basketball

Semester pattern of eligibility	Number of PC	Cumulative GPA without PC	Cumulative GPA
SS 1&2	0		2.84
SEM 1	2	2.33	2.57
SEM 2 (spring)	1	1.81	2.27
SS 1&2	1	1.96	2.39
SEM 3	1	1.64	2.13
SEM 4 (spring)	2	1.6	2.23
SS 1&2	1	1.65	2.28
SEM 5	0	1.77	2.28
SEM 6 (spring)	1	1.74	2.2
SS 1&2	2	1.74	2.29
SEM 7	3	1.64	2.34
SEM 8 (spring)	4	1.62	2.3

[a]The football player left after the seventh semester.

Note: SEM = semester; PC = paper class; SS = summer sessions.
These two tables show the impact of paper classes on the eligibility of one representative football and one representative basketball player.

Table 3. Paper-class advantage to grade point average

Total GPA	Number of PC	GPA in other courses
2.3	15	1.64
2.3	18	1.56
2.9	13	2.15
2.6	14	2.14
2.6	12	1.93
2.3	14	1.54
2.3	9	1.90
2.2	6	2.04
1.9	6	1.72
2.1	9	1.82
2.1	7	1.73
1.6	12	0.90
2.2	4	1.98
2.2	5	2.03
2.6	5	2.49
2.5	3	2.38
2.4	11	2.02
2	10	1.68
1.9	8	1.51

Sample of paper-class impact on GPA.

sage that Crowder was no booster with "extremely close ties" to the Athletic Department; Crowder's and Nyang'oro's status as gung-ho UNC sports fans went unmentioned in his seventy-four page report.) Consistent with the overall tenor of his report, Martin sought to account for motive by inventing an alternative explanation that had literally nothing to do with athletics. "We noted the possibility," Martin said, "that an emerging department would be motivated to increase its enrollment."[23] Julius Nyang'oro, in other words, had perhaps devised this grand and fraudulent scheme in order to make AFRI/AFAM look like a department with robust enrollment figures.

Here the governor seemed to be grasping at straws. The AFRI/AFAM Department had long been considered an enrollment "success story" in the College of Arts and Sciences, and its enrollments had remained healthy throughout the Nyang'oro era. AFRI/AFAM had become a department in 1997 largely because of its enrollment figures, not in spite of them. And Martin's own numbers offered scant support for the idea that Nyang'oro had sought and found a surefire technique to make AFRI/AFAM look like an enrollment driver in the college. The Martin and Baker-Tilly figures showed that at the end of an eight-year period that preceded the introduction of the university's new general education curriculum in 2006, annual enrollments in AFRI/AFAM had grown 13.6 percent. By contrast, in all other departments of the College of Arts and Sciences over that same eight-year period, annual enrollments had increased 13 percent.[24] The enrollment increase in AFRI/AFAM, in other words, was consistent with the overall increase in the size of the UNC student body beginning in the late 1990s. Nyang'oro had attracted a few more students than might have been expected if he had been running only normal courses, but the difference in numbers was statistically negligible. Besides, much other evidence from the period suggests that Nyang'oro was unusually irresponsible in attending to broad departmental interests—including enrollments—during the scandal years.[25]

At the BOT meeting where Martin announced his results, Chancellor Thorp was subdued but also visibly relieved. Craving closure, like everyone else in the room, he began the meeting by assuring the BOT that "the hard questions have been asked and answered." He knew that the illusion of thoroughness that Martin and Baker-Tilly had crafted would position the university well to "move on" from scandal and embarrassment. The elated, mirthful reactions of the board members who sat listening to Martin's summary findings suggested that, indeed, the university stood poised to turn a corner.

In truth, however, the Martin report, together with a UNC Board of Governors review that affirmed and celebrated Martin's findings a few months after, crystallized a UNC cover-up that had been driven all along by the imperative to protect the Athletic Department, whatever the cost. Suspicions and unanswered questions would therefore continue to fester. Within hours of the Martin report's release, close readers were poking holes in the governor's reasoning, wondering about the incompleteness of his statistics, and questioning the strategy behind his analysis. The criticism that followed the report's publication was withering, and after a Baker-Tilly spokesperson admitted that the critical claim about the Faculty Athletics Committee's assurances to the ASPSA in 2002 and 2006 had no evidentiary basis—any conversations had taken place "sort of offline," she said—the governor had to issue an official retraction of that important piece of exculpatory evidence.[26]

Before the retraction, however, university leaders had already demonstrated their fealty to Martin and his report. Members who had served on the Faculty Athletics Committee in 2002 and 2006 had noticed the libelous treatment Martin had given them. At a January 2013 meeting of the Faculty Council, one of the former members of the committee—History Department chair Lloyd Kramer—disputed Martin's claim that the FAC had ever had a discussion about anomalous independent study courses in 2002 or 2006. Pressing Holden Thorp and faculty chair Jan Boxill, he asserted that "faculty have a duty to correct this finding and to dispute the suggestion that faculty would let academic fraud continue under the guise of academic freedom." He asked about the process for amending the report or registering an official dissent from this key finding.[27]

What followed was an amazing display of evasiveness and dishonesty. Holden Thorp, of course, knew better than anyone in the room why Martin had asserted so confidently that the FAC was guilty and the ASPSA was therefore innocent. Whether through acquiescence in a dishonest scheme devised by others or through excessive trust in others, Thorp had been the one who polluted the information stream that flowed into the FEC report back in July, and he and others had clearly made sure that Martin fastened on the importance of the Blanchard-Mercer story as the governor went about crafting his own overall interpretation of the UNC scandal. (Thorp's role in this episode had just been revealed by the N&O two weeks before this faculty meeting.)[28] Thorp, like Martin, had never bothered to verify the story's veracity, but he had clearly recognized its utility. Now, at the Faculty Council meeting, Thorp declined to show any remorse for having promoted a story that was on the verge of being publicly discredited. Instead, he simply asserted that Martin's report had been an "independent" one, just as "everyone wanted," and its conclusions therefore could not be challenged. "We embrace the report," he said. So close to the finish line, with the cover-up nearly secured, Holden Thorp was ready to declare Martin's report definitive; he was in no mood for do-overs.

Those who joined Thorp in his warm embrace of the Martin report also chimed in. Jan Boxill, who praised Martin's report for its thoroughness, challenged the accuracy of Kramer's memory. Did minutes from the Faculty Athletics Committee meetings not prove that the discussion about the strange independent study courses had taken place? (In fact, the minutes showed no such thing.) When Kramer reminded her that he was in the room at the time and recalled no such conversation, she responded that "faculty do not precisely remember conversations that occur in committee meetings." Kramer had probably just forgotten what he and the FAC had done. The current chair of the FAC, Joy Renner, jumped up to agree with Boxill. Memory was an uncertain thing, and conversations can always be "interpreted differently." When Jay Smith asked Renner whether even one piece of evidence suggested that course anomalies had ever been discussed at the FAC, Holden Thorp thought it appropriate to intervene: "Joy wasn't even present at those FAC meetings," so her comments should be taken only as commonsense speculation. Anthropology professor Vincas Steponaitis added his voice to the chorus. Even if what Kramer said was perfectly true, he noted, it was time to move on. "How does what happened at a meeting in 2002 and 2006 affect moving forward? In my mind it doesn't."[29]

The "move forward" brigade carried the day. Kramer was at least able to enter a letter of dissent into the Faculty Council minutes at the next council meeting in February.[30] The letter bore the signatures of most of the faculty who had served on the FAC during his tenure, and no committee member—not even the conspicuously silent Jack Evans—ever publicly supported the Blanchard and Mercer account of what had happened in 2002 and 2006. But Martin's general conclusions, it had become clear to everyone, were not going to be reopened for discussion if Thorp, Boxill, and their allies had any say in the matter. Those conclusions protected the ASPSA and diverted attention from athletic admission practices, and that fact trumped all others.

When the Athletic Reform Group proposed at another strained faculty meeting in March that the Faculty Council should call for a series of "town hall" meetings that would finally make it possible to air conflicting views about the scandal and to seek accountability from deans, coaches, and administrators, Boxill demurred. Although she and her supporters acknowledged that public discussions about controversial issues often happened on university campuses, in this case there had already been a whole lot of talk after all. Biology professor Greg Copenhaver, after objecting to the disrespectful tone of chief university critic Jay Smith, claimed that the problems at UNC had all been the fault of two academic officers anyway, so he was unsure about what was to be gained by further discussion. He said something about the removal of the few "bad actors" and the impressive virtues of UNC "student-athletes," a comment that drew shouts and applause from the council. Steponaitis said that he did not object to having further public forums, but he insisted that if any public discussions were to take place, the organizers would have to make sure that the conversation not become overly critical. "All points of view" had to be evenly represented.

The chancellor noted that American Association of University Professors president Hunter Rawlings would soon be coming to town and that he would lead a panel discussion of some sort. Wasn't that enough? (Acting as a careful tactician, Thorp had arranged beforehand that the Rawlings group he called into being would look only toward the future in its consideration of the intersection of academics and athletics. The August 2013 Rawlings report, with its long list of worthy recommendations, said scarcely a word about the University of North Carolina at Chapel Hill. There was not even a suggestion that a scandal had occurred there.) Boxill finally expressed support for the idea of town-hall discussions, at least in principle, but she carefully avoided making any commitments.

The rest of the spring semester frittered away. The following fall semester came and went. Boxill never organized a town hall–style discussion for the UNC campus. When newly embarrassing revelations in the spring and summer of 2013 raised still more questions about who had known what and when during the UNC scandal, university dignitaries simply refused to acknowledge the relevance of the questions. (UNC president Tom Ross, whom Bill Friday had assumed would listen eagerly to Mary Willingham, politely declined her invitation to have a conversation about athletics in June 2013.)[31] The new provost, James Dean, flatly rejected another call for public town-hall discussions in October 2013.[32] The university's leaders had simply decided that this case was closed. Governor Martin's verdict— "This is not an athletic scandal"—was not subject to appeal. After all, agitated public discussion "could raise further NCAA issues," as Jan Boxill had noted back in the summer of 2012, "and that is not the intention" of anyone who loved Carolina athletics.

. . .

The Martin report contained valuable data and analysis. Martin had shown that the fraudulent activity was not an invention of the Butch Davis era and that it stretched at least as far back as the late 1990s. The report exposed the scope of the "unauthorized grade change" practice in AFRI/AFAM, noting that at least 560 grade changes had been illicit. (The university never made a move to correct any of the fraudulent grade changes.) And the report very helpfully confirmed that no AFRI/AFAM faculty other than Julius Nyang'oro bore responsibility for the egregious course manipulation that had gone on for more than a decade.

None of these positive outcomes of the Martin inquiry changes the brute fact that the governor's report is a woefully inadequate account of the UNC experience with athletic-academic fraud. Martin and Baker-Tilly neglected to pursue course and grade records dating to the period before 1997; they claimed, wrongly, that those records could not be accessed without difficulty. The "red flags" Martin and Baker-Tilly used to identify suspect courses in AFRI/ AFAM and elsewhere proved to be unduly limiting. Courses that did not see an unusual number of grade changes, for example, flew right under the radar of the Baker-Tilly number crunchers. Perhaps most troubling of all, the seemingly scientific jargon of the Martin report ("Type I anomalies," "Type II anomalies") masked the omission of what may well have been the biggest of all categories of contaminated courses in the AFRI/AFAM experience: the courses that Julius Nyang'oro admitted to having taught. The irregularities that accounted for the construction of the Type I and Type II categories were strictly bureaucratic in nature. Only courses whose instructors of record had denied teaching them (Type I) and courses for which the instructor of record could not be identified (Type II) were considered anomalous. Martin and Baker-Tilly found 216 of them—an impressive number, to be sure.

This meant, however, that all the courses that Nyang'oro confessed to teaching in his two-decade tenure were presumed to be perfectly legitimate. The courses in which unacceptable double standards had applied to athletes (and perhaps others) but which nevertheless met the minimal bureaucratic standards of normalcy were given the all clear. Martin, for example, flagged only 10 independent study courses over eighteen years as having been "anomalous." They were tagged as anomalous because of bureaucratic irregularities involving signatures on grade forms.

The presumption of normalcy in the absence of red flags suggests that the Martin report vastly underestimated the degree of fraudulent academic favoritism that afflicted the AFRI/AFAM Department during Nyang'oro's years of leadership. Whereas the typical tenured faculty member teaches 4 courses per year, Martin's own figures showed that Nyang'oro always taught somewhere between 10 (in 1994–95) and 24 (in 2006–7) during the height of the scandal. (His name was attached to the class rolls of 239 courses between 1994 and 2012, a period during which other tenured faculty members would have taught an average of between 65 and 75 courses.)[33] Given what had now been established about Nyang'oro's standards, and given the centrality of athlete enrollments in his courses from his earliest days on the faculty—a fact that Martin could easily have established had he tried to do so—why did he assume that acceptable pedagogy had characterized most or all of Nyang'oro's regularly scheduled classes?

Jim Martin helped to expose an academic fraud shocking for its enormity. But he underestimated just how enormous the problems really were, and he failed to notice or refused to acknowledge the role of the Athletic Department in creating the conditions that called those problems into being. The real sources of those problems, and the Athletic Department's long-standing strategies for finessing or working around them, form the core of the next chapter.

Seven

"No one ever asked me to write anything before"

This chapter begins with a story. Sometime between 2003 and 2010, a UNC football recruit—let's call him Reg—had trouble establishing his eligibility to play an NCAA sport. Each spring thousands of high school athletes have their credentials reviewed at something called the NCAA "clearinghouse," where officials verify that students have met minimal academic standards while completing their high school educations. Those minimal standards are set on a sliding scale. If the combined SAT score is 820, for example, the high school GPA can be as low as 2.5. If the high school GPA is a barely acceptable 2.0, then the SAT needs to be 1010 or better. In addition, students have to take a set number of courses in a "core" high school curriculum.

In some way or another, Reg's high school records had been deficient. He failed to make it through the clearinghouse. Unlike all other football recruits at UNC, he therefore missed out on summer orientation. He took no summer classes. He missed the screening tests typically done for athletes confirmed as having, or suspected of being at risk for, certain learning disabilities. He formed no helpful relationships with academic support personnel.

Reg nevertheless made it to practice in August, and he was in his seat on the first day of classes in the fall. Either because UNC had successfully lobbied the NCAA for an exemption or because the student had taken summer courses that made up for whatever the high school transcript lacked, he earned eligibility just under the wire and was able to join the team in time for the fall season. (First, of course, he had to win admission to the university—but that apparently presented no great obstacle.) Reg was expected to make major contributions to the football program. His coaches therefore welcomed him to campus and began working to get him up to speed on the playbook.

Early in the fall semester Reg found himself being directed to the office of learning specialist Mary Willingham, who worked particularly with the UNC athletes who struggled to read and write. Having never met the player, Willingham prepared for her first encounter with him by reviewing his high school dossier. What she saw when she opened Reg's folder left her dumbfounded. The player had never—not once—passed a general competency test during his primary and secondary school years. His reading skills (and writing and math skills) had consistently fallen below minimum standards. Year after year he had been promoted to the next grade not by passing benchmark exams but through the exceptional process known as compiling a "portfolio"—an assemblage of written work, accompanied by teacher testimonials, that ostensibly prove a student's sufficient mastery of the basic skills measured on end-of-grade or end-of-course tests.

Willingham's first reaction on confronting this summary of Reg's academic history was to question the admissions process at UNC. What could possibly have justified the admission of a student so obviously unprepared for college? One whose high school experiences had given pause even to the permissive NCAA? A student who had never passed a reading test? After her anger subsided—she would later share some of that anger with the admissions director—she began to think about pedagogy. Would she need to start by having Reg sound out three-letter words and vowel sounds, as usually happened with the most desperately behind athletes? (In fact, preliminary diagnostic tests indicated that Reg could handle at least some multisyllabic words, though he would be facing a steep uphill climb.) Willingham saw that Reg was going to require much help; she worried about whether she would be able to give him the time he needed.

Reg's first semester was painful. He could not make it through English 100, Basic Writing, the sole course offered at the university that might be construed as "remedial." He earned Cs and Ds in his other courses. The spring semester was scarcely better, though he would benefit from being retroactively dropped from a summer session math course in which he had earned an F. (This was an oft-used trick that showed the complicity of academic personnel in the eligibility games played at UNC.)

In the spring semester of his first year in college, however, one bright spot emerged from Reg's transcript. He got a good grade in AFRI 520, Southern Africa. Clinging to that life raft, he subsequently entered into the AFRI/AFAM course stream and went on to take ten paper classes in the Nyang'oro-Crowder curriculum, including three in the summer that followed his difficult freshman year. He did well in all three. In his sophomore year Reg would also find safe harbors in Education in American Life, Portuguese Literature in Translation, and other fail-safe courses. But it was the parallel AFRI/AFAM curriculum that proved indispensable to his academic fortunes, at least in the short run.

The blatant favoritism began early. Since Reg faced a deficit in credit hours after failing (and subsequently withdrawing) from that math class in the first summer session following his freshman year, his handlers had to get creative. In the second summer session he took a makeup math course, one paper class, and a two-credit-hour independent study in AFRI. The two-hour course would have been a highly unusual arrangement even under normal circumstances, since independent study courses, like most courses, typically involve three credit hours. But at UNC only students with GPAs of 2.0 or better are permitted to take as many as nine credit hours (the equivalent of three courses) in a single summer session. Most take between three and six hours. Reg could take no more than eight hours if he did not want to call attention to himself; any more would require the approval of a dean. So, needing a boost in both his credit hours and his GPA, Reg's academic counselor requested that Debby Crowder put him in a "variable hours" independent study course and to adjust the hours down to two so that the player could schedule a strangely out-of-balance eight-hour summer session. Even this schedule, had it involved legitimate course work, would have been unusually burdensome for a student stuck with a 1.5 GPA at the end of his first academic year. But the friendly AFRI/AFAM manager naturally obliged her colleagues in ASPSA, even though Reg was not an AFRI major and even though any objective academic would have regarded independent study as a seriously inappropriate course choice for a student who had struggled so much in standard classes. Reg got his two-hour independent study. He pulled down an A-.

Reg had friends in AFRI/AFAM and in several other places, and he always stayed eligible to play football. But the learning gaps he had brought with him to UNC—gaps that were never adequately addressed and that the university would still be loath to publicly acknowledge—ultimately proved insurmountable. He accumulated eleven more Ds and Fs after his freshman year; most courses outside of the Nyang'oro-Crowder curriculum proved too difficult for him. (Notably, however, he managed a B+ in English 100 in the fall of his sophomore year, after having failed it in his first fall term. Had he really learned to write so well in the space of a single year? One can only assume that by his sophomore season, he was receiving untold amounts of illicit "academic support" from someone.) Reg finally left UNC without a degree. He also left without having his name called on draft day. He never found a career in football. Today his exact whereabouts are unknown.

Reg's story epitomizes the failing system of big-time college sports, and it shows why system reform is so urgently necessary. All of the ingredients for academic failure and the cynical exploitation of a student's physical gifts were present in Reg's case. Start with a high schooler who has been poorly educated—simultaneously neglected and pampered, consistently "portfolioed" to advance through the K–12 experience. Send him through an eligibility "clearance" process that is eminently manipulable, a place where low standards can always be moved lower. Next, send him to a highly regarded university where the normal admissions process is intensely competitive and where the curriculum is designed to serve students with 4.5 high school GPAs and average combined SAT scores of 1350. Send him to a place, in other words, where he will never find a student peer group outside of athletics and where the university authorities he heeds and respects will not be professors and researchers but rather coaches, trainers, and athletic administrators. Finally, hand him over to the architects of the local eligibility machine whose first purpose is to keep him on the field while he is guided through a "special" curriculum that leads to subpar or nonexistent learning experiences and to no meaningful degree.

This was Reg's experience. It is the experience of far too many profit-sport athletes. This chapter probes the depths of the problem. Focusing on the UNC experience, it shows the forms of accommodation that are required to maintain the pretense that college athletes are "students first." And it shows why UNC's leaders had always insisted—to the point of false consciousness—that "this is not an athletics scandal."

Diamonds in the Rough

At UNC, as at many other places around the country, the athletes who play in the profit sports of basketball and football often come from challenging school and home environments. Life in their communities conditions them to be smart, perceptive, and resilient, but it does not always prepare them well for college. In the same recruiting class that yielded Reg and his clearinghouse difficulties, for example, one other football player had a high school attendance record that almost defies belief. His admissions folder revealed that he had been counted absent for 360 days in high school. Since a school year has only 180 days, this means that his rate of absence over his four-year high school career was precisely 50 percent. Yet this student, who would have had trouble mastering much of anything in classes that he missed or skipped every other day, somehow earned the grades he needed to get promoted year after year. A star on the high school football team, he evidently never had to worry about being suspended from the team for performing poorly in the classroom. Once he arrived at UNC, his academic counselor simply continued the pattern and tried to protect him from his academic deficiencies. The player made it into four paper classes, but the healthy grades earned in those four courses could not quite offset the deplorable performance in all other UNC courses; seeing the writing on the wall after a disastrous semester in which he had earned only Ds and Fs, this player decided to leave the university long before his senior year.

Although the attendance record for that player was certainly unusual, the experience of casual neglect that lay behind it was not at all uncommon. One starting basketball player told Willingham that his high school guidance counselor informed him that he really did not need to come to school—except on game days. (According to school policy, players had to sit out games if they had been marked absent earlier in the day.) This favorable star treatment in high school contrasted with the bullying treatment he had received in primary school. In fifth grade an angry teacher had once told him in frustration, "You'll never learn to read. You might as well give up." The forms of treatment this player received throughout his years in public school—coddling on the one hand, contempt on the other—would seem to have been spurred by different motivations. But in fact, they sprang from the same complex of attitudes. Research has shown that teachers have a strong tendency to assume that black male students are either troublemakers in need of disciplining or athletes who will get by on their physical prowess. The intellectual abilities and interests of black male students are likely to be dismissed and discounted, if not actively discouraged.[1]

Whether confronting condescension or coddling, the black athlete too often finds that his academic needs and prospects are neglected. The basketball player whose absences were noted only on game days coasted through his classes in high school, learning little along the way, while his athletic fortunes continued always to rise. "No one ever asked me to write anything before, Mary," he told the UNC learning specialist. Nor had he ever read a book from beginning to end. He was a charming young man and an eager learner once his mind was properly stimulated, but in his youth he had been consistently let down by those around him. Academics proved to be a constant battle in college. He made only slow, if steady, progress in developing his reading skills. Simple pride prevented him from taking paper classes, however. He told Willingham, "I can't even write a three-page paper. Why would I even try to turn in a twenty-page paper?" This player worked to stay eligible for basketball through other means.

A background colored by poverty complicated the lives of many UNC athletes. (One football player spent seven of his eighteen preuniversity years living in a car with his mother; keeping the car running, registered, and on the road presented a major hurdle all its own.) Deprivation affects academic performance in many measurable ways, as educators have long known.[2] Just as debilitating as the actual experience of material want, however, are the low expectations and lack of nurturing that tend to characterize so many impoverished schools and communities. One female athlete we will call Tina also struggled academically. Early in Tina's collegiate career, Mary Willingham noticed that she squinted whenever she worked to decipher words on a page. When asked whether she had worn glasses in the past, Tina responded that her eyesight had never been checked. She had spent years in North Carolina's public schools, compiling a mediocre academic record and struggling to stay at grade level with her reading, but no one had ever noticed the strain in her eyes whenever she held a book in her hand.

Willingham reported this discovery to Robert Mercer, the director of the Academic Support Program for Student Athletes. After doing the research necessary to find whether eyeglasses would constitute an "impermissible benefit" in the world of the NCAA (they do not), Mercer and others in the ASPSA arranged for the purchase of Tina's glasses—the first pair she had ever possessed. Her reading comprehension expanded almost immediately, and she worked hard to prove wrong the many teachers and classmates from her past who, she said, "never thought I could do it." Although she enrolled in many AFRI/AFAM paper classes and "directed readings" courses in Exercise and Sport Science and elsewhere, she did finish her degree and was reading reasonably well by the time she left UNC. What she might have accomplished had she been fitted for eyeglasses and given proper encouragement in elementary school is anyone's guess.

As Tina's case suggests, admission to UNC could be transformative for athletes from modest backgrounds who have the requisite academic ability and initiative—even leaving aside the small minority who also use their UNC experience as a springboard to lucrative athletic careers. But introduction to the Chapel Hill community could also bring a form of culture shock. One profit-sport athlete who had grown up in a house with limited plumbing found himself in an alien environment during a drama class in his freshman year. The requirements of the course included student attendance at one play. This player, who had never seen the inside of an actual theater, was unprepared to interpret the verbal and physical cues that are encoded in dramatic performance and read as second nature by practiced theatergoers. During the performance, when one of the actors looked toward the audience and beseeched his listeners for help, the player responded to what he understood as a personal invitation. He walked up onto the stage. After hearing gasps and seeing the startled responses of everyone else in the auditorium, the athlete recognized his faux pas. He descended the steps, grabbed his backpack, and fled the theater in shame. For this particular athlete, as for many of his underprepared teammates, the "learning experiences" that form the daily life of the university proved to be not only academically challenging but also psychologically and emotionally draining. He never finished his degree. (He also never played in a professional league.)

In addition to posing unaccustomed challenges, the university can also seem like a uniquely unwelcoming place. In an English composition course in the mid-2000s, an instructor asked her students to write a composition about some particularly memorable childhood experience. One athlete decided to share a searing memory. When he was nine years old, he recalled, he spent part of an afternoon rolling around on the floor wrestling with his dog, who enjoyed the occasional bout of rough play. On this occasion, though, the dog became rambunctious and bit the player's six-year-old sister in a fit of excess enthusiasm. The bite drew blood, tore a significant amount of flesh, and moved the girl to hysterics. (Her scream, her brother wrote, was "the worst sound I ever heard.") The event traumatized the whole family. In reaction, the distraught mother ran to a neighbor's house to borrow a baseball bat. When she returned, she handed it over to the nine-year-old. "Here, go take care of that dog." "What do you mean?" the boy asked. "Take this bat and go kill that dog. We can't have it biting someone else." (The mother was moved at least as much by economic pragmatism as by anger; she could not afford what a veterinarian might charge to euthanize the animal.) Not wanting to disobey his mother, the boy took his beloved pet into the backyard and, with heart sagging, proceeded to beat it to death. He remembered feeling guilty about this act of cruelty years later. He was unable to get the image of the helpless dog out of his mind.

When the athlete turned in his paper, the instructor reacted unexpectedly. She read his account and, instead of feeling sympathy or pity for the boy turned young man, decided to report him to the authorities. The player was reported not to the police or to the Anti-Cruelty Society but to the academic authorities at UNC. The instructor considered the player a menace to the community. His essay displayed violent tendencies, and she suspected that he was mentally unbalanced. She worried about the safety of the other students in her classroom. Should this player really be at the university at all? (In this class, as in his other classes, there had been no behavioral problems to speak of.) Despite the attempted mediation of a skillful assistant dean, the student was indeed pulled from his composition class. He also had to abandon a special transition-to-college summer program in which he had been enrolled; he would prove to be one of the last football players ever to participate in the program. Watched very closely by his handlers in the wake of this incident, the player was made to feel just how "different" he was. Why a child who had grown up in stressful poverty should have been expected to relate only sunny memories in his university English class was never explained to him.

Later, Mary Willingham was given her own unexpected lesson in the alternative composition styles of her most challenged students. A football player came to her one day with a question. "Mary, will you help me with something I've written?" Thinking it was an essay for a composition class, she reminded him that she could only proofread and make suggestions. She tried to be mindful of the rule against altering the content of students' essays. When he turned his "essay" over to her, she found that the piece was not an English paper at all. It was a letter addressed to a judge. With his mother sitting in jail awaiting a court date, the player was trying to make a desperate appeal for her release. He explained in this letter that his younger siblings were receiving care from an ailing grandmother and that his mother's continued detention would force him to drop out of school to return home as caregiver. When Willingham realized what she was reading, she decided she would give the player extra help, fixing a few words and cleaning up the punctuation. She even used the office fax machine to send the letter to the courthouse (a probable impermissible benefit). The mother won her release from jail, and Willingham's student was able to stay on campus. The ultimate happy ending proved elusive, however. Although this player ultimately did make it across the graduation finish line, he continued to struggle in the classroom. And he never caught on in the NFL.

All of these incidents were experienced by discrete individuals, and many more eye-opening stories could be added to the list. The point in relating these experiences is not to embarrass blameless students or to suggest that they were somehow undeserving of an education. Every student is educable. The reason to emphasize the often rough conditions from which these athletic diamonds emerged is simply to underscore the intersecting forms of desperation that are integral to the world of big-time college sport in its current configuration.

First, the athletes themselves are often desperate to escape the environment of dead-end deprivation in which they and their families have become trapped. (One basketball player who would play in the NBA expressed this reality bluntly: "I'm my family's lottery ticket," he told Willingham. "I have to succeed.") Their desperation leads them to focus, often from a very young age, on developing the skills they believe might open the door of opportunity. For black students in particular, this means that their sports often take priority over other concerns. At every turn they are encouraged to dedicate themselves to athletics. America's entertainment culture encourages them to identify with and emulate athletic superstars; fellow students make them the big men on campus; teachers and administrators overlook absences or poor grades (and in some cases their obvious needs); coaches talk up their potential; tournaments for the Amateur Athletic Union give them a taste for travel and feed their dreams. Even their own families can contribute to the perception that athletic achievement holds more promise for them than simple hard work in the classroom. A 2004 study found that fully "66% of all African American males between the ages of 13 and 18 believe they can earn a living playing professional sports."[3] Year after year youngsters desperate for success and enlivened by the thrill of sport pour disproportionate energy into athletics. Too often, their academic performance remains an afterthought for them and for all of the critical people in their lives.

The second type of desperation that helps form the infrastructure of fraud is the desperation of coaches who feel pressure each year to recruit as many blue-chip and second- and third-tier players as they can find. The pressure to recruit well is intense in all sports, but football is the worst because football is the revenue engine that drives the train. Football coaches are therefore the most vulnerable coaches in any Athletic Department. In 2012 alone 30 of the 125 major-program "football schools" either fired their head coaches for not winning enough games or saw their coaches recruited away from them because they had won too many. When Texas head coach Mack Brown was forced into retirement at the end of the 2013 season, the Texas AD, Steve Patterson, was candid in outlining the criteria for success by which he would be measuring candidates to replace Brown. In addition to noting the importance of experience in college coaching and an ability to hold up well under pressure, he simply added: "You've got to win. You've got to win big."[4] Brown was the second winningest active coach in the nation at the time of his firing (Virginia Tech's Frank Beamer ranks first). One national championship and fifteen winning seasons in a sixteen-year tenure were just not enough for the Longhorn faithful.

Football coaches are desperate men. They identify every talented athlete they have a reasonable chance of recruiting, and they go hard after each one. Because their squads are so large and injuries so frequent, football coaches have to bring in dozens of new players each year, replenishing the "depth chart" for each position on the team. Walk-ons and "preferred walk-ons" (meaning walk-ons who are effectively promised that a scholarship will be granted to them in the near future) help to meet the demand, but the big-time coaches who want to win and retain their jobs also have to land their share of the three-, four-, and five-star recruits who have caught the attention of every coaching staff in the country. The coaches and their large staffs pull out all the stops to make their recruits feel loved and to assure them that they will be happy and contented if only they make the "right" decision. The players are invariably shown a good time when they make recruiting visits to the campus—even to the point of being teamed with comely coeds who flirt with them, engage in provocative banter, and serve as "eye candy" for the duration of the campus visit.[5]

In addition to whatever athletic inducements they are offered during their stay—playing time, future championships, television appearances, first-class facilities and trainers—they are also promised the moon academically. Recruits are typically told that they will receive "world-class" educations and that these educations, for all their world class–ness, will be easily acquired. As a football recruit at one southern university recalled in a study published in 2000, he was both "depressed and relieved" when he was informed during his recruiting visit that he would not need to exert himself in the classroom. "When I first got here—I remember when I was being recruited, there was a couple players, . . . and they said, 'You don't have to go to school, because the teachers are going to take care of you.'"[6] Another player, a senior looking back on his academic experiences, thought he would have done much better in the classroom "if it weren't for coming in and having a group of people say, 'This is the minimum you need to do,' and holding your hand here and holding your hand there." Another athlete in the same program remembered what it was like registering for classes in his first semester. He had thought about some classes he was interested in taking and showed up for his advising appointment ready to talk about them. He found that his courses had already been selected for him. "I mean, when you come there, to say 'Well, I already have a list of classes you should take' . . . . And you're like, 'Well I don't want to take that.' And they're like, 'Well I've already registered you.' [You feel] like you have no control, and that's not letting you grow up, that's not letting you become what you want to do."[7]

Nurturing young students, developing their interests, seeing that they "grow up" intellectually, preparing them well for a life outside of sport: these objectives, unfortunately, are not the goals coaches have foremost in mind. Coaches need bodies. They need to restock their teams with well-conditioned, docile, compliant, high-performing bodies. (Minds matter mainly to the extent that they need to be trained and disciplined.) Needing athletic "diamonds," they will mine every vein in search of the talented players who can improve the team, raise the university's visibility, boost the coach's fortunes, and enrich the many beneficiaries of the profit-sport enterprise. Because academic performance will remain a strictly secondary concern even after matriculation, the diamond miners pay relatively little attention to the academic preparation of their targeted recruits. If they cannot help noticing that some of the students are grossly unprepared, the recruiters overlook the problem and ask others to do the same. (Much the same is true in basketball, of course. When Roy Williams was asked about reports that one of his players was a nonreader, he told ESPN's Andy Katz that he really simply could not say. "That's not my world.")[8]

And so the recruiting desperation of coaches converges with the desperation of all those dreaming high school athletes to produce an elaborate admissions process that is rife with fraud and fakery. The quantitative metrics imposed by the NCAA in the clearinghouse process lend themselves to endless gaming. The list of enablers of the codependent relationship that has formed between high school athletes and university coaching staffs is a long one. It includes high school teachers (who fatten GPAs preemptively), guidance counselors (who massage transcripts as needed), the operators of diploma mills (who hand out fake credentials in an emergency), faculty review committees at universities (who find reasons to look the other way), admissions officials (who work closely with coaches and really enjoy their time in the luxury boxes), athletic directors (who distract attention from the underbelly of their operation by pretending that the purpose of an Athletic Department is really to support the "Olympic sports"), NCAA propagandists (whose measures of success provide a license to defraud), and even unques-tioning fans. All work toward the same overarching purpose of providing necessary cover for dishonesty, exploitation, and—when necessary—outright fraud.

When Mary Willingham confronted one athlete whose feeble reading ability squared not at all with his better than 500 SAT read-ing score—"How did you do so well on that test, Sean?" she asked—"Sean" responded to her with disarming candor. "Oh, I didn't take that test." Who did? Willingham asked. Sean grew reticent. "I would rather not say." (Another athlete who had overheard the conversa-tion helpfully chimed in: "In my state that happens all the time!") In truth, abundant circumstantial evidence suggests that this aspect of the NCAA clearinghouse vetting process is frequently subverted. Legendary University of Nevada at Las Vegas basketball coach Jerry Tarkanian echoed the UNC player: "It happens all the time." The most notorious recent case unfolded at the University of Memphis, which had its 2009 Final Four appearance struck from the record books after an anonymous tipster revealed that current NBA star Derrick Rose had hired a replacement to take his SAT for him in 2007. Memphis also later acknowledged that another of their bas-ketball players, Robert Dozier, had also entered an SAT score so sus-picious that the university itself had disallowed it. But Memphis is not alone. Deshawn Stevenson, when he was being recruited by Roy Williams and the Kansas Jayhawks, followed a dismal 450 combined SAT test score with an impressive 1150. So great was the disparity between the first and second tries in this case that the Educational Testing Service, which administers the SAT test, refused to certify the score. (A disappointed Williams complained at the time about the "raw deal" Stevenson had been handed.)[9] Mary Willingham, in her time in UNC's ASPSA, saw more than a few suspicious improve-ments in SAT verbal scores, with improvements of 200 points or more on second- or third-try attempts. She always wondered about the authenticity of the results.

But even when scores and GPAs and high school curricular expe-riences have not been directly tampered with, the enablers of the system remain guilty of self-delusion at best and willful hypocrisy at worst. While doing their part to get athletes admitted into institutions that are ill-prepared to serve them, and which often have little desire to serve them, they pat themselves on the back for providing "opportunity" and for defending "diversity." They then turn the athletes over to caretakers who shepherd them through a set of academic experiences whose first function is to disguise. Let's have a closer look at the nature of the "opportunity" that UNC has provided its profit-sport athletes.

By the Numbers

Alternative academic standards for star athletes are nothing new at UNC. Lawrence Taylor, the Hall of Fame linebacker who played in Chapel Hill from 1978 to 1981, boasted in his 1987 retrospective that he had beaten the academic system at UNC by finding the many courses "ready-made for football players."[10] The go-to courses in the 1980s included Chinese Civilization, Arts and Crafts, and those hardy perennials, the French Novel in Translation and Education in American Life. The Athletic Department used them religiously, counting on the gift grades in these classes to balance out those dreaded GPA killers from math, science, and foreign language. But even the gifts would not necessarily be enough. One teaching assistant (TA) who was a graduate student in communications in the early 1980s still remembers a painful encounter she had with a first-year football player in a large survey course. He had turned in a short and shockingly unsophisticated paper that reminded her of some of the creative writing done by a smart third grader she knew. She asked the player to come to her office hours to talk about his writing and how it could be improved. He showed up punctually, but what this teaching assistant still recalls vividly is how deeply ashamed the player was. He was apologetic about not doing good work, but he explained that "none of this was ever important to me before," and he had therefore floated through school without learning how to write.[11]

Julia Wood, Lineberger Distinguished Professor of Humanities Emerita, tells a similar story about a basketball player who took one of her smaller courses in the 1980s. He was an earnest young man who came into her course fully intending to make every effort to perform well. In the first weeks of the semester, he was always alert for the beginning of lecture. By the end of most classes, how-ever, he had tuned out. He often put his head down on his desk; occasionally, he caught up on his sleep. When Wood stopped him after class one day to ask him about his obvious disengagement, the player apologized for his inability to follow along. "I just don't understand what you're saying." This was not an especially difficult course, and Wood refrained from using theoretical language in her lectures, she recalls, but the athlete just found the vocabulary set at too high a level. When Wood asked him if he would like to visit her during office hours, it became clear that he had not yet looked at the syllabus and knew nothing about her office hours. Two weeks later, when she asked him again whether he had plans to come in, the player responded that he "really didn't have the time" to visit. Resigned and defeated, he went on to fail the course.[12]

Other faculty sometimes navigated through such situations by showing excess sympathy for the athlete concerned. Another teaching assistant who completed his PhD in French around 1980 recalls that his supervising professor once overrode a failing grade and gave a B- to a star football player in a summer French-literature course. He did this—to the great surprise of the teaching assistant—even though the player had scored a miserable 16 out of 100 on his final exam.[13]

Such were the conditions in which Julius Nyang'oro, Debby Crowder, and Burgess McSwain forged their working relationship at the end of the 1980s. Several of the earliest beneficiaries of Nyang'oro's gen-erosity had registered SAT reading scores at or below 300. At least one athlete who took classes with Nyang'oro in the first half of the 1990s had scored 200 on the SAT reading test—the lowest possible score, a score that required no correct answers.

The other continuity that links the 1980s to UNC's more recent experience with academic fraud is that the educational outcomes in all cases were predictably bad. Few of these players from the 1980s went on to graduate. As with the significant number of foot-ball players in the 1990s and 2000s who flunked every course in their final fall playing season, they all understood that the "oppor-tunity" they had been given was the opportunity to play hard and prove themselves on the field or court. Some of them had very much wanted a degree, and they labored to earn it to the extent that their schedules and abilities allowed. But their academic wants and needs had been systematically subordinated to the individual and team goals of athletic achievement. Their academic deficiencies, and their need for serious catching up, were either ignored or masked by their stewards of eligibility and the university faculty and staff who were always willing to "work with" them.

This sad reality is amply demonstrated through the experiences of nearly two hundred athletes whose reading and writing abilities were measured in a study conducted by Mary Willingham between 2008 and 2012. In early 2013 the study became the focus of controversy on the UNC campus, after Willingham shared a summary of her findings on a CNN broadcast. Those findings, which cast doubt on the academic readiness of a large percentage of so-called committee-case admits, were quickly denounced by the university's provost at a highly charged Faculty Council meeting. UNC's Institutional Review Board, meanwhile, developed concerns about the data-collection methods used in the research and rescinded Willingham's permission to continue the study. The IRB also forbade discussion of the study's details, which precludes in-depth reporting in this chapter. But the basic profile of Willingham's pool of athletes, as revealed through statistics and commentary already made part of the public record, still presents an eye-opening picture.

The SAT scores of the athletes in question were among the data points the university had hoped would never be revealed. Thirty-four of the approximately 180 athletes who underwent testing in the Willingham study had SAT verbal scores below 400, some of them landing far below 400. SAT scores by themselves are poor predictors of academic performance, but reading scores that fall more than 200 points below the twenty-fifth percentile ranking of UNC's admitted students—as indicated by UNC admissions office statistics for 2013—point to classroom adjustment problems that will almost inevitably mar the experiences of those with so much catching up to do.[14]

The university's provost and other officials have fiercely disputed Willingham's claim that academic underpreparedness, and the shortcuts they require in an environment where true remediation is not an option, presented a massive challenge to academic integrity at UNC. The provost even hired three experts to analyze one portion of Willingham's statistics and to declare, on the basis of their partial reading of the Willingham data, that a majority of the athletes in the study pool—85 percent of whom were football or basketball players—were reading *at or above* college level when they arrived at UNC. Even most committee-case athletic admissions, according to the provost's experts, would seem to have been more than ready to tackle college-level work when they arrived in Chapel Hill.

The extreme unlikeliness of this proposition is underscored by national statistics. In 2012 the organizers of a UNC-sponsored literacy summit at the School of Library Sciences pointed to the existence of a national literacy crisis. Drawing on studies of the National Assessment of Educational Progress (NAEP), they noted that only "14% of African American 8th graders performed at or above the proficient level in 2009." (Equally surprising: only one-third of *all* students tested in 2009 met the "proficient" threshold.) The literacy gap affecting black students directly correlated with a range of disproportionately negative outcomes for male youth, including unacceptably high rates of unemployment, incarceration, and homicide.[15] In his *Minority Students and Public Education*, author Michael Holzman shared state-by-state statistics on reading levels that should shock the conscience—especially for inhabitants of southern states. The NAEP assesses students as reading at the advanced, proficient, basic, or "below basic" level. In North Carolina in 2011, fully 54 percent of black male eighth graders were judged to be reading at the "below basic" level, with only 7 percent reaching proficiency and none achieving the advanced level. Those dismal scores placed North Carolina thirty-second out of the thirty-eight states for which 2011 statistics were available.[16] Critics of Mary Willingham's study would thus have the world believe that UNC recruits its African American scholarship athletes only from among the 14 percent (and 7 percent in-state) who were reading proficiently when they entered high school. The two-thirds of American students who have reading deficiencies of some sort are simply ignored by football and basketball recruiters in Chapel Hill. Or so UNC officials would like to claim.

If this were the case, however, UNC would have no way of explaining the most sobering measure evinced in the Willingham study: classroom performance. More than half of the students in Willingham's pool had UNC grade point averages under 2.3. (A great many had GPAs under 2.0; one had an abysmally low 0.86 GPA.) A comparison with a more representative cohort of students at the university underlines just how unimpressive a C grade point average really is. In the fall of 2008, the faculty's Educational Policy Committee studied the phenomenon of grade inflation at UNC–Chapel Hill and found that the average GPA of undergraduates from across the university was 3.21, a solid B.[17] In the humanities fields, where many of the athletes screened by Willingham pursued their majors, the average GPA was a bit higher, at 3.27. (The average grade earned in African studies in 2008, 3.52, was one of the six highest averages in the College of Arts and Sciences.)[18] Yet more than half of the athletes tested by Willingham between 2005 and 2012 had GPAs that fell somewhere below a 2.3. And the grades that produced that strikingly unimpressive figure, it must be remembered, included those earned in hundreds of paper classes. Officials at UNC may not wish to admit it, but the majority of the students in Willingham's group constituted a cohort for whom continuing eligibility and long-term graduation prospects remained a constant, nagging concern. They lived continuously on the eligibility bubble, worrying from semester to semester whether their final exams would leave them in dire straits and in need of significant academic help before the next playing season.

Historical records from the Academic Support Program itself prove that this phenomenon was nothing new. In 1990 football academic counselor Brian Davis reported to coach Mack Brown on the classroom performance of his first-year players. The report could not have buoyed Brown's spirits. First-year scholarship players had earned a mediocre 2.09 GPA in 1989–90, and those who had actually played (that is, who had not been redshirted) averaged a slightly lower 2.05. Worst of all were the committee-case players, who had pulled down a troubling 1.86 GPA in their first year on the

UNC campus. (Davis found a silver lining around this particular cloud, however, noting that the 1.86 was actually "almost .5 higher than their average predicted first semester GPA.")[19] The experience of observing the struggles of such students put the then director of the Academic Support Program, John Blanchard, in a reflective mood in the spring of 1992. In his end-of-year report, he noted that "students who do not have a reasonable chance to graduate and are admitted to this academically rigorous university can have a difficult experience." Their classroom difficulties often become so severe, he observed, that "it impacts every area of their lives." Blanchard averred, "College athletics is too big an enterprise," one that creates a "tremendous amount of pressure" even for academically prepared athletes. He therefore recommended that faculty admissions committees exercise greater care in rendering admissions decisions, since "the integrity of this great university is challenged when students who have limited chances of competing in the classroom" gain entry.[20]

The realities that lay behind Blanchard's concerns can hardly be said to have improved over the next twenty years. The deep frustrations felt by the more challenged individuals who worked with Mary Willingham are at least suggested by the numerical profiles of some who stayed at UNC for four or more years but never walked down the aisle on commencement day. Consider the senior who seems to have made a good-faith effort to pursue his degree after entering the university with a combined SAT score in the mid-800s. After compiling more than 150 credits with the help of a dozen paper classes, a sub-2.0 GPA nevertheless left him academically ineligible and facing an uphill climb to meet the minimum requirements to earn his diploma. Another student with an SAT score around 900 racked up more than 130 credit hours at UNC, but his 1.78 GPA made his cause a hopeless one; he will never be able to earn enough As in his required courses to close his GPA deficit. Another challenged player with a combined SAT score under 650 somehow managed to compile 134 credit hours at UNC. But getting through his required math and science courses proved too high a hurdle for him. He, too, left the university without his diploma.

Table 4. Academically close but no degree

GPA	Hours	Academic standing
1.98	139	AI
1.95	152	AI
1.8	138	AI
1.91	138	AI
1.9	141	AI
1.8	119	AI
1.9	115	AI
1.778	132	AI
2.1	141	*
1.98	140	AI
1.879	144	AI
1.933	120	AI

Note: AI = academically ineligible; * = student could not pass math requirement. Figure shows athletes leaving academically ineligible. 120 hours required for a degree.

Careful and honest examination of the curricular experiences that lie behind such stories—at UNC and elsewhere—is long overdue.

"Opportunity" Knocks

An idea of the special classroom challenges faced by so many of the students who worked with Mary Willingham is conveyed in the recollections of two teaching assistants from the Department of History. These advanced graduate students, who taught in the department between 2003 and 2013, tried earnestly to help the profit-sport athletes who took some of the broad survey courses that drew in legions of first-year and sophomore students at Carolina. Their teaching experiences ultimately made them question the basic morality of the big-time sport enterprise.

Julia Osman remembers a large Western Civilization class in which several athletes were enrolled. All of the athletes in this particular class were at least a bit behind their classmates in general ability, but one football player faced severe deficiencies. When preparing for an early midterm exam, the player questioned Osman about acceptable ways of answering identification questions. (ID questions prompt students to provide basic facts about an item—say, the Gutenberg Bible—by situating it in time, placing it geographically, explaining its significance, and so on.) He wanted to know whether writing in full sentences was a requirement. Would a few words with bullet points be okay? Osman told him that the professor did indeed require complete sentences, but the player's midterm ID answers nevertheless contained only isolated words and sentence fragments. "He couldn't even write, 'The significance of Martin Luther is . . . ,'" remembers Osman. His responses to the essay questions on the exam were even more disturbing. They offered "a conglomeration of key words and phrases" that pointed in the direction of an answer but were "not articulated in any coherent fashion."

Later, students in the class had to write a short paper about Machiavelli's *The Prince,* and the player came to Osman for help. The text "seemed incomprehensible to him," and Osman had to put in extra time during office hours to help him decipher at least some of the meaning of that innovative and challenging Renaissance text. It proved to be a real struggle and a major time drain. But when the due date rolled around, this player turned in a passable C paper, replete with fully formed sentences in flowing succession. "I knew there was no way he could have written that paper," says Osman, but "since there was no way to prove he was not the author," the TA and her supervising professor declined to report the suspected cheating to the Honor System. Throughout her time in Chapel Hill, Osman volunteered at the Durham County Public Library, where she helped lead weekly workshops for Durham's middle school and high school students who had an interest in writing but no real outlet for creative work at home or in school. She recalls that those students, even those who came from poverty and showed up more for the snacks than for the writing exercises, easily outperformed the weakest athletes she encountered at UNC, including the one who seems to have sought illicit help for his Machiavelli paper.

Anne Berler taught several athletes in American history survey courses, and she gained added perspective from serving for a year as a history tutor in the ASPSA. She recalls one especially painful tutoring session, during the first of her two semesters on the job, during which she tried to prepare four football players for an upcoming in-class history exam that would require one essay and several short ID answers (the questions having already been distributed to the class in advance). Finding it impossible to elicit from them potential thesis statements for the essay, she decided to simplify the session by focusing on the shorter and more basic ID questions. "Take out your notes," she said. They all stared at her blankly. "You have no notes? Well . . . okay, let's look at the textbook. We can find the por-tions of the text in which the ID items are discussed." They slowly dragged out their texts and located the chapter that focused (to the best of her memory) on the Monroe Doctrine. "Okay, so how would we want to define the Monroe Doctrine?" More silence. "Here's a start. Let's take a few minutes to write a one-sentence summary for each of the three paragraphs that talk about this item. Then we'll see how we might put them together in a meaningful whole." After leaving them on their own to write for a bit, Berler came back to see what they had come up with. Three of the four were finishing up, but the fourth was concentrating intently, hunched over his note-book. Peering over his shoulder, she noticed that he still had not managed a sentence. "Having some trouble? Well, just read this key sentence here out loud. What would you say is most important in there?" As the player began to fumble over the first words on the page, Berler suddenly realized that the striking physical specimen in front of her was a nonreader. Sensing his embarrassment, and feeling embarrassed herself, she immediately changed direction so that the player's teammates would have their attention shifted elsewhere. "Okay, everyone, what did the professor say about the Monroe Doctrine just last week?"

The next morning Berler expressed her concerns to Beth Bridger, the chief academic counselor for football. She explained that she was having a serious problem reaching one of the players she had helped the night before, and she had no idea what to do about it. Bridger, unmoved, responded with smiles and encouragement. "Just keep at it. I'm sure he's getting something out of it." But Berler felt no encouragement. In fact, by the end of one semester of tutoring, she felt that she was defrauding the university even by accepting payment for services rendered. "I wasn't helping those guys. They were never engaged anyway, but tutoring just wasn't what they needed. I didn't know how to teach someone to read. I felt like a failure." She stayed with it for one more semester, but she left the ASPSA demoralized and haunted by a nagging question: "How are these guys passing their classes? How are they surviving?"

These classroom and tutoring experiences were obviously awkward and even humiliating for the athletes who had to endure them, and the academic counselors in the ASPSA, understandably, were inclined to minimize their pain. Like academic counselors everywhere, they formed bonds with the athletes they helped. They rooted for them and wished them the best. They and the staff tutors who worked with them often made extraordinary efforts to teach lessons that would help the athletes in the classroom. Most of the counselors, one can assume, also sought to remain at least outwardly "compliant" with NCAA rules against impermissible help and academic fraud.

But academic counselors also understood that they had to keep players eligible, preferably while minimizing their academic discomfort. Hotly recruited athletes in the profitable and visible sports of football and basketball are not brought to campus to sit on the sidelines or to spend ineligible semesters repairing their GPAs. They are expected to devote themselves to their sport and to be ready to play on game day. The time demands alone are enormous. A 2007 NCAA survey found that football players work forty-five hours per week at their sports during the season, while also carrying a full-time academic load. A more recent study estimates a weekly time commitment of fifty-three hours per week for home games alone.[21] The National Labor Relations Board (NLRB) of Chicago found in 2014 that Northwestern players devoted up to sixty hours a week to football during fall training camp.[22] (Basketball players have it better, but not by much. The 2007 NCAA survey found that they put in an average of thirty-seven hours per week.)

Off-season football is scarcely less demanding than in-season. In a recent email a UNC football player outlined his typical February routine. Up at 5:00 a.m., conditioning drills at 6:00. Classes from 8:00 until 2:00 p.m., including a break for lunch. Off to the weight room from 2:15 until 4:00 p.m. Position meetings (running backs, defensive linemen, and the like) from 4:00 to 5:00 p.m. Dinner around 6:00, followed by mandatory study hall from 7:00 to 10:00 p.m. Finally, off to bed so the cycle can be repeated bright and early the next morning. The few free minutes built into his schedule would evaporate in March, when the team had to get ready for spring football, with three practices a week in addition to regular conditioning. "Football," he said, "is a year-round sport—the best way to stay in shape is to never get out of it!"[23] This extraordinarily capable athlete harbors realistic dreams of medical school, but many football and basketball players endure this exhausting grind while also struggling to comprehend the vocabulary of Machiavelli and while laboring to compose sentences that will somehow pass muster in English 101.

To help athletes manage these conditions, sympathetic and pragmatic academic counselors exploit every loophole they can find. They identify every curricular soft spot in existence. They cultivate every friendly faculty member or program that might be willing to "help out" athletes in need. One UNC football counselor, who came to the university after having worked in similar positions at several other universities, admitted candidly in an interview that "the first thing I did when I arrived at all of these places was find out which courses were the ones we used."[24] At UNC, this counselor quickly discovered, AFRI/AFAM was the most hospitable of all academic programs. This is why counselors were constantly on the phone with Debby Crowder, asking her to get certain courses on the schedule and to get certain athletes in those courses.

But Julius Nyang'oro and Debby Crowder were hardly alone in signaling their willingness to help athletes, and it would be a mistake to assume that corner cutting and athletics favoritism were restricted to a single "rogue" faculty member in a single department. Allies were scattered across the university. In the Department of Romance Languages, the longtime instructor of the French Novel in Translation, recently deceased, expected to serve so many athletes in his class that he specified at the bottom of his syllabus that all students—even the nonathletes (!)—were invited to attend the end-of-semester review (which was held in the Kenan

Field House, home to the ASPSA). He also offered the occasional "directed readings" course for athletes, and his French Theater in Translation course offered a perfect double-dipping opportunity for athletes in need of easy GPA boosts; counselors typically registered their weakest students for both courses. The instructors for various Portuguese literature-in-translation courses also hosted many athletes each year, generally distributing high grades to them. Many challenged athletes wound up in both Portuguese and French literature-in-translation courses, with some compiling as many as a half-dozen such courses. They took these literature courses even though they took no French or Iberian history classes; evinced little other interest in France, Portugal, their languages, or their civilizations; and never showed any interest in other literature courses such as Major American Authors or Shakespeare. They took FREN 40 or PORT 70 because the instructors were known to go easy on athletes who made some effort.

Another course that has long had great appeal to athletes is Women in Sport. According to a fall 2014 report in the *Daily Tar Heel*, 85 percent of the students enrolled in Exercise and Sport Science 260 in 2011–12 were athletes. The grading distribution in all courses taught by the instructor, Barbara Osborne, helps explain the high concentration of athletes. The popular website Blinkness .com, which provides course-profile information for UNC students, indicates that 90 percent of the grades distributed in all Osborne courses are either A or B.[25]

Help could also be found outside the College of Arts and Sciences, and counselors actively exploited it. The revered instructor for Education in American Life, a course offered in the School of Education, gave good grades to athletes who routinely caught up on their sleep while spread out in the back of his classroom. He even gave tests for which answers left blank would not enter into grade calculations. (Only answers *attempted* would be marked right or wrong.) Later, a School of Library Sciences course called Finding and Retrieving Information (popularly called "the Google course") would become another perennial favorite for athletes needing to pad the transcript. A is by far the most common grade awarded in INLS 200.

Back in the College of Arts and Sciences, still other instructors offered frequent directed-readings courses on demand. Certain professors in the Departments of Philosophy, Exercise and Sport Science, and Geography were especially generous in this regard. Jan Boxill frequently offered directed readings in philosophy, especially during the summers, and 67 percent of her students earned As (virtually all others earning Bs) between 2003 and 2009.[26] Throughout the 1990s and into the early 2000s, it would have been difficult to find an athlete who had not taken Geography 95, Topics in Geography. This independent study–style course was joined to other favorites—for example, Philosophy 47, Ethics of Sport; Philosophy 46, Philosophical Issues in Feminism; and Exercise and Sport Science 83, Physical Education in the Elementary School—in addition to the French, Portuguese, and education courses already noted. In the 2000s new courses entered into the standard rotation: Exercise and Sport Science 260, Women in Sport; another School of Education course, Navigating the Research University; as well as drama courses galore. (Says Ben Smith, a UNC nonathlete and aspiring journalist who wandered into some slide courses on his own: "The drama department . . . is notorious for several professors who simply read off slides" and engage in little real teaching.)[27] For a short time, a course called Naval Weapons Systems also attracted disproportionate numbers of athletes—after a part-time instructor showed up in the ASPSA office to advertise his no-test course and to drum up enrollments.

None of the courses just discussed was fraudulent in the sense that the Nyang'oro-Crowder no-show lecture classes were fraudulent, but they were all either notoriously easy or known to be athlete friendly. (It must be said, however, that many of the directed-reading and independent study courses undoubtedly set an exceptionally low bar for academic achievement; they proceeded on the basis of informal, ad hoc arrangements and involved only those professors who enjoyed "helping" or spending time with athletes.)[28] What made all of these classes attractive for academic counselors was the simple fact that any athlete who showed up and gave it the college try was assured a helpful grade. These classes, combined with the even friendlier paper classes in AFRI/AFAM, therefore constituted the profit-sport athlete's course of study. Thanks to deliberate strategizing by their counselors, who studied grading patterns and longitudinal course "success" rates carefully, challenged athletes effectively had a special curriculum constructed just for them. All of the academically challenged athletes, virtually without exception, took the same courses to meet their science and math requirements. (It was evidently taken as gospel that Geology 11 was the only science-with-lab course in the curriculum that could be successfully completed by an academically challenged athlete.) They also took the same set of mismatched and intellectually unrelated courses to meet their elective and distribution requirements.

University officials have insisted that there is nothing unusual or unethical about a course-selection process that leads athletes from Stagecraft to the French Novel in Translation to Finding and Retrieving Information to Ethics of Sport to Education in American Life to paper classes to as many directed-readings courses as friendly faculty are willing to schedule. Senior associate dean for undergraduate education Bobbi Owen replied to a query from the *Raleigh News & Observer* by explaining that "students drift to places where they understand they will be accommodated." "Word of mouth," she said, is powerful, and there is really no explaining how individual students wind up in a particular course.[29] Technically, it is true, of course, that with the exception of the fake courses in AFRI/AFAM, all of the other courses mentioned in this chapter were real courses. It is also true that athletes had every right to take them. Other students knowingly take easy courses on occasion, after all, and they rely on word of mouth to find such courses.

But what makes the athletic shadow curriculum so troubling, and administrators' disregard for its existence so shocking, is that "drift" and "word of mouth" had nothing at all to do with its creation. The shadow curriculum pursued by profit-sport athletes was a product of engineering. (As the senior associate dean for undergraduate education certainly knows, until 2012 profit-sport athletes at UNC were typically registered into their courses by the academic counselors in the ASPSA. The athletes provided minimal input, and counselors remained always in control of the process.)[30] Not only were athletes steered overwhelmingly toward the same unde manding courses, but they were also housed within the same two or three majors, even though the university offers close to a hundred major possibilities. On the 2013 UNC football team, for example, 75 percent (49 of 65) of the players who listed majors on the Athletic Department website majored in either communications (COMM) or exercise and sport science (EXSS). (After the academic fraud in AFRI/AFAM was exposed in 2011, counselors suddenly abandoned the department; only 1 football player—1 out of 122—listed a major in AFRI or AFAM in 2013.) The 2013 men's basketball team showed a little more variety, but of the 8 scholarship players with declared majors, 5 were in either COMM or EXSS. Meanwhile, among the eleven other majors pursued on the much larger football team, walk-ons were dramatically overrepresented. Walk-ons, with fewer eligibility pressures and usually no NFL aspirations to pursue, represent a different population of athletes and therefore have access to a more variegated set of educational experiences.[31]

No regular UNC student would ever dream of compiling the odd assortment of courses that show up on a typical scholarship football or basketball player's transcript, nor would they tolerate having such a limited set of educational options available to them. But the NCAA and its member institutions have constructed a system that facilitates the recruitment of academically weak or uninterested athletes to the university and ensures their cynical "processing" through curricular paths of least resistance. Julius Peppers, Michael McAdoo, "Reg," Marvin Austin, and the basketball player who had never been asked "to write anything" before he arrived in Chapel Hill shared one thing in common. Like so many other profit-sport athletes in Carolina's recent history, they marched in lockstep through an impoverished educational itinerary that not only denied them access to the full menu of intellectual possibilities available to their nonathlete classmates but—even worse—left many of them in the same undernourished state in which they had arrived on campus. This form of educational malpractice stems from the university's willingness to accept the subordination of athletes' academic needs and interests to the evidently more important needs of the big-time sport machine. Regular students can pursue educations and intellectual enrichment; athletes must focus their academic efforts on eligibility and healthy team Academic Progress Rates (APRs). The next chapter reviews the many under-the-radar techniques that have been used by the Athletic Department and the ASPSA to ensure that athletes stay in line and stay out of academic trouble.

Eight

Tricks of the Trade

In 2007, not long after Butch Davis had taken over as the head coach of the UNC football team, a visibly agitated Beth Bridger stepped out of the office of Wayne Walden, the counselor for the basketball team. A football academic counselor, Bridger was angry about the courses available to her football players for the upcoming semester, and she blamed the basketball team for the dearth of options. "We deserve the same help and the same treatment that basketball gets when choosing classes. We bring in more money!" What she specifically had in mind, recalls Mary Willingham, who overheard the conversation, were slots in paper classes. Too often, Bridger thought, basketball got all the preferential treatment. She insisted that football players should have equal access to the independent study and no-show classes offered by Julius Nyang'oro and Debby Crowder, the classes that the basketball team had taken by the bushel over the previous several years. (An undergraduate seminar in Portuguese literature would be packed with football players and baseball players in the fall of 2008, but it enrolled not a single basketball player; the PORT program was certainly friendly territory, but no department worked as well for athletes as the department of Nyang'oro studies.)

Bridger's concern about basketball's privileged position in the UNC sports hierarchy captures well the distorted values that have come to structure the big-time sport enterprise. The justification provided for Bridger's anger—"We bring in more money!"—points to the root cause of universities' neglect of the educational well-being of their athletes. Instead of wringing her hands about her players' lack of access to music courses, Burch Field Research seminars, study-abroad opportunities, textbooks they could fully understand, and postcollegiate careers outside of sports, she worried about their lack of access to fake courses that would impose no academic burden on them. Why? Because what evidently mattered most to Bridger, and to too many of her colleagues, was that the players be kept eligible to play on Saturdays, eligible to contribute to the university's gate receipts, eligible to make the coach look good, eligible to draw attention to whatever NFL potential they possessed, eligible to participate in the enormous business-entertainment enterprise that, for some, dwarfs in importance the university's real mission of educating students and disseminating knowledge. The educational quality provided to the athletes in question, and the learning outcomes of their classroom experiences, scarcely registered as concerns.

A glance at the class roster of one course offered at the height of the course-fraud scandal—AFRI 520 (Southern Africa) from the spring semester of 2007—suggests that Bridger really had little to complain about even before she expressed her concerns outside Walden's office. Although this course was not identified by Governor Martin as an anomalous course (another sign that Martin may have greatly underestimated the true number of substandard courses), the fall 2006 version of the same course *was* tagged as anomalous, and the registration pattern in the spring 2007 version of the course suggests that it functioned in the very same way as its predecessor from the previous fall. Of the fifty-two students enrolled in the course, 50 percent, or twenty-six students, came from the football and men's basketball teams. And the football players greatly outnumbered the basketball players—twenty-one to five. The five members of the basketball team made up nearly a third of the entire roster, it is true, but the twenty-one people on the football roster were probably the very players who most needed the good grades on offer in AFRI 520 (though the same may also have been true of the basketball team).

One other feature of the AFRI 520 class in the spring of 2007 underlines the sheer banality of corruption amid the "normalization of deviance" in university athletic programs.[1] The total number of athletes in this class was not twenty-six but rather thirty-four (out of the total of fifty-two students). And quite a few other teams were represented, including women's basketball, wrestling, men's lacrosse, and women's soccer. Most intriguingly, although several of the other players who came from teams other than football or basketball were academically challenged—either with low board scores, low GPAs, or with GPAs propped up by the paper-class curriculum— several others were not. At least three were excellent students. They were in this course only to benefit from free time and lax standards, to take a sip of the draft enjoyed by so many other UNC athletes over the years. Julius Nyang'oro and Debby Crowder offered a cornucopia of easy As and Bs, and in the 2000s multiple academic counselors from multiple teams made sure that some of their players received invitations to the banquet.

This chapter captures the broader institutional context for UNC's academic-fraud scandal. Its subject is the systematic nature of the Athletic Department's threat to academic integrity at UNC in the period between 1990 and 2012. Through various tricks of the trade, academic counselors and their complicit partners or unwitting enablers in academic offices across the university managed to manipulate the curricular machinery so as to maximize benefits for athletes. They did this especially, but not exclusively, for athletes who otherwise would have had their eligibility imperiled. The paper-class scheme was only one dimension of an all-out assault on educational quality and institutional integrity.

Dropping, Adding, Lying

UNC professors who have athletes in their classes are sent "academic progress" forms three times each semester. They are asked to record on these forms the basic indicators of a player's academic performance. Does the athlete attend class regularly? Has he or she received grades on tests, quizzes, or papers? What percentage of the total grade is represented by these marks? The compliance rate on these forms has always been poor—Mary Willingham estimates that only about one-third of instructors returned the forms by the announced deadline during her tenure in the ASPSA. But they none-theless perform two valuable functions. They create the impression that counselors in the ASPSA monitor athletes' academic work with the intention of intervening with additional help or encouragement whenever warning signs present themselves. (This is helpful for the purpose of cultivating strong relations with faculty.) More impor-tant, the forms can be used to shape the "drop" strategies of at least some of the more academically challenged athletes.

Profit-sport athletes typically register for one course in excess of those needed for the semester schedule. Needing four classes and twelve credit hours for a full-time schedule, they will often regis-ter for five courses, expecting to drop one along the way. This prac-tice is hardly specific to athletes. Many students discover that their eyes were bigger than their stomachs on registration day, and they, too, often decide to drop a course or two in the middle stages of a semester. What makes athletes' course-management strategies different is that they are formulated by academic counselors who always have one eye trained on the likely eligibility outcomes of athletes' course experiences. Academic progress reports that seem designed with educational interests in mind are in fact often used to decide which academic experiences will be strategically abandoned.

In some cases the dropping of a course had to be offset by the adding of another—either because the athlete would otherwise fall below the minimum twelve hours to qualify for full-time status or because the dropped course would have met a need that now had to be addressed through other means. This meant, during the long fraud years, that paper classes were sometimes added to athletes' schedules halfway through a semester or even later—thus add-ing a delicious accent to the bogus nature of the courses in ques-tion. (Dropping a challenging geology course and compensating for the loss by picking up a no-show AFAM 395 [Field Research], for example, would have been a very helpful transaction for eligibil-ity purposes. The educational costs of the transaction were never considered.) Such course additions had to have been approved by officials in academic advising, though it is at least possible to imag-ine that such approvals were granted precisely because there were no suspicions about the course being added. Still, why any academic official would approve the adding of a course at week six of a semester or week three of a summer session is a question unlikely to bring a satisfying answer.

Officials' awareness of the eligibility numbers game, and their gradual on-the-job acclimation to the sort of administrative favoritism that such eligibility issues sometimes necessitated, surely would have contributed to their inclination to be generous or helpful. In the ASPSA the pressure to accommodate eligibility needs was omnipresent. In one unforgettable incident, Mary Willingham participated in an unethical action the sole purpose of which was to preserve a football player's eligibility for a single game. The player had come to his counselors in tears after learning that a failing grade in one of his fall courses would leave him ineligible for the bowl game his team was scheduled to play in two weeks' time. (Compliance officers eagerly await end-of-semester grades so that they can "certify" the eligibility of players headed to postseason and postsemester bowls or tournaments.) This one failing grade would so impede the player's "academic progress"—the Academic Progress Rate, being one of the metrics the NCAA uses to measure academic performance—that he would be forced to sit on the sidelines for one of the most important games of his career. This player was a favorite among the ASPSA counselors, so they sprang into crisis mode as they brainstormed to wriggle free from this bind. Some wanted to pressure the professor to reconsider the grade he had assigned or to lobby for a second-chance final exam. (Carl Carey had used this stratagem successfully for one of Julius Peppers's drama courses in 1998.) Someone else mentioned a possible appeal to the NCAA. But Willingham calmly found the easiest solution to the problem. Since this player, like most of his teammates, had a large stockpile of paper classes and AFRI/AFAM independent study courses on his résumé, with good grades in all of them, Willingham realized that if the player merely dropped his current major and switched to AFAM, he would be able to show the necessary "progress" toward his degree that the compliance office required. Because of all those excess AFAM credits on the transcript, the failed course would not impede "progress" in the same way if he simply pretended to switch majors.

Paper classes had never so dramatically saved a player's eligibility before; high fives were exchanged all around when the counselors realized the great efficacy of this little trick. Perhaps the best part of it all was that they needed to misrepresent the player's major only for about an hour, while the compliance process speeded to completion. As soon as the player was certified, his major was switched back to his preferred field of study. The NCAA would never know, nor would they care. Catastrophe had been averted with a few keystrokes and the lapse of an hour's time. (One other effect of this incident was that it helped to awaken Mary Willingham's conscience; it was not long after this event that she began to speak up more aggressively about an unethical environment that had made her feel increasingly uncomfortable.)

As the strange case of the major-switching football player demonstrates clearly, the fall and spring semesters concealed multiple booby traps for athletes concerned with preserving their eligibility. During those grueling fourteen-week terms, the athletes in football and basketball were devoting forty- and fifty-hour weeks to their sports, carrying full course schedules, and plowing through at least some demanding classes. Many student GPAs sustained real damage in the fall or spring. This is one reason so much athletic course work was completed in the summer, when schedules were less hectic and the academic terrain more forgiving.

Endless Summer

Athletes, particularly in the profit sports, take a disproportionate number of their classes in the two summer sessions that run from mid-May to the end of July. In principle the practice is unobjectionable. It even makes good sense, given the great time demands placed on football and basketball players during their respective fall and spring playing seasons. But the dynamics that drive summer school offerings each year create ample room for corner cutting and built-in athletics favoritism, and the ASPSA has traditionally exploited those dynamics to the hilt.

One of the defining features of the UNC summer school, for example, is its stand-alone operating budget. (This funding scheme is one of the reasons summer courses are administered by an autonomous dean presiding over a separate administrative office.) Because the summer school controls its own budget and cannot rely on university overhead or the occasional infusion of money from the College of Arts and Sciences or the professional schools, summer courses have to be funded almost entirely through tuition money. This means that enrollment numbers matter.

A faculty member who is scheduled to teach a summer course, and who looks forward to drawing a salary supplement in compensation for the additional teaching, runs the risk of having his or her class canceled at the last minute if it fails to attract the minimum 10 student registrations usually needed to justify the cost of the course. The premium thereby placed on student demand—after all, what instructor would want to forgo that six-thousand-dollar salary supplement that was going to pay for the family vacation?—provides a perverse incentive to acquire for one's summer courses a reputation for being easy, fun, or just not too demanding. (In fairness to UNC faculty, it bears stressing that not all instructors who teach during summer school act on or would even acknowledge this incentive.) Summer courses are, almost by definition, somewhat watered-down versions of courses offered during regular semesters; there is simply no way to cover in less than five weeks the amount of material normally covered in fourteen. But the desire to make one's courses sufficiently "likable" to attract healthy numbers also tilts the playing field in favor of athletes in one other way. Faculty (and the summer school dean) will often be grateful for the existence of a ready-made clientele who can be recruited for the classes on offer. The temptation to recruit actively for one's classes, or to happily address an existing demand for certain kinds of courses, is bound to affect instructors who regularly teach in the summers and have come to depend on the sometimes significant salary supplement that the summer sessions provide. (This same basic temptation to ensure a robust enrollment in a spring course led a temporary naval science instructor to round up bodies in the ASPSA during the fall registration period. After promising a course with no tests, he got 30 athletes to enroll in his Naval Weapons class; that version of NAVS 302 drew 38 students in total.)[2] Some instructors head into the summer expecting and very much hoping for robust athletic enrollments in their classes.

Apart from these generic features of the typical summer school course—a subtly lower degree of difficulty and instructors who are eager to maintain healthy enrollment figures in their classes—the ASPSA has found more specific attractions in the summer sessions. Because the summer school allots teaching opportunities to academic departments based partly on previous enrollment patterns, faculty or programs that annually attract large numbers of athletes are ensured of having plenty of courses on offer—including many of the courses in the shadow curriculum that protects the academically weakest athletes. The regular summer availability of AFRI, AFAM, and SWAH courses has already been noted. Recreation (Leadership and Group Dynamics), Exercise and Sport Science (Women in Sport), Drama (Perspectives in the Theater), and the School of Library Science's "Google course" (Finding and Retrieving Information) also annually attracted athletes in droves. Some courses could be scandalously likable. In the 1980s the summer school allowed some correspondence courses to be completed in a week, by athletes and others. When the provost discovered this pattern, he addressed the problem by making a personnel change.[3]

An idea of the way in which a reputation for likability could provide distorting incentives to faculty can be gleaned from the summer history of the French Novel in Translation. A course on the French novel would not seem to possess any special cachet among students of the twenty-first century. French departments around the country are struggling to maintain enrollments in their language classes, as the popularity of French (like that of other European languages) continues its steady decline in college classrooms. Yet so popular was the French Novel in Translation that a single class section accounted for 90 percent of the total French Department enrollments in the second summer session of 2003; French 40 supplied 185 seats out of the total 206 French seats taken. (In that same summer session, other English-language literature courses—on Shakespeare, Chaucer, and the chief romantic poets, for example—struggled to fill. One had just 7 students, and few had more than 20.) The inflated figure for French 40 in 2003 was no anomaly. In the second summer session of 2004, French 40 drew 191 students, while courses in the French Department as a whole, French 40 included, drew 218. Not all of the students in the course were athletes—French 40 was widely notorious—but the ready-made athletic clientele in second summer sessions at UNC assured Professor Fred Vogler that he would always be permitted to teach in the summers.[4] Mutual benefits were to be had in a system in which athletes needed to pad their transcripts with GPA boosters before the fall.

One basketball player in the 1990s, for example, used the opportunity afforded by summer sessions to load up on courses from the shadow curriculum of that era. In addition to the many Nyang'oro-sponsored courses he took during the summers, he also took summer versions of Ethics of Sport, Movement for the Actor, and the French Theater in Translation (he aced it). Sometime later a football player compiled a summer course record that included Basic Writing, Education in American Society, Elementary P.E. Methods, the French Theater in Translation, the French Novel in Translation, and assorted AFAM and EXSS courses. (This course lineup was virtually identical to that of countless other football players.) A women's basketball player who entered the university sometime after 2000 also managed to find hospitable courses in abundance. Besides the many hours of AFRI and SWAH she pursued in the summers, her summer course record also included a geography independent study and a philosophy directed-readings course. (Faculty chair Jan Boxill offered directed-readings courses virtually every summer between 2002 and 2010, the years for which the summer school has maintained enrollment records; she also taught Ethics of Sport to scores of students most summers. The course was by far the most popular course offered by the Philosophy Department in summer sessions.) It goes without saying that the grades athletes earned in all these courses were uniformly high. Summer was a happy time.

With the most at-risk (or most favored) athletes, counselors in the ASPSA sometimes used summers for a quite specific purpose: padding the GPA before the first real semester began. The story of Marvin Austin, the prized defensive lineman who came to UNC as Butch Davis's first star recruit, illustrates the eligibility games of summertime at their most perverse. Mary Willingham recalls how disturbed she was to learn that Austin was going to be removed from English 100 (Basic Writing) at about the midpoint of the second summer session in 2007—a maneuver that required special approval. She regarded English 100 as the athletes' most valuable course, the lone opportunity for the counseling staff to identify any deficiencies and develop skills that would be needed at the university. But attendance issues had hampered Austin's performance in the English course, so it was arranged that he would be added to a class that did not require his presence—an advanced paper class, AFAM 428. He pulled a B+ in that 400-level (meaning graduate- and advanced undergraduate-level) course, thus preserving his freshman-year eligibility and helping to ease his transition into the rough-and-tumble world of real university classes. Austin's long-term educational interests were cynically sacrificed for the purpose of GPA maintenance. This preemptive plumping of the GPA was useful in the first year, since athletes did not enjoy priority registration for their first semester on campus. The priority registration system, a version of which exists on almost every campus in America, gives athletes a jump on registering for their favored courses. But no such privilege existed for the first fall semester, since students already in residence had begun their own registration process in March. This meant that athletes often had to register for a series of challenging courses in the fall; a cushion carried over from the summer could be most helpful.

The distributors of soft grades sometimes acted on the best of intentions, to be sure. They felt sympathy for the athletes who worked such long hours and often seemed overmatched by the university course work they were asked to do. Others—perhaps Nyang'oro and Crowder among them—deliberately sought to compensate for a system they regarded as inequitable. But others were put in the position of "taking care" of athletes because of their own vulnerable positions at the university. Not all individuals and programs enjoy the same security and the same protections in the university hierarchy. A program like Portuguese, for example, which saw its graduate program abolished in 2005 because of "low productivity," and where undergraduate enrollments have flagged in recent years, would have had an obvious incentive to serve the needs of the athletic program and thereby prove to the dean of the college its continuing utility for undergraduates. (Modern Brazilian Literature in English Translation was another summer staple that enrolled healthy numbers year after year.)

Individual instructors, too, could be placed in unenviable positions. Classes in the English composition program are routinely taught by advanced graduate students, the great majority of them female. These instructors lack not only the protection of tenure but also the status of faculty and the deference automatically accorded faculty—especially male faculty.[5] English composition classes are often packed with athletes, since successful completion of English 101 and 102 (and since 2013 the single-course English 105) has long been the one graduation requirement that applies to every single student at UNC. English 100, Basic Writing, is another course through which many athletes must pass, and it is offered every summer.

The English instructors for all of these courses are more vulnerable to subtle forms of harassment than regular faculty, and in the past some received the occasional agitated phone call when a bad grade placed an athlete in peril. But killing with kindness always worked better than outright harassment, and academic counselors carefully cultivated their relations with English instructors. So critical was the composition program to the academic fortunes of athletes that, Willingham recalls, "we spent a lot of time 'courting' the TAs and the entire program." The grad assistants were invited to the ASPSA in August, before the beginning of the fall semester, and "we gave them Carolina T-shirts and told them to call us anytime for help if they wanted to go to games. It was a total scam." When UNC went to Notre Dame for an away football game in 2006, the director of the composition program, Todd Taylor, traveled with the team. (He went as Willingham's guest.) He satisfied a lifelong dream by kicking a field goal during warm-ups—in the shadow of Touchdown Jesus. Many of the graduate instructors in the composition program routinely accepted the blandishments sent their way by the Athletic Department: game tickets, guest coaching assignments, travel opportunities. Through such measures the Athletic Department sought to keep the personnel in this critical "gateway" curricular program sympathetic to its needs.[6]

The ASPSA's method of combining ingratiating kindness with

veiled intimidation tactics is vividly illustrated in a 2005 incident involving one of Mary Willingham's challenged students. Willingham remembers that a relatively inexperienced instructor called a meeting for an athlete who seemed to be in danger of failing English 101. Since the player was reading far below grade level and worked with Willingham regularly, she decided to accompany him to the meeting. The player, a nice guy who understood that he was in way over his head academically, was literally shaking from fear as they walked to the meeting. But once they arrived, Willingham took charge and proceeded to paint the instructor into a corner. "Look, we need to help this guy so he can stay and get an education here. If he can't get past 101, he'll have to go home. I know you don't really want that. We understand that this really isn't the class for him right now, but it's the situation we're in. We have no choice. He's willing to work, he comes into our office whenever he has free time, and we're doing everything in our power to get him up to speed. Can't you work with us?" Without really meaning to—she had intended simply to use her considerable charm to appeal for human sympathy and an academic lifeline for a student she desperately wanted to help—Willingham applied difficult-to-resist pressure to a graduate student who was just trying to make her way. The twentysomething instructor, who had never had an official from the Athletic Department in her office before and probably wanted this to be the last such visit, acknowledged the impossible situation in which the student found himself. She saw what needed to be done, and she indicated a willingness to help out.

In the end the player not only passed the course but got a B. In fact, Willingham recalls that during her tenure in ASPSA, the academically challenged athletes tended to earn high marks in the composition courses—higher marks than in most of their other nonfraudulent courses. That such grades did not necessarily reflect unusually high verbal aptitude is suggested by the subsequent pattern of their course selections. With the exception of the composition courses, English courses were virtually absent from the course records of profit-sport athletes.

English instructors and graduate students could be wooed, leaned on, and "worked with." At UNC, however, perhaps the clearest example of opportunistic exploitation of the vulnerable came not in English courses but in the Swahili program. Alphonse Mutima is an untenured instructor in the AFRI/AFAM Department who has been widely praised as a good and passionate teacher of the Swahili language. David Pizzo, who teaches at Murray State University and pursued his doctoral studies at UNC in the early 2000s, remembers Mutima as "a very hard worker" and an "excellent" teacher. But he says it was quite obvious, in his own Swahili courses, that "the athletes were sort of dumped on Mutima" and that either because of direct pressure or because he understood that he had to operate "in the environment Julius [Nyang'oro] had created," he got the message to "just pass them." (According to a faculty member aware of the dynamics Mutima had to endure, at least one academic counselor from the ASPSA pressured Mutima directly, and on more than one occasion, to make sure that certain athletes got through his courses.) Mutima was frustrated by the presence of the athletes, says Pizzo, because their hearts were not in it and their performance was "kind of terrible"—not because they necessarily lacked ability, he says, but because they were so often physically exhausted, uninterested in the language, and fully aware that these were "padded hours" they needed only to get through. Listening to the athletes make the same grammatical errors and struggle with the same basic vocabulary words day after day caused general embarrassment and hampered the classroom atmosphere. "I could see that Mutima just wanted to pull his hair out. . . . He seemed very overworked, very stressed out, and very powerless."[7]

Pizzo's recollections match those of Rye Barcott, who was a Reserve Officers' Training Corps student and UNC undergraduate in the late 1990s. He has published a memoir that recounts his role in founding the nongovernmental organization Carolina in Kibera, and in it he recalls fondly the passionate teaching of Alphonse Mutima. His Swahili course, however, was held in the most "polarized" and "bifurcated" classroom Barcott had ever entered. "A dozen male athletes and a few guys looking to complete their foreign-language requirement with as little work as possible sat in the back rows. Separated by a no-man's land of barren desks, the rest of us, about eight students, sat in the front." Mutima "did the best he could" with his two very different clienteles. Barcott, like Pizzo, zestfully drank in Mutima's every word and learned a great deal about both Swahili and the recent history of central Africa. But Mutima simply "dealt with" the guys in the back of the room, though "he had little respect for them" because they seemed to take the gift of education for granted.[8] Still frustrated in 2010, Mutima would later contact a tutor in the ASPSA during one summer session to see if someone there could arrange for one struggling football player's transfer to a paper-class version of intermediate Swahili.[9] For instructors dedicated to their students but assigned a role to play in the NCAA eligibility machine, summer could be a trying time.

A World Apart

The overreliance on summer courses—many profit-sport athletes earn between one-quarter and one-third of all their credit hours in the summer, which makes them strange outliers in the UNC undergraduate population—is only the most obvious sign of the segregated educational tracks that have been constructed at the university. The five most popular majors offered at UNC are communications, psychology, biology, political science, and economics. Athletes cluster in communications, but recruited profit-sport athletes are effectively excluded from four of the five fields of study to which their nonathlete classmates are most attracted. Similarly, the music and art courses that so many UNC undergraduates take in fulfillment of their fine-arts graduation requirements are terra incognita to football stars; they work on stagecraft instead. If a starter on the football or basketball team ever expressed a desire to study abroad, he would most likely be laughed out of the locker room. As Anthony Kelly of the University of Washington (UW) put it in 2010, "There are these unwritten rules that you have to follow to make sure that the coaches are okay" with any slightly unorthodox behavior, including the expression of interest in certain academic pursuits. "I really just looked at it as an issue of control."[10]

Despite the pieties spouted by the NCAA and its many defenders, recruited athletes in the profit sports understand all too well where and how they are expected to invest their time and labors at their respective universities. Academics are "important" and promoted to the extent that they do not interfere with team activities and objectives (and, even more to the point, to the extent that they facilitate athletic eligibility), but elite players who are recruited to a university to play a sport are expected to make their sport their priority. As former Maryland basketball star Laron Profit puts it, "We're not student-athletes, we're athlete-students." As reported by journalist Dave Zirin in a 2011 interview, Profit likened the recruitment process, in which lip service is always paid to academics, to a game of bait and switch. "[As] soon as we walk onto the campus, we're told expressly what we're there to do, and that's be athletes first, students second."[11] University of Missouri football player Sean Coffey concurs. He recalls that his coaches, in general, never encouraged him "to do anything outside of football." The inner-city kid from Cleveland was shuffled off to the agriculture major "because it was easy." About the academic staff in the Missouri Athletic Department, Coffey says, "They know every class and which ones are easiest." Their job "is to keep us eligible." They may claim to care about a player's postathletic future, but "it's evident and glaring that's not really the case."[12]

That the eligibility machine forces athletes to subordinate academic needs and interests to the priority of participating in their sport does not escape the attention of the athletes themselves. One former UNC football player who played in the Butch Davis era, and who wishes to remain anonymous, shared in an email to the authors his disgust with the exploitative system under which he labored. Detailing all the corruption he saw at UNC "would take pages and pages for me to convey," he wrote, but he especially remains indignant over the neglect of the educational needs of so many of his teammates. Whatever the academic deficiencies of some of the guys on the team, he noted, "All that matters to the powers that be are pushing them through and keeping them eligible to play and pass the classes." As for the goals consistent with the stated educational mission of the university—"having these athletes actually improve, learn, and correct [their reading] problems"—this player saw them consigned to "the very bottom of the list."

One of the key figures in the UNC scandal, football player Michael McAdoo, would certainly agree with this assessment. After first being suspended from the team for committing academic violations he had come to regard as strictly business as usual (the copying of text from an Internet source and the acceptance of excess help from a tutor who worked in the home of the head coach), he was later steered to the notorious AFAM 280 paper class by a football academic counselor in the summer of 2011. UNC eventually succeeded in winning the dismissal of a lawsuit filed by McAdoo in part by insisting that the university had honored its commitment to the player by facilitating his education even after his suspension from the team; that "education," however, included his enrollment in yet another paper class, McAdoo's fourth. He now complains bitterly that he was "done wrong" by the university. When recruiters first talked to him, McAdoo says, they told him that "academics is the first thing they were going to push—'You are going to do academics and then play sports.' But come to find out it just felt like it was all a scam."[13]

Athletes in the profit sports live with structural constraints and forms of discipline that should really leave no doubt in their minds about the level of the university's commitment to their educations. Their academic schedules and major choices are largely determined by their practice schedules, and their financial-aid agreements—in uniquely perverse fashion—actually require that they skip classes. But in addition to the basics of course scheduling, which always subordinate academic to athletic needs, athletes find themselves always in the iron grip of athletics personnel who exercise constant discipline and surveillance over them. "Virtually every detail of their lives," write Robert McCormick and Amy Christian McCormick, "is carefully controlled by coaches and athletic staff, not only during the season but year around." During the summers football and basketball players are typically "required to remain on campus during the week and may leave only with the advance permission of the coach." And their every move is monitored by compliance officials who reinforce continually the athletes' identities as (amateur) athletes. The fact that "coaches alone may decide not to renew a player's scholarship for any reason or no reason (and can even terminate the scholarship mid-term for cause), only cements the coach's control."[14]

It all comes down to "an issue of control," remembered Anthony Kelly of Washington. A stark expression of this effort to control players' bodies and minds, and to command their loyalty to the machine, is found in the locker room of the UNC football team. As revealed in the documentary film *Schooled: The Price of College Sports*, the coaching staff at Carolina uses players' NFL aspirations as leverage against them when needed. Posted on a door in the locker room is an infantilizing sign that identifies misbehaving individuals and reminds the rogues who their master is. "ATTENTION NFL SCOUTS: I will not discuss the following players. They are selfish, lazy, and have NO concept of team. They cannot help you win football games."[15]

The very existence of that sign makes a mockery of the oft-repeated claim that college football players are "students first." Not only is it offensive that UNC would allow the bullying and intimidation of aspiring professionals within its student body—coaches threaten to brand players as malcontents and egotists in the eyes of NFL scouts and prospective employers—but the overarching message conveyed by that locker-room sign is wholly incompatible with the values of a university. The threat of having to wear the dunce cap inevitably chills free speech and autonomous thinking. It discourages the formation of strong, forceful opinions. It effectively preempts the questioning of authority. It therefore directly undermines the lessons imparted in university classrooms, even as it ensures the coaching staff's "control" over students supposedly engaged in an "extracurricular activity." The message of that sign—conform, obey, and shut up, or else—might be appropriate to some sorts of employer-employee relationships, but it could never be appropriate to the relationship between an educator and a student on a college campus.

The UNC coaching staff cannot really be held responsible for this state of affairs, of course. In treating players like children without mature minds of their own, and in freely acknowledging (and exploiting) the fact that their players came to the university because they hope to play in the NFL, the coaches are only showing their firm understanding of reality. Most coaches, to be sure, are well intentioned. Most care genuinely about their players, and they surely hope that all players will take advantage of the educational "opportunity" given to them. But they also know that their recruits are under their control, and they will deliberately use that control to squeeze out of them every ounce of athletic effort. Behind closed locker-room doors, where they are free to drop the pretense that the enterprise they run is really all about education, coaches continually reinforce their players' identities as athlete-students who must perform physically, prove their dedication to their sport, and keep the coaches happy.

And the players gradually get the message. Although they typically enter their universities with idealistic hopes about their academic futures, longitudinal studies have shown that athletes in football and basketball grow "increasingly cynical about and uninterested in academics" the more time they spend on campus.[16] Anne Berler, the history graduate student who spent a year as an ASPSA tutor and taught many an athlete as a teaching assistant in history survey courses, remembers being struck by the passive, disengaged affect of most of the profit-sport athletes with whom she worked. In class discussions, she recalls, the athletes almost seemed to be participating in a contest to see who could be the quietest. In one recitation section that had a large representation from the football and men's basketball teams, eliciting comments from the athletes was like pulling teeth. (Sadly, the one football player who remained relatively engaged stifled his enthusiasm so as not to draw the attention and derision of his teammates.)

In tutoring sessions, too, the athletes typically planted themselves in their chairs and waited to be filled, like empty vessels, with whatever wisdom they needed to get through the next test. Berler recalls that their own feeble mastery of the material never seemed to bother them much. "There was always a sense that they knew someone would pull their chestnuts out of the fire," she says. Indeed, one reason football and basketball players flock to courses where exams are few and papers are many is that papers can always be written by someone else—including, in at least some instances, by academic counselors. Mary Willingham recalls that Beth Bridger frequently served as stenographer for football players; she would have them talk to her about the paper they wanted to write while she did the actual composing. Willingham, too, offered help in sentence construction that she now realizes went beyond the bounds of permissibility. But trying to pull paragraphs out of severely under-prepared students is exhausting work; it left her in tears on more than one occasion.

In her time as a tutor Berler frequently received the subtle message, both from the athletes themselves and from at least one academic counselor, that it was really perfectly all right if she wanted to do some of the athletes' work for them. There were many formal restrictions on the amount and type of help tutors could provide, and tutors were officially informed about the need for scrupulousness. But reality has its own imperatives. Berler always managed to resist the temptation to do players' work for them, but she remembers being made to feel guilty about it. Jennifer Wiley was simply one of the tutors who succumbed to the subtle pressures applied within the walls of the ASPSA. Unwilling to feel guilty for not helping, she instead took on a kind of guilt that her superiors were all too happy to accommodate. (Remember, Wiley, not Berler or one of her like-minded colleagues, won the 2008 "Outstanding Tutor" award.)

Disciplined, "controlled," guided, and protected, recruited profit-sport athletes are conditioned to regard their academic lives as secondary to their proper university function: playing hard, winning games, and striving to make the pros. The people who are theoretically in a position to advocate for them, and to protect their long-term interests, are in fact servants of the eligibility machine. Living in a world apart from the real university, they resort to countless tricks in order to game the system, pulling the wool over the eyes of the athletes themselves in the process. The whole "academic support" complex, Sean Coffey has told *Sports Illustrated*, constitutes a world of groupthink in which players function like "blank-faced 'assembly-line workers' doing whatever they [are] told."[17] What they are told, in so many subtle and not-so-subtle ways, is that they should regard their academic experiences either as a necessary evil or as a fringe benefit to enjoy only as time allows.

The Silence of the Rams

Since 2010 the sporting rivals of UNC have predictably and understandably focused their ire on the competitive advantages that Carolina sport teams enjoyed as a result of the university's egregious academic misconduct over a period of decades. The unfair advantages were indeed many. Paper classes kept many grade point averages artificially inflated, allowing athletes to focus on their athletic endeavors in a way that athletes at other universities could only dream about. Paper classes also served purposes that were arguably more nefarious—boosting graduation rates and protecting Academic Progress Rates (even, as we have seen, for players who majored in AFAM for only one hour), creating summer sessions in which six credit hours would be awarded to a player who actually focused entirely on physical conditioning and guiding departed players over the graduation finish line long after they had left the campus. (One effect of the UNC scandal is that skeptics will always wonder, and reasonably so, whether "returning" players who finished their degrees after leaving for the pros ever returned to anything like a real academic grind. Were they effectively handed paper-class diplomas so that UNC could maintain its stellar APR?)

Chapters 7 and 8 have shown that athletes at UNC received many illicit or questionable "benefits" even outside the offices of Debby Crowder and Julius Nyang'oro—slide courses in many departments, drop/add policies that could be cynically manipulated, priority registration, retroactive withdrawals from courses in which Fs were earned (in addition to the routine grade changes that Crowder and Nyang'oro also effected in many semesters), access to helpful ghostwriters, academic counselors who exploited vulnerable faculty and curricular soft spots wherever they could find them. The football team, it is worth noting, profited from one other cynical maneuver that seems to have been specific to the sport. A small percentage of football players over the years simply checked out academically during their final fall playing seasons, flunking all of their courses so they could focus on football and prepare for the NFL draft. With eligibility no longer in need of protecting, they tanked every course they took and dropped the pretense that they had ever been student-athletes.[18]

In short, a great many victories, and probably more than one national championship, owed something to UNC's scandalous academic permissiveness and its acceptance of a double-standard curricular system that shielded athletes (particularly in the profit sports) from the full burdens and risks imposed by a normal course of study at a university. Duke and NC State fans have every right to be angry.

Whatever the justifiable anger over the competitive advantages enjoyed by UNC since the early 1990s, however, by far the greatest scandal that has unfurled since Julius Nyang'oro enrolled his first athlete in an independent study is the educational defrauding of so many Tar Heel football and basketball players. By shepherding recruited profit-sport athletes through a shadow curriculum that spared them the academic rigors their nonathlete classmates routinely endured, a shadow curriculum that also enabled the university to circumvent its obligation to remediate the academic deficiencies of many, the university simultaneously denied them access to real college educations. Not all of the athletes who were processed in this cynical manner were academically disadvantaged. Many a bright and capable star athlete was guided through the same bogus course of study that also kept the poor students eligible. That course of study saved time for more important priorities, it kept them safely on the conventional path toward the pros, and it sometimes even rewarded them with a diploma of dubious value. But whatever the level of academic preparedness of the profit-sport athletes who came to Carolina between 1990 and 2011, almost all who matriculated in this era should be seen as victims of a fraud. The scholarship agreements they signed—documents that promised them educations in exchange for their athletic labors—lured them to the campus under false pretenses; the university to this day has refused to acknowledge this structurally conditioned breach of contract.

Why has the university doggedly stuck to its strategy of obfuscation and denial? More important still, why did no one, until November 2012, speak up about the academic misconduct they had witnessed? Countless officials in athletics, and a considerable number of officials in academic affairs, had to have known or suspected that athletes were receiving preferential gifts that subverted academic standards and thereby made players' lives easier in the short term. How did so many live with the hypocrisy for so long?

Race is the third rail of university politics. It is an issue that almost everyone studiously avoids discussing, in part because comments about race can easily be misconstrued. Even the most sincere and sensitive talk about racial issues becomes unavoidably painful to all concerned. The easy thing to do is to pretend not to notice either continuing racial inequities or the imperfect and superficial fixes that have been devised to combat them through the years. A deceptive but reassuring aura of political correctness and mutual congratulation has imperceptibly taken the place of honest thought and searching discussion.

Unfortunately, at UNC this long-term reticence allowed insidious forms of institutional racism to take deep and permanent root. Start with the history of the AFRI/AFAM Department and the look-the-other-way attitude with which college administrators approached their responsibilities with regard to that department. A succession of deans had to have known about Julius Nyang'oro's international travel habits, which made him a de facto absentee department head for many years. They had to know that the man never answered an email. (This anomaly formed the subject of running jokes in other administrative offices around the campus.) They had to know that Nyang'oro governed his department without relying on the sorts of consultative bodies and democratic procedures that character-ized departmental governance everywhere else in the College of Arts and Sciences. (If they did not know this, their lack of curios-ity about what was going on in a fledging department constitutes an embarrassing failure of its own.) Deans seem not to have wor-ried that an absentee leader might see fit to rule through expedi-ence, procedural shortcuts, and a disregard for protocol and the opinions of others.

Deans oversaw the AFRI/AFAM Department, in other words, with an attitude of benign neglect. They kept reappointing Nyang'oro as chair, even as other candidates joined the faculty and developed their own visions for the department's future. In 2007, according to one member of the faculty, the dean reappointed Nyang'oro after all the other members of the department had first been told by Nyang'oro himself that he was preparing to step down. One day, with his col-leagues having assembled to discuss the future of the department and its leadership needs, Nyang'oro simply walked in and stunningly announced to them that "the dean and I have worked it out after all, and so I will be renewing."[19] This most anomalous reappointment procedure—elsewhere in the College of Arts and Sciences, deans routinely poll or interview faculty to hear their thoughts and preferences before selecting a new chair—assured Nyang'oro his fourth consecutive five-year term as chair.

Deans apparently never asked themselves why a person would want to serve ten or fifteen or twenty years in a position that most faculty regard as both thankless and tiresome. Was this indifference not a sign that deans had an instinctive low regard for the department and its role in university life? At least two former faculty members think so. Michael West of Binghamton University, who worked at UNC for eight years before his departure in 2002, notes that it was always clear to him and his colleagues that AFRI/AFAM "was not considered a valued part of the university." He pointed to Nyang'oro's long reign as proof. (Another telling sign: the college's lack of interest in establishing a graduate program in AFRI/AFAM.) "A person should never remain in a position of leadership for [twenty years] at any institution," West observed. "It's not good for anyone." He noted the deans' very different manner of dealing with leadership transitions in other departments, and he asked himself why only the department dominated by black faculty could go ignored for so long. "It's just impossible to imagine this happening in Biology or English or History." West liked Nyang'oro personally and still regards him as a friend, but he saw Nyang'oro's uninterrupted stewardship of the department as a clear "sign of neglect" on the part of the administration.

Other signs of neglect were cited by Professor Walter Rucker, now of Rutgers University, in an interview conducted in 2014. Rucker noted that AFRI/AFAM had never in its history gone through what is known in higher education as an "external review." Such a review involves a visitation by a panel of respected peers from across the country who audit every facet of a department's performance—its teaching, its research output, its budget, its organization, its plans for the future, in addition to the morale of its students, faculty, and staff—before writing a lengthy and considered evaluation of its strengths and weaknesses. These external reviews typically shape strategic plans at the departmental level, and college deans periodically remind chairs of departments of their need to plan and carry out such reviews each decade. All departments with graduate programs—which AFRI/AFAM lacked—are required to conduct such reviews. Yet no such review was ever contemplated for AFRI/AFAM while Julius Nyang'oro served as chair. Just as surprising, observed Rucker, was that some faculty members in the department seem to have been exempted from what is called "post-tenure review"—a peer evaluation of faculty research productivity and teaching practices that takes place every five years after the granting of tenure. Only in the aftermath of scandal did the university consistently meet its basic administrative obligations.

How can the college justify this record of neglect? Would deans ever have dreamed of treating other departments similarly, of failing to ensure standards, of failing to secure and advance a department's reputation, of failing to cultivate administrative leaders for the future? "If UNC is a plantation, as has been frequently said," notes West, "the Department of African and Afro-American Studies was the slave quarters." The department was regarded by administrators, he says, as a "service unit." By that he means, principally, that the department was seen as an enrollment winner, a department that filled many student needs, but he also acknowledges the possibility that the "service" provided by the department's courses involved the special needs of the Athletic Department. West was sympathetic to the athletes themselves. The schedules of two football players he once spoke to were "horrendous. . . . They just had no time to study." But because his courses were not easy, he encountered very few athletes throughout his tenure at UNC. More to the point, he regretted that his department had become a depot for students who had to be processed; the department should have become so much more.[20]

Between the early 1990s and 2011 the Department of African and Afro-American Studies appears to have been on the receiving end of a form of racism that most often goes unacknowledged, a patronizing racism rooted in low expectations. Although they have rebounded impressively from the scandal since 2012, the many conscientious scholars and teachers who work in the newly named Department of African, African American, and Diaspora Studies still suffer the effects of this unfair history of administrative neglect. The university's refusal (as of 2014) to have a candid discussion about the sources and nature of this administrative failure will perpetuate those ill effects indefinitely.

One of the more ironic and tragic dimensions of the entire Nyang'oro course-fraud scandal is the fact that the AFRI/AFAM Department grew out of the anguished cries of black UNC students who demanded, in the late 1960s, that the university meet its moral obligations to educate one and all. In a 1968 manifesto that began the process that led to the establishment of the curriculum in African and Afro-American studies, leaders of the Black Student Movement found UNC "guilty of denying equal educational opportunities to minority group members of the local community, the State of North Carolina, and the nation at large." Among their demands, which included the widening of athletic recruitment to include black athletes and the adoption of more sensitive admissions procedures that would take into account the biases of the SAT, the BSM called for a Department of African and Afro-American Studies, preferably one to be staffed by black scholars. From the very beginning, in other words, the founding of the department was envisioned as a means of redressing UNC's past sins: the denial of equal educational opportunities to Americans of African descent.[21]

Yet the form of residual prejudice that unfairly constrained the institutional development of the AFRI/AFAM Department appears also to have extended to perceptions of black students. This helps to explain why educators and administrators could develop and so easily accommodate themselves to a set of segregated academic experiences that challenge the core principles enunciated in *Brown v. Board of Education*. It is not only the uninformed and secretly racist sports fan who believes that African American athletes should feel "lucky" even to be on a college campus. Such sentiments find expression in faculty lounges and all across the big-time sport universe. Why would UNC tolerate a 51 percent graduation rate among black male athletes (versus 89 percent for the student body as a whole) unless its officials assumed that lower levels of achievement were to be expected of black students? Staying with the 51 percent of success stories, why did academic counselors and the people to whom they reported direct so many UNC graduates to an AFRI or AFAM major where, they knew full well, classes in the Nyang'oro curriculum contained no tests and no meaningful instruction?

There is a widespread belief at UNC, as at many universities, that it is acceptable to hand black athletes counterfeit educational credentials since real credentials will lie forever beyond their grasp. At least they were given the "opportunity" to spend time on a college campus, goes the thinking. (Self-satisfied and privileged whites tend to chalk up classroom shortcomings among black athletes to laziness, lack of drive, and "cultural" issues.) These attitudes are insulting, offensive, and destructive, but the fact that they simmer just beneath the surface of polite university discourse helps explain both the institutional refusal to take AFRI/AFAM seriously and the long-term toleration of the department head's solicitous care taking of athletes and other students (many but not all of whom were black). Despite the excellence of so many of its faculty, the department was regarded by some as a cargo bay for students who had somehow to be "cranked through" the system. The cranking through was the thing, since this helped not only athletes in need of eligibility, but also university graduation rates and minority retention rates that factored into national rankings. The intellectual content or caliber of the instruction provided in AFRI/AFAM (much of it very high indeed) was regarded with indifference. Only the numbers mattered; quality control was completely ignored.

The actions of key players such as Jan Boxill, John Blanchard, Jack Evans, and Holden Thorp between 2010 and 2012 suggest another reason, of course, why Tar Heels remained silent in the face of athletics favoritism and defective educational outcomes for so many: in Chapel Hill athletic success is valued for its own sake. The imperative to preserve that unsullied record of athletic success, and a powerful desire to spare the Athletic Department punishment and embarrassment, led administrative and faculty leaders to engage in a cover-up that could shield the operations of the ASPSA from public and NCAA scrutiny. If preserving the myth of athletic innocence in the AFRI/AFAM course-fraud scheme meant that faculty all across the university had to pay for the sins of Julius Nyang'oro, if protecting the athletic brand required a thorough overhaul of academic procedures that placed new burdens on faculty and department chairs whose salaries remained frozen for four years (while athletic salaries continued to grow apace), and if the resumption of athletic business as usual required the subtle defaming of the entire AFRI/AFAM Department, well, everyone has to take one for the team now and then.

Even those who knew better, who had pangs of conscience, who felt queasy about what they had observed, would have necessarily remained reticent to speak at UNC–Chapel Hill. Naked cronyism, blind loyalty to the powder blue, incestuous relations across administrative units, and a craven desire to protect one's position and future prospects in the administrative hierarchy virtually ensured that staff would look the other way if they sensed that things were amiss. Looking the other way was part of the institutional culture of the place. One former staff member who worked in academic advising for years beginning in the late 1990s says bluntly: "Everyone who worked in Steele Building [the home of academic advising] knew all about AFAM. The no-show classes, the admission of athletes who could not handle regular work, the use of independent studies. All of it. Everyone knew."[22] One senior graduation adviser echoed this sentiment in a March 2014 conversation. "We all knew. Of course we did."[23] Other advisers and staff members whose sincerity cannot be doubted have insisted that they knew nothing at all, and so the truth must lie somewhere between these two poles. Yet clearly some, and perhaps many, knew something was wrong but never spoke up to object. Why?

Leaders determine whether a work environment will be characterized by openness, candor, and the freedom to voice concerns. There are reasons to suspect that *openness* and *candor* were not the watchwords of Steele Building operating procedure. Sometime between 2004 and 2009 an experienced academic adviser began questioning some of the more byzantine procedures and policies that governed the Office of Undergraduate Education. She was particularly concerned about undergraduates' often seemingly aimless course selections; she wondered whether they were getting the truly substantive advising they needed in order to construct a coherent course of study for themselves. When she took her concerns to senior associate dean Bobbi Owen, she was rebuffed. When she raised similar concerns a second time, the dean made no attempt to hide her impatience. The baffled adviser finally blurted out: "Bobbi, what do you want me to do if I see a problem, or if an error has been made, or if something needs to be corrected?" Owen responded, "If no one has complained about it, it's not a problem."[24] The adviser made the decision to leave her job not long after that dispiriting conversation.

The tendency to go along just to get along was hardly confined to the Office of Undergraduate Education. UNC's former director of diversity education and assessment Cookie Newsom remembers that the outrageous recent story about a UNC housekeeping supervisor who routinely demanded sex from his female subordinates had quite the scandalous underside. That particular supervisor's history of aggressive sexual harassment, which was publicly exposed only in a 2011 lawsuit, was discussed in the corridors of UNC administration long before the public learned a thing about the man's serial victimization of vulnerable (and often non-English-speaking) employees. Even the Office of Human Resources knew details about the inexcusable behavior and the suffering of many university employees, but no one there moved to put a stop to the abuse. The recent athletic-academic scandal, says Newsom, "was a symptom of an institutional disease." The Tar Heel faithful, she remembers, like to congratulate themselves for their long-standing reputation for doing things right—for following the "Carolina Way." Says Newsom, "I have a whole other concept of the Carolina Way. The Carolina Way is secretive, nontransparent, [and] . . . amazingly unethical. That is the Carolina Way. Keep your mouth shut, do what we expect to be done, which is the same old, same old, and don't make anybody mad who could possibly be important." Newsom recalls that while she served at the university, between 2003 and 2012, she rarely saw a good deed go unpunished. "If you do something at Carolina, you're going to get in trouble. If you do nothing, you'll be fine. . . . The culture at Carolina is: keep your mouth shut."[25]

Hence the silence of the Rams.

. . .

The fraudulence and the petty corruption exposed at UNC in 2011 and 2012 were egregious. The university owes the state of North Carolina and the entire world of college sport a show of exceptional contrition. But the pressures and conditions that made the scandal possible—the admission of athletes who need serious catching up in basic skills, the priority given to athletic achievement in the lives of so-called student-athletes, the insulated and largely autonomous institutional mechanisms available to big-time athletic departments, the ingrained hypocrisy of academic leaders, the complaisant complicity of too many faculty—are endemic to the college-sport enterprise. The problems created by these entrenched conditions are all the more serious at institutions that court reputations for selectivity and research prowess. The incentive to turn a blind eye, to wallow in denial, is all the greater when high reputations are at stake. A review of the college-sport landscape over the past decade or so shows that UNC manifested severe symptoms of a true pandemic of corruption.

Nine

Echoes across the Land

The UNC course-fraud scandal was unusual for its long duration, for its scale, and for the sheer volume of illicit academic benefits distributed to athletes between 1990 and 2011. But the disposition to render misguided "favors" to athletes, which was deeply ingrained at UNC, is hardly uncommon in the big-time sport universe. The past fifteen years have seen a steady succession of scandals involving friendly faculty, unauthorized assistance from tutors, ghostwritten papers, corrupted curricula, and fraudulent academic credit. The circumstances have varied—though the commonalities between these other cases and the UNC experience are also striking—but taken together the scandals point to a very troubling phenomenon. Everywhere, it seems, university faculty and other employees have been willing to actively subvert the real educational mission of their institutions. They have placed the needs of the athletic machine, and the eligibility needs of individual athletes, above their professed commitment to educational integrity.

The independent studies scandal that came to light at Auburn University in 2006 has drawn more national attention than most other cases of academic failure.[1] In a lengthy exposé, Pete Thamel of the *New York Times* detailed the Athletic Department's exploitation of directed-readings courses in sociology throughout the early 2000s. As at UNC, where a department chair facilitated the distribution of free credit hours, so at Auburn the head of the Department of Sociology, Thomas Petee, supervised a scheme predicated on the cutting of corners. In one academic year alone, 2004–5, Petee supervised 250 students in independent study projects. Not all were athletes—in fact, three-quarters of the beneficiaries of Petee's brand of benevolence were not athletes—but there can be little doubt about which students profited most from the directed-readings courses he offered. As former Auburn defensive back Carlos Rogers said of Petee, "He's the kind of teacher that, you know, he wants to help you out, not just pile a lot of stuff on you."

Petee helped a lot, and he rarely piled on. The faculty member who eventually blew the whistle on the department head, fellow sociologist James Gundlach, found that eighteen members of the 2004 Auburn football team had taken ninety-seven hours' worth of directed readings with Petee (nearly two three-credit courses per player). They earned a GPA of 3.31 in Petee's classes (roughly a B+), but their collective GPA in all other Auburn courses was 2.14 (C). So helpful was Thomas Petee to the football team—one player took seven courses with him, three took six, five took five—that Auburn jumped to the top of the NCAA's Academic Progress Rate rankings, even though the football team had a disappointing 48 percent graduation rate. An idea of Petee's importance to the squad can be gleaned through later developments. Between 2006, when Petee's practices were first uncovered, and 2011, by which time the university had closed some gaping academic loopholes, Auburn's APR dropped from 4th in the nation to 85th out of 120 programs. (This plunge was a *good* thing, because it showed that Auburn was again playing by the rules.)

Petee had helped players with registration techniques that mimicked the practices used in Chapel Hill. When one player had to drop a course late in the fall 2004 semester, putting him behind the eligibility eight ball, an academic counselor simply pointed him to Petee, who allowed him to register for a "one-assignment" directed-readings course in the "ninth or 10th week" of the term. And like Julius Nyang'oro and Debby Crowder, who allowed football players to take paper classes to satisfy foreign-language requirements, Petee offered challenging statistics and theory courses in the independent study style, which even he admitted to the *New York Times* was "not usually" done. When Gundlach went public with the academic corner cutting he had found, many on the Auburn campus were shocked. One sociology professor lamented that his department had become "a dumping ground for athletes." An exasperated David Cicci, who then served as chairman of Auburn's Faculty Senate, admitted that "I have never heard of anything of this magnitude in any discipline at any university." (Cicci, of course, knew nothing about the mind-boggling corruption unfolding a few hundred miles to the northeast even as he spoke.)

Tellingly, however, the university's administration reacted to the Gundlach revelations first with denial—his superiors refused to launch an investigation when he first confronted them with information about Petee in 2005, and the provost initially allowed Petee to continue in his role as department head even after the scandal went public—and then with the familiar declaration that the whole thing was an academic issue having little to do with athletics. (Indeed, UNC personnel may have patterned their later behavior on the amazingly effective precedent set at Auburn.) In announcing new and more restrictive policies on independent study courses in August 2006, Auburn's acting president, Ed Richardson, "stressed that athletes were not shown special favor," according to *OnlineMontgomery*. He insisted that "athletics is a minor player" in the whole affair. A resigned Gundlach responded, "I expected them to do everything possible to clear athletics."[2] His expectations were realized.

Although the Auburn case is small potatoes compared to two decades of fraud and thousands of bogus grades, it clearly shares the DNA of the UNC scandal. A friendly faculty member helped disproportionate numbers of athletes by offering virtual no-show classes in which As were handed out—in the Auburn case—at an 81 percent clip (though 17 percent of the athletes had to settle for Bs). At both places regular procedures and normal curricular expectations were thrown to the winds. The NCAA ultimately looked the other way because nonathletes had also enrolled in the courses. University administrators denied that eligibility pressures or a desire to help out the Athletic Department had much at all to do with the fraud (though Auburn's Petee was enough of a fan that he asked for the autograph of star running back Carnell "Cadillac" Williams, whose last semester at Auburn consisted solely of two directed-readings courses with his favorite sociologist). At Auburn as at UNC, academic officials were forced to bear the responsibility for the corruption of the curriculum. Petee was eventually forced to leave the university, and one other professor was also disciplined. The whistle-blower, Gundlach, was subjected to abuse by boosters and retired prematurely after leading his crusade for integrity.

Thomas Petee's favoritism was shocking, and his practices eerily foreshadowed what was later to be revealed at UNC. But other recent events from across the country provide evidence of big-time corruption every bit as sobering as the developments at Auburn, and the institutional parallels between UNC and many of the other universities recently rocked by scandal are in some ways more revealing than the comparison with Auburn. Auburn is, after all, a school from the Southeastern Conference where football has always been king. Although it is a fine institution, Auburn has long had the reputation, however fairly or unfairly earned, for allowing its love of football to undermine its commitment to academic excellence. Athletics-induced corruption at Auburn, some would be inclined to say, is only to be expected.

The athletic programs at the Universities of Michigan, Washington, and Minnesota, by contrast, were long regarded as places that "did things right," as institutions where sports remained in their proper place. All of those universities, moreover, share with UNC the aspiration to be regarded as among the very best public universities in the nation. With highly ranked programs, star faculty, and hard-earned reputations for research prowess, these universities present to the world a carefully cultivated image of academic rigor and seriousness, an image that helps them to attract their share of the best students and enters into the algorithms that produce annual college rankings.

How telling is it, then, that each of these outstanding universities has recently had its own experience with embarrassing academic misconduct carried out for the benefit of athletes? Seen collectively, their experiences bring two questions to the fore: Are big-time athletic programs compatible with high academic standards? Does the existence of high academic standards at big-time universities actually *increase* the incidence of corruption and hypocrisy? The experience of the past decade and a half would seem to yield depressing answers to these fundamental questions.

The Teflon Team

Rick Neuheisel's University of Washington football team had a remarkable 2000 season. During a thrilling 11-1 campaign, they won more than half their games by six points or less. In an early-season contest on national television, they kick-started their glorious year by defeating a highly regarded Miami team in a game decided only in the final minutes. And they capped the season with a convincing victory over Drew Brees and the Purdue Boilermakers in the Rose Bowl, finishing the year as the third-ranked team in the country. At the dawn of the new century, the Washington Huskies had reclaimed their place among the nation's elite football programs, where legendary coach Don James had first taken them in the 1980s.

Because of Ken Armstrong and Nick Perry's searing profile of Washington's 2000 football team, *Scoreboard, Baby*, sports fans also know that the University of Washington provides an object lesson in the moral costs of big-time sport success. The 2001 Rose Bowl championship team was defined as much by its off-the-field lawlessness as by its on-the-field exploits. Defensive back Anthony Vontoure, who suffered from mental illness and would die a tragically premature death at the age of twenty-two, had frequent violent outbursts and once nearly beat a nineteen-year-old Chico State student to death at a birthday party that he had crashed with friends looking for a fight. Future NFL tight end Jerramy Stevens appears to have raped an incapacitated freshman coed only weeks before the 2000 season began. He was also convicted of assault during his first semester on campus (for stomping on a young man's head and breaking his jaw), he spent several weeks in jail after a marijuana bust in the summer before his freshman year, and he drove so recklessly and so often inebriated that he was responsible for two separate hit-and-run accidents during his Washington playing career.

Strong safety Curtis Williams, known for his ferocious hits on the field, had trouble containing his violent impulses when he was outside the lines. On many occasions he punched, threatened, choked, bloodied, and battered his wife, Michelle, the mother of his young child. She usually tried to cover for him, as victims of domestic abuse so often do, but by the fall of 1998 Williams already had three separate assault convictions on his record, he had been incarcerated for several months, and he had to withdraw from the university during his sophomore season because he was unable to do schoolwork in his jail cell. Despite the pattern of irresponsible behavior and the obvious menace he posed to his wife, Williams was never removed from the football team (though Coach Jim Lambright at one point apparently wished to do so), and the local media repeatedly covered for the player by withholding from news reports any of the details about his various convictions or incarcerations. When Williams's playing career came to a premature end in the fall of 2000—he was paralyzed while making a tackle—Washington fans had not the slightest idea that their tragic hero was a convicted felon. *Seattle Times* columnist Blaine Newnham even gallingly reported in the wake of Williams's accident that "friends of Curtis said [wife] Michelle was more abusive than he."[3] Multiple additional warrants for Williams's arrest still hung over his head at the time of his accident. (One such arrest warrant had been issued because of eight hundred dollars in unpaid parking tickets—a misdemeanor infraction for which numerous UNC athletes would later gain notoriety.)

Williams's friend and teammate Jeremiah Pharms compiled perhaps the most shocking record of lawlessness of anyone on the Washington team. A frequent drunk driver like Stevens, a perpetrator of domestic battery like Williams, a serial abuser of animals, Pharms also nearly killed a man while carrying out a premeditated theft. After purchasing some marijuana and spying the storage methods of the dealer, Kerry Sullivan, Pharms later returned to Sullivan's apartment wearing a mask, accompanied by a friend, brandishing a firearm, and intent on stealing the remaining marijuana stash. After the men forced their way inside, a stunned Sullivan, who had been quietly studying for a calculus exam, impulsively lunged for the masked man's gun. Pharms whipped Sullivan over the head with the pistol and then shot the victim as he fell. A single shell traveled through his thigh and into his chest, narrowly missing his liver before puncturing a lung. Luckily for Sullivan, one of his roommates was a nursing assistant who immediately stopped the bleeding after Pharms and his accomplice made their getaway. Doctors were never able to remove the bullet from his chest cavity, however. Ten years after the event, Sullivan still suffered shortness of breath and a deep ache in his shoulder.

To put it mildly, the behavior of many Washington football players between 1996 and 2000 was atrocious; at least two dozen members of the 2000 team were arrested at some point during their Washington careers. But more shocking than the bad behavior of these wayward young men was the cold indifference of the authority figures around them. Armstrong and Perry provide a portrait of permissiveness and denial that is simply breathtaking for the tentacles of complicity it reveals. Representatives from every vital constituency in the Washington community—coaches, administrators, students, faculty, the district attorney's office, the local media—helped keep quiet about players' wrongdoing and thus prevented the Huskies' magical season from being disrupted by arrests, trials, jail time, or any of the other usual consequences of bad behavior.

The community's collective handling of the Stevens rape case is telling. Stevens was regarded as a critically important offensive weapon for the Huskies in 2000, and after his arrest journalists fell all over themselves to lament the possible impact on the team of a prolonged Jerramy Stevens absence. Everyone agreed that Washington's season would be in jeopardy without the sturdy tight end. Happily for the Huskies, Stevens never missed a game, and his good fortune resulted in part from the favorable treatment he received from the authorities. King County prosecutor Norm Maleng led a dilatory investigation that lasted more than three months. (Just one year before the Stevens case, in 1999, Maleng had declined to charge three football players involved in a brawl outside a fraternity house, even though the city attorney for Seattle quickly proceeded to prosecute the three players for the same incident; later, in 2002, Maleng would decline to charge another football player accused of rape.)

In October 2000, more than halfway through the Huskies' season, Norm Maleng rendered a public decision that eerily foreshadowed the notorious press conference dedicated to the case of Florida State quarterback Jameis Winston thirteen years later. Maleng announced that there was "insufficient evidence" to bring charges against Stevens in the alleged rape. He made this determination despite the presence of a highly credible accuser, on-the-record testimony from a casual eyewitness to the assault, irrefutable DNA evidence, and many witnesses who could testify to the rag-doll condition of the drugged victim. Leaving all that aside, and refusing even to malign Stevens's conduct on the night of the incident, Maleng would only say, "What this case demonstrates is what we've always known . . . Excessive drinking can lead to poor choices."[4] In other words, the girl should have stayed away from the punch bowl.

The victim—identified in *Scoreboard, Baby* only through the pseudonym Marie—had not suffered her last indignity. When she proceeded to file a civil lawsuit against Stevens and the University of Washington, the university showed an unseemly and uncharacteristic determination to drag her name through the muck. When she filed the suit, she identified herself only by her initials. As Armstrong and Perry point out, this is "not uncommon in litigation alleging sexual assault or molestation; plaintiffs in such cases often want to protect their privacy." Universities, it should be stressed, are ordinarily quick to invoke the privacy rights of their students in order to shield themselves from public scrutiny and to justify withholding embarrassing information from curious citizens. UNC, for example, draped itself in the Family Educational Rights and Privacy Act banner throughout its many scandal-related battles with the press and public interest organizations between 2010 and 2014. In the Stevens civil suit, however, the University of Washington demanded that Marie's full name be disclosed in the court file. In an action that would seem to have been driven by spite, the university moved to reveal Marie's name because it was "axiomatic" that "secrecy obstructs the public's view of government." Happily, the university failed in its effort to embarrass the victim.[5]

That Washington was willing to show a vindictive streak in its treatment of a person who threatened to embarrass both the Athletic Department and university administrators was only one of many strange parallels between the UW and UNC cases. Perhaps the most obvious similarity linking the two scandals was the corruption that undermined Swahili language instruction at the two institutions. Swahili is an important language spoken by more than 140 million people. It functions as a lingua franca throughout southeastern Africa, and its instruction is vital to African studies programs everywhere. It is no small irony, then, that the athletic program at Washington thought to use an untenured lecturer in Swahili as its lifeline to continued academic eligibility for at-risk athletes. This strategy must have stemmed from the racist assumption that an instructor in an African language who worked in the Department of American Ethnic Studies would just *naturally* be inclined to help athletes in need.

Unlike the unfortunate Alphonse Mutima at UNC, who resentfully acquiesced in Athletic Department demands because he was subject to various forms of coercion, Seyed Maulana indeed appears to have been a willing participant in the degradation of his own courses. During away games Maulana would fax examinations to coaches; he would later receive faxed answers in return. What those answers contained (not to mention who wrote them) is anyone's guess, since a full year of Swahili instruction generally left Maulana's students able to utter only a few elementary greetings. "I tend to focus more on the structure of the language," Maulana would later explain. Whatever the focus of his exams, the grades were always good. Appreciative of his teaching philosophy, football and basketball players flooded into Maulana's courses in such numbers that "other students could wait three or four years" to get into Swahili classes.[6]

The popularity of these courses is easy to understand, since they restored or preserved eligibility on many occasions. As early as 1992 Washington quarterback Billy Joe Hobert had taken fifteen credits' worth of Swahili in one summer session; he thereby regained his footing on a path toward the football field. Five years later, when Curtis Williams found his scholarship in jeopardy, he followed the Hobert precedent and took fifteen credits in a single course—Intensive Swahili (probably similar in its intensity to UNC's accelerated Swahili 1–2 sequence, but nevertheless worth nine more credits than the UNC course). Williams earned fifteen credits of B with Maulana's course, boosting his GPA from 1.84 all the way to 2.06 and thus preserving his eligibility for his sophomore year. As was the case at UNC, Williams also found other friendly courses (independent study, Dinosaurs, and so on), joined them to his thirty credits in Swahili—the equivalent of ten courses, which would add up to a major at most universities—and used the soft grades to counterbalance all his failing grades in real courses: Introduction to Psychology, Introduction to Astronomy, Sociological Methods, Appreciation of Architecture, and more. The same basic pattern also held true for Anthony Vontoure. With his twenty-five credits of Swahili and generous grades in a number of other courses favored by football players—Dinosaurs (again), Introduction to Dance, Sexuality in Scandinavia, and so on—he always kept the eligibility hounds at bay.

Above all, the University of Washington case shows how deeply and widely the acceptance of double standards for athletes extends throughout university communities. Assault, theft, reckless endangerment, attempted murder, rape, drug use, and (it goes without saying) academic corner cutting that approached outright fraud: all of these football-related activities were tolerated, facilitated, and covered up by virtually everyone who learned about them. (UNC, by contrast, had no serious problems with lawlessness, but Carolina athletes in the profit sports also clearly understood that they played by different rules; they enjoyed luxury rental cars, the occasional cash loans from agents, the favors of "party organizers," and the indulgence of campus parking officials—all while UNC compliance officers slept on the job.) With the exception of some powerless victims and a few indignant police officers, the Greater Seattle community simply looked the other way as Washington football players implemented their reign of terror; as fans they preserved the excitement of Saturday afternoons in Husky Stadium at all costs. Meanwhile, the educational destinies of all the young men on the Washington football team—the example of the enterprising Anthony Kelly and his trips to South Africa notwithstanding—were neglected, cynically managed, or left to chance.

In Seattle the desire to field a championship football team induced otherwise good people to countenance very bad things. But Washington was not alone. Willful blindness has become one of the pre-conditions to athletic success in the big-time arena. Consider the many things not seen in Ann Arbor, Michigan.

Friendly Faculty and Friendlier Administrators

Between the fall of 2004 and the fall of 2007, John Hagen of the University of Michigan's Department of Psychology offered at least 294 independent study courses in addition to his regular teaching load. At least 251 of those courses, some of which were individual-ized and some of which involved small circles of students, enrolled varsity athletes. These figures are intriguingly Nyang'oro-esque, and one might expect them to have arisen from a secretive and under-cover scheme to subvert Michigan's curricular standards. Yet one of the more shocking aspects of the Michigan independent study story, which came to light because of some remarkable investiga-tive reporting at the *Ann Arbor News* in 2008, is that Hagen and many of his colleagues and superiors defended and endorsed his practices when confronted by dumbfounded journalists at the local newspaper.[7] Hagen, when asked whether his courses were used in an effort to preserve eligibility for certain athletes, dismissed the suggestion as "ridiculous." Associate dean Bob Megginson, who investigated Hagen's independent study practices in 2006 (in the wake of the furor over the Auburn story), happily reported back to his boss that Hagen's courses were "academically sound" and that the "eminent social scientist" was doing "exactly (what) we hope faculty will do" with their students. The dean of the College of Lit-erature, Science, and the Arts, Terry McDonald, repeated Meggin-son's sentiment and carried it even further when the *Ann Arbor News* sought him out. He hailed Hagen's independent study classes as exemplary courses that represented the very best of what Mich-igan had to offer. "This is the kind of faculty experience we aspire to provide for all of our students," he told one undoubtedly slack-jawed reporter.

Michigan's reflexive defense of Hagen's teaching opens a win-dow onto the accommodationist mentality that prevails at so many big-time sport universities in the twenty-first century. McDonald, in heaping praise on Hagen for his impassioned pedagogy, was like an architect who, standing amid smoldering ruins, admires the scorched pediment over the burned-out doorway. No impartial academic could react to the results of the *Ann Arbor News* investigation with anything other than head-scratching disbelief; that Michigan officials rushed to spin the story into an example of university teaching at its best speaks volumes about the instinct for denial that has burrowed deeply into university administrations across the land. Deans, provosts, presidents, and many faculty are increasingly loath to admit that the dynamics now driving athletic programs place severe pressures on the academic infrastructure of America's universities and leave far too many athletes scandalously underserved by their schools.

Hagen may be a capable teacher and a first-rate scholar, but the testimony collected by the *Ann Arbor News* makes clear that his independent study courses were university courses in name only. Two football players were able to add a three-hour Hagen independent study course with only four weeks to go in a fourteen-week semester. They could get away with this because there was not much catching up to do anyway. Wide receiver Greg Matthews reported that he had to meet with Hagen only "a couple of times" in the course of his entire independent study experience, and hockey player Danny Fardig told the *Ann Arbor News* that his three independent study courses with Hagen were conducted primarily through email. Other students reported spending all of fifteen minutes a week in Hagen's office, even though a three-credit-hour course is supposed to require an average of six hours of work outside the classroom in addition to three hours in class each week. Usually, it would seem, relatively little was going on outside of class. Some students wrote papers, but the expectation was not universal. Most of the students who talked to the local newspaper during its investigation admitted that their independent studies with Hagen "involved little to no research." As football player Shawn Crable put it, Hagen was not "really a guy who is work-oriented, he's not just bringing you in to write papers and all that stuff." Athletes at Michigan had found that rare professor who was not "work-oriented."

Just as Carlos Rogers had said of Auburn's Thomas Petee that he "wants to help you out, not just pile a lot of stuff on you," athletes at Michigan had nothing but kind words for Hagen and his work requirements. Hockey player Chad Kolarik said of Hagen that "he's not one to yell at you if you don't bring your assignment in. . . . He really likes the athletes." (Hagen was a courtside regular at Michigan basketball games.) Football player Rueben Riley, one of the two athletes who added a Hagen course after ten weeks had already elapsed in the semester, noted that "you can come up with your own assignment, that was kind of Hagen's style." To the extent that his independent study courses were organized around themes, Hagen tended to focus his lessons on such things as time management, keeping a calendar, "learning to study," and note-taking techniques. Former defensive tackle Alan Branch used his Hagen independent study to learn "how to use a day planner." "At the end," says wide receiver Mathews about his independent study, "we had to make a calendar about the remainder of the semester. It was about a month-long calendar. It was one of the easier classes. It was a class I'd recommend for any freshman student."

Freshmen or not, many athletes found themselves steered in Hagen's direction by academic counselors in Michigan's Academic Success Program (ASP). When Perry Dorrestein faced a sub-1.8 GPA at the end of his first year in Ann Arbor, an academic counselor sent the offensive tackle to Hagen's office to request a summer-session independent study. Hagen obliged. Dorrestein took a four-credit-hour version of the course, earning an A, and thus bumping his GPA back over the 1.8 threshold required by the Big Ten for sophomore athletic eligibility. His story was not unusual. "[Hagen] was used as a safety net," one former employee in the Academic Support Program told the *Ann Arbor News*. "The Hagen thing wasn't a secret. One of the first options, probably the first option always . . . was John Hagen. 'See if we can get John to take another.'" So popular were Hagen's courses that the directors of the ASP had to serve as gatekeepers. The football and basketball players particularly had to be controlled, because "their whole team would be [in] there if you let them." (Beth Bridger at UNC had known all about gatekeeping and its attendant frustrations.)

The Michigan case resembles the North Carolina case in all its essentials—the ASP's exploitation of a friendly faculty member who liked sports, the bending or near abandonment of academic standards in virtual no-show classes, the manipulation of drop/add policies, the gaming of eligibility rules, the favoritism to athletes mixed with an acceptance of nonathletes in the gift courses on offer. But the most troubling similarity of all is found in the reactions of university leaders to the misconduct that was finally uncovered. In neither Chapel Hill nor Ann Arbor did responsible parties honestly acknowledge the issues in play. Indeed, Michigan's faculty and administrative leaders even went to lengths of denial that UNC and Auburn could not fathom. Whereas Holden Thorp and Ed Richardson had at least acknowledged academic wrongdoing at their schools, in part so as to confine the damage to academic affairs and thereby insulate the athletic program from any recriminations, Michigan went one better. It denied the existence of any questionable behavior at all. Rather than apologize for a breakdown in standards, Michigan insisted that substandard pedagogy was exemplary pedagogy.

The mechanics, the breadth, and the audacity of Michigan's strategy of denial are most impressive. When the *Ann Arbor News* confronted the chair of Michigan's top-ranked Psychology Department and provided her a mountain of anecdotal evidence that students were gliding through Hagen's courses, she responded by insisting that "we have a very clear set of standards" in the department. Independent studies always involved fifteen- to twenty-page research papers, she said, and if students were saying otherwise, it could only be because they did not realize how hard they were being pushed. "My experience is that students, when they're doing independent studies that they like, really underestimate what they're doing." (This department chair, Terri Lee, had been the undergraduate studies head in 2006, and it was largely on the basis of her word that Bob Megginson, the associate dean, had given Hagen the all clear in August of that year.)

When Scott Paris, a faculty colleague in psychology, became curious about Hagen's activities and began reviewing records and listening to student scuttlebutt, he went first to the provost and then to Megginson to report that Hagen's students had told him that "[Hagen] simply talks about athletics and the university and his projects" in his courses and that little real work seemed to be going on in all those independent study classes. When Megginson told Paris that the issue had already been settled, he was struck by the dean's lack of curiosity and his eagerness to move on. "It became clear to me," said Paris, "that he hadn't really talked to students, he hadn't done the research, he hadn't looked back into the record of enrollments. . . . He basically saw no problem because he didn't look for it." (At UNC officials steadfastly refused to examine enrollment records from Julius Nyang'oro's earliest days on the faculty, and they went to court to prevent the *Raleigh News & Observer* from gaining access to some of those same records.) Paris took his complaints to the executive committee of the Psychology Department (executive committees provide advice and guidance to the chair), and he asked for a real investigation.

What he got was more whitewash. The six-member committee examined samples of written work that Hagen himself had selected, they interviewed the professor (but no students), they looked at grade distributions, and they then issued a report claiming that Hagen "did not favor athletes." They also declared the content of his independent study courses "appropriate." Paris called the report "laughable," but the executive committee was destined to have the last word. The department, Paris believes, was "more interested in explaining away a potentially embarrassing situation" than in finding out why so many athletes flocked to John Hagen's courses. Too many people had already publicly vouched for Hagen, his classes, and departmental policies; by 2008 confessing to negligence and uncovering a pattern of corruption seem no longer to have been an option. As a defensive dean McDonald would finally tell the *Ann Arbor News*, "This is the No. 1 psychology department in the country telling us that they have vetted this and that they are in conformance" with standard procedures. Hagen's exemplary service was therefore beyond reproach. "This is not Auburn," huffed the curiously incurious dean.

But the *Ann Arbor News* had many more revelations to share, and what the newspaper would come to call Michigan's "culture of denial" was clearly not limited to the Psychology Department or to a couple of deans. Michigan's eligibility machine was well oiled indeed. Athletes pursued a foreign language (Ojibwe, a Native American language) in which little foreign-language instruction seems to have occurred, and—for a time—the profit-sport athlete's curriculum included a tailor-made program in kinesiology that was created and partly paid for by the Athletic Department. The program had lower admissions standards than any other academic unit at the university, and it saved scores of admissions slots for athletes each year. When the sport management track in the kinesiology program raised its standards significantly in 2002, a new curricular path emerged to take its place. At-risk athletes still got admitted through the kinesiology program, but after the first year or two at the university they transferred out in droves toward a new favored major—general studies—in which profit-sport athletes (but no one else) clustered in large numbers. When confronted with questions about these suspect practices, faculty and administrators at Michigan—with a few notable exceptions—clammed up, ran away, or offered Pollyannaish assurances that all was well.

The tendency to deny reality—to find rationales for accommodating the eligibility needs of athletes who were underprepared or undermotivated and almost universally underserved—is especially acute in Academic Support Programs, where employees form close bonds with the athletes they seek to help. When football academic counselor Shari Acho, who served as codirector of Michigan's Academic Success Program at the time of the *Ann Arbor News* series, was told that athletes had reported to the newspaper that she encouraged them to pursue the general studies major, she simply denied it. "I don't think encouraged is the right word," she said. Every student, she insisted, decides his or her own major. When asked to explain why scholarship athletes clustered in general studies in such large numbers, she had no explanation for the phenomenon. Yet whenever football recruits visited the campus, the *Ann Arbor News* learned, Acho arranged for presentations that featured the general studies major. And the players clearly got the message from someone—if not from her, from others—that general studies was the place to be. In 2004 fifty-eight of seventy-four recruited football players—fully 78 percent of the total—listed general studies as their academic concentration. (General studies has no foreign-language requirement and no natural science require-ment, and it allows for the inclusion of a disparate set of classes from across the university.)

Clearly, one of the great advantages of the general studies degree at Michigan, apart from the scheduling flexibility that came with its exponentially larger selection of available courses, was the ability to incorporate all the known "friendly" faculty and classes within the typical course of study. John Hagen's independent study courses (and other Hagen courses) could be used, as could the Ojibwe lan-guage courses, an education course on mentoring (in which ath-letes averaged an A grade), and an ancient history course that had long been a favorite of athletes—classics professor David Potter's Sports and Daily Life in Ancient Rome. (Both Potter and Hagen served on Michigan's Advisory Board on Intercollegiate Athletics; this eighteen-member group, dominated by faculty, is feted at the Michigan football team's bowl game each year.)

Academic counselors at Michigan, like those at North Carolina, routinely steered football and basketball players toward the same constellation of courses. Of the eighteen freshmen football players who were recruited in 2004 and who stayed at Michigan long enough to choose a major, all but one wound up in general studies—even though several had come to the university expressing interests in other fields. Basketball player Brent Petway reported that in 2005, a year he spent academically ineligible, he had had no say at all in choosing the courses for which he was registered. At times, an inter-nal Michigan audit would eventually discover, academic counselors even changed athletes' course schedules without their knowledge or consent. When asked to comment on the audit findings, and on the athletes who had reported being steered into courses by academic counselors—including defensive lineman Gabe Watson, who said that Shari Acho picked most of his classes for him and also helped write his papers—Acho again could only respond with a shrug: "I don't know . . . I don't know why they would say that."

Academic counselors behaved in this way, of course, because eligibility rather than education was their foremost priority. The imperative to maintain eligibility led counselors to hunt down the easiest available courses and to find the most easily manipulated major. Kinesiology professor Jay Basten, who taught many under-prepared athletes in his first years on the Michigan faculty and who was largely responsible for the tightening of standards in the sport management program in 2002, was asked by the *Ann Arbor News* whether the university could afford to allow its highly recruited athletes to pursue "an academic experience similar to that of a typical student." His response was swift and emphatic: "No." The learning gaps were too great and the time demands placed on athletes too powerful to overcome. A former Athletic Department employee, who spoke with the *Ann Arbor News* only on condition of anonymity, shared Basten's perspective. What many of the athletes really needed, he said, was "some basic, targeted instruction, like basic skills remediation. There really wasn't the opportunity to do that." So counselors instead directed athletes to general studies and to a menu of John Hagen courses. (When Michigan's vice provost, Phil Hanlon, was asked whether athletes were handled in this way, he simply dismissed the premise of the question. "I don't think there are any easy courses at the university," he insisted.)

The most dispiriting example of Michigan's culture of denial came in the wake of the *Ann Arbor News* series. The Senate Advisory Committee on University Affairs (SACUA), "the elected executive arm of faculty governance," deputized two faculty members—physics professor Keith Riles and law professor Richard Friedman—to look further into some of the issues brought to light by the local journalists. The two faculty members drew up a list of questions for the vice provost, Phil Hanlon, and asked for a meeting at which their investigative plans could be hashed out. But the meeting with the vice provost never took place. The investigation never happened at all. Internal dissent on the SACUA and a familiar administrative instinct to stonewall derailed the faculty probing before it began, thereby effectively preserving the status quo.[8]

The details behind the squelching of the faculty review are most illuminating. Riles and Friedman clearly took the newspaper reports seriously. The preliminary list of thirty-three questions that they sent on to Hanlon in preparation for an expected mid-April meeting addressed the steering of athletes to particular courses, the reservation of athletic admissions slots in kinesiology, the nature of faculty advising in the general studies program, and the standards for monitoring independent study courses. They also made clear that they hoped to review transcripts of a large sample of athletes so as to do a statistical analysis of course-selection patterns and performance records in the favored courses. "We took the investigation seriously," Riles would later say. They were therefore determined to ask "probing and relevant" questions.

But the chain of events that unfurled when this list of questions landed in Hanlon's in-box on April 9, 2008, tells us a lot about how athletic departments escape accountability at big-time institutions. Although Hanlon had initially indicated his willingness to meet with Riles and Friedman, he saw trouble when he opened the document they had sent. He immediately forwarded it to the provost, Teresa Sullivan (now the president at Virginia). Sullivan, in turn, arranged a meeting the very next day, April 10, with two faculty members with close ties to the Athletic Department—pharmacologist Charles Smith and classicist David Potter. Potter taught one of the courses popular with athletes, and both he and Smith sat on a number of committees that addressed athletics issues, including SACUA itself but also the Advisory Board on Intercollegiate Athletics (the group that gets free room and board and transportation to bowl games) and the Academic Performance Committee, which examines the eligibility status of athletes with marginal academic records. (Smith and Potter were joined on that committee by the ubiquitous John Hagen.)

When Smith and Potter saw the Riles and Friedman questions that the provost brought to the meeting, they balked. What they most obviously objected to was the fact that Riles and Friedman intended to look directly into the *Ann Arbor News* allegations. "They were all questions about what happened in the *Ann Arbor News*. 'Can you substantiate?'" Smith later recalled. Smith considered the document "highly offensive." Potter complained that the questions went "far beyond any discussion of the BGS [bachelor in general studies]." Smith maintained that Riles and Friedman had no authority to ask such questions and that their real motive was "to do damage" to the university administration. (Minutes from the SACUA meeting show, however, that Riles and Friedman were formally asked to "look into the uses of the BGS degree.") Smith and Potter both later acknowledged to the *Ann Arbor News* that they just "didn't like the approach the investigation was taking." (Recall UNC leader Holden Thorp's concerns that the very word *investigation* might "set off alarm bells and push an inquiry in the wrong direction.") Smith and Potter therefore raised questions in Hanlon's mind about the scope and legitimacy of the Riles and Friedman inquiry, and the vice provost backed away from the edge of the cliff. He canceled the scheduled April 15 meeting with Riles and Friedman and told them that certain unidentified faculty members had communicated to him "a different notion of how SACUA wanted to proceed" in its questioning of athletic practices. Riles and Friedman subsequently gave up, and the Michigan Athletic Department dodged a dangerous bullet—thanks principally to its key protectors among the faculty.

The Michigan case throws into relief one of the greatest obstacles to reform in the world of collegiate sport. At big-time institutions, key administrative and faculty committee positions tend to be dominated by the compromised and the co-opted. Such individuals are inevitably predisposed to protect the athletic machine. In many cases, because of benefits and favors they themselves have received, they feel threatened by the inquisitive; they assume an indignant posture when confronted with the most commonsense questions. In other cases, they simply do not want to see the sport-entertainment complex endangered and will do what it takes to nip troublemaking in the bud. Why would Phil Hanlon, on seeing the list of questions submitted to him by SACUA faculty delegates, become so nervous that he immediately contacted the provost, Teresa Sullivan? Why would Sullivan immediately reach out to athletics-friendly faculty for a second opinion? Why did those faculty work to obstruct a fact-gathering mission they chose to interpret as "offensive"? Why did deans, a department head, and a Faculty Executive Committee rush to the defense of John Hagen's athlete-friendly teaching? Why did University of Michigan president Mary Sue Coleman repeatedly refuse to sit down for an interview with local reporters conducting an exposé of Michigan athletics? *Ann Arbor News* columnist Jim Knight said it best: "U-M's top leaders . . . have no interest in talking to people who ask hard questions. Unless you've drunk the Everything's OK Kool-Aid, you're viewed as an adversary."[9] Too many powerful people on too many big-time sport campuses have become silent partners in a plot to defraud. Having convinced themselves of the fundamental virtues of college sport, and of their own underlying probity, they work to deflect critical attention from practices whose ugly realities cannot be spoken out loud.

One of those ugly realities—athletes' dependency on good-hearted academic support personnel who frequently cross the line to offer them "impermissible" help—was exposed most unexpectedly at the University of Minnesota in the late 1990s. The truth rose to the surface not because leaders elected to lead but because a subordinate with a conscience decided she could no longer live with the hypocrisy.

Ghostwriter

A bombshell disrupted the University of Minnesota basketball team's trip through March Madness in 1999. On March 10, the day before the Minnesota Golden Gophers were to play their first-round tournament game against Gonzaga, the *St. Paul Pioneer Press* reported that Jan Gangelhoff, a former office manager for the Academic Counseling Unit in athletics, had confessed to having written papers for at least nineteen basketball players over a period of five years. She estimated that she had directly contributed to more than four hundred assignments, some of which she had composed in their entirety. Included among the beneficiaries of Gangelhoff's illicit assistance were several players on the current team, as well as members of the 1997 team that made it all the way to the Final Four. Because of the possibility that four players from the 1999 team would later be shown to be ineligible, the university suspended them from Minnesota's first-round game. Two starters and two subs watched from the bench as the Gophers were summarily bumped from the NCAA Tournament.

Academic support staffs are filled with people who identify with and feel sympathy for overburdened and academically challenged athletes, and Gangelhoff exemplified the type. Although she herself was not an academic counselor, the athletes gravitated to her, and she mothered them. Like UNC's Burgess McSwain, who dedicated the last decades of her life to nurturing UNC basketball players, Gangelhoff developed close relationships with the Minnesota players. She welcomed them into her home, gave them Christmas gifts, and looked out for their interests as she understood them. (Also like McSwain, Gangelhoff was unmarried, had a quiet home life, and had the time to devote herself entirely to the needs of the athletes she helped.) Her concern for athletes' well-being meant that she did what she could to keep them eligible, to keep them with the team and on campus. Sometimes this required extraordinary efforts. "They bring in these high-risk kids, and they know that everything they did in high school was done for them."[10] Although the players never directly asked her to write their papers for them, and although her complicity in an obvious cheating scheme was never discussed openly, she found herself doing the athletes' work. "I kept getting new kids and they said 'Can you help me with this course, can you help me with that?'" To protect her own time, and to provide the help that was needed, she streamlined the process and just did the work herself.[11] (She had players recycle some of the same papers for different classes. "I did that all the time," Gangelhoff would say.)

Basketball coach Clem Haskins and other athletics officials seem to have been fully aware of the kinds of help Gangelhoff was providing. "The coaches knew. Everybody knew," said former player Russ Archambault. "We used to make jokes about it. . . . The coaches would be laughing about it."[12] But the academic situation in which many players found themselves—either because their abilities lagged or because they just needed the break—was really no laughing matter. Haskins himself once noted in a conversation with another tutor that one of his players "needed a lot of help," and he told academic support personnel about the grades needed to maintain eligibility in certain select cases.[13] Gangelhoff always chipped in when asked, and she assumed that when she was shown favors in the Athletic Department—the office manager was flown to Hawaii for a pre-season tournament in 1995, for example, and she was a frequent guest at banquets, parties, and other team events—the kindnesses were done in compensation for all the writing she had done for the team. "Why else do you think I got to go to some of the places I did?" Gangelhoff responded when asked whether she had received extraordinary compensation from the Athletic Department.

Gangelhoff's decision to speak to the press followed months of difficult soul-searching. "I came to the conclusion that something has to change," she explained to the *Pioneer Press* reporters. Unless forced to change its culture, Minnesota would "continue to bring kids in and then throw them away." Gangelhoff's revelations set off a chain reaction that exposed deeply corrupt academic support practices at Minnesota, particularly within the basketball program. Three academic support employees ultimately confessed to writing papers for basketball players, but at Minnesota, as at UNC, the actual acts of cheating were the least offensive of all the misdeeds exposed by the investigative reporters who eventually swarmed to the story. More troubling was the high-level malfeasance that came to light as witnesses began to speak out and as emails and internal memos trickled into the public domain. The evidence showed Athletic Department personnel regularly ignoring or covering up problems and actively plotting to subvert academic standards. Faculty and administrators, meanwhile, were far too inclined to accept excuses and to look the other way.

Already by 1992 Haskins was working to place academic advising for basketball under his direct control and beyond the auspices of the general academic counseling program. The director of the general program, Elayne Donahue, complained to the men's athletic director that "basketball players are only allowed to interact with the academic staff that has been anointed by the coach, and the coach only anoints those he can co-opt."[14] Far from reacting as they should have to this disturbing news, university officials acquiesced in the coach's wishes and formally placed basketball advising under Haskins's personal control in 1994. The predictable consequences of this organizational scheme were already visible by 1995. In that year a faculty member complained to academic counselor Brian Berube (who still reported to Donahue in the general academic counseling shop) that a basketball player had apparently cheated with his written work. (Two years later this same professor would complain to Berube that another player, Courtney James, had just turned in a paper that was "the best [he] had seen in his nearly forty years at the university"; since James normally struggled with written work, the professor detected fraud.) Berube reported the incidents to the basketball academic counselor who worked for Haskins, Alonzo Newby, and he also contacted a tutor to inquire about her possible involvement in writing one of the papers.

The basketball program's handling of the professor's allegations, and of Berube's reporting of them, was telling. No one ever contacted the professor, and no form of investigation into the alleged academic wrongdoing was ever initiated. Instead, Haskins and his henchmen attacked Berube—a counselor who did not work under Haskins's supervision—for holding conversations about basketball players with people who were not among the coach's "anointed." Berube was soon "confronted on the street" by an assistant basketball coach, and he was the recipient of multiple hostile memos from Haskins and the assistant. Worse, they cynically played the race card so as to intimidate and silence a person of integrity who merely did his job by reporting allegations of wrongdoing. Haskins complained that Donahue and her office perpetuated "racist assumptions about black athletes." The player in question, Haskins wrote in a letter to Donahue, "is intelligent enough to write a good paper if given time." He added that he resented the way the matter had been handled, "and I want it stopped immediately." Haskins' assistant, meanwhile, berated Berube: "I have lost all respect for you as a man and as a person who has the best interest of young people at heart, especially people of color."

Haskins "want[ed] it stopped immediately," and he and his assistant threw down the chilling charge of racism, because both wanted to ensure that there would be no prying into the practices of the basketball academic support operation. Alonzo Newby, for example, had been exploiting something called the InterCollege Program (ICP)—wherein students design their own majors in a manner similar to that of Michigan's general studies degree—to enable academically challenged basketball players to circumvent demanding academic schedules and to pile up grades that helped with eligibility. Athletes were repeatedly given "special favors" in being admitted to that program.[15]

Meanwhile, sociology graduate student Alexandra Goulding, who served as a tutor in athletics and worked with some of Haskins's players, had found that a failure to be "helpful" could lead to the loss of one's job. According to reporting by the Associated Press, Goulding's very first day on the tutoring beat was an eye-opening one. Basketball star Courtney James came to her while working on a one-page paper about "his goals in school." (The assignment sounds similar to the bar-lowering tasks devised by Michigan's John Hagen.) Finding that James "was not proficient in typing or putting his thoughts to paper," Goulding sat down and started typing with James at her side. "From yes and no statements from him," she would later say, "I created the sentences." Afflicted by her conscience, she immediately went to academic counselor Newby to tell him that "you will have to get [James] some remedial tutoring." Unless James could be brought up to speed, he and his tutors would have to resort to dishonesty, and Goulding refused to go there again. "I cannot and will not write his papers." She later went to Haskins to communicate the same message to the head coach. She was drawing a line in the sand. But in exchange for her integrity, she got the boot. Newby soon came to her to tell her that "she would not be offered a contract to continue" her work as an Athletic Department tutor.[16] (Recall the case of the study-hall monitor who was dismissed at UNC because she had witnessed wrongdoing and had dared to report it to her superiors.)

What Haskins and Newby expected of their tutors, of course, was what loyal soldiers like Gangelhoff provided them: cover from the academic storm for the players and a public disguise for the Athletic Department's single-minded pursuit of athletic success. Haskins was deliberate and methodical. Gangelhoff remembered that he once came to her to remind her that the papers she churned out for the players needed to have the sound of an undergraduate's prose. "Just remember, Jan, you can't be too good. The papers can't be too good." (He might have had in mind the Courtney James submission that unfortunately came across to his professor as the best paper he had seen "in nearly forty years.")[17] Haskins's efforts to bring academic counseling for basketball under his direct personal control was an early sign that he knew exactly how delicate the academic management of his overworked and sometimes under-prepared players would need to be if Minnesota wanted to compete for conference and national titles.

And for the longest time Haskins had little reason to worry about interference from academic officers at the university. A faculty dean had noticed the apparent gaming of the ICP program in 1993, and she reported her concerns to the university president, Nils Hasselmo, in 1994. But when Alonzo Newby simply ignored the problem, to which he was alerted more than once, President Hasselmo and the dean failed to follow up. Elayne Donahue warned high-level Athletic Department administrators that Gangelhoff was violating university policy by tutoring players, since that was not part of her job as an office manager, but when she was ignored she let the issue drop. The professor who flagged the apparent paper fraud of Courtney James in 1997 likewise went away after he initially reported his suspicions; James never faced any disciplinary action. When the men's athletic director, Mike Dienhart, heard from Haskins that Brian Berube was alleging that some basketball players had committed plagiarism, Dienhart was more inclined to discipline Berube than to look into the allegations of cheating. Berube later remembered how "baffling" it was that he had been called in for a meeting with the athletic director to address the concerns voiced not by a faculty complainant but by the irritated Haskins. "At no point did anybody express concern that there was a faculty member expressing concern about academic impropriety. They were shooting the messenger."

Jan Gangelhoff's courageous disclosure of her own wrongdoing violated Minnesota's unspoken code of silence and acceptance, and it paved the way to redemption for the university, which rededicated itself to honest and transparent practices after absorbing heavy punishment from the NCAA. But the deep-rooted instinct to shoot the messenger surfaced as soon as Gangelhoff opened her mouth. McKinley Boston, who served as vice president of student development in the Athletic Department, immediately tried to discredit Gangelhoff by questioning her truthfulness. "Some of her current allegations seem to be inconsistent with statements she made in the past," he told the *Pioneer Press*. Other people had earlier complained about Gangelhoff, he noted, but her own allegations were "new stuff."[18] Haskins, when confronted with Gangelhoff's claims, struck an indignant posture that he clearly hoped would close down the questioning. "I've been here thirteen years, don't you know me, what I stand for as a man, as a person?" The university president, Mark Yudof, was obligingly effusive: "I think the world of Clem Haskins."

Even Governor Jesse Ventura got into the act. After the *St. Paul Pioneer Press* revealed the Gangelhoff allegations, the governor pronounced the whole thing "despicable"—and he referred to the journalism, not to the university's corruption. Ventura's main concern was that the basketball team's tournament fortunes had been sacrificed in the name of journalistic "sensationalism." (The newspaper had in fact only nailed down the story, and secured written proof of Gangelhoff's allegations, a few days before publication; delaying publication for the sake of wins on the court would only have taken the reporters into a different sort of moral quagmire.)[19] But the editor who gave the green light to publish the story on the eve of the NCAA Tournament, Walker Lundy, maintained his bearings and stood firm by his decision to publish, even though disclosure of the wrongdoing was destined to bring great embarrassment to the university. "They had corrupted the basic reason a university exists, which is to educate people." (Russ Archambault later confirmed the point. "In the two years I was there [at Minnesota]," he recalled, "I never did a thing.") At Minnesota, Lundy properly concluded, the institution's failure "to educate people" deserved to be dragged into the sunlight at the first opportunity, when public attention would be piercing and when a collective sense of outrage would have the best chance to effect real change.

. . .

Common threads connect the sobering stories from Auburn, Washington, Michigan, Minnesota, and UNC (to which could be added other examples from UC-Berkeley, Stanford, Florida State, Tennessee, Fresno State, Southern Cal, and most recently Notre Dame).[20] At all of the schools discussed in this chapter, a long-cultivated culture of willful blindness permitted the systematic degradation of the academic standards on which they based their impressive rep-utations. Co-opted or indifferent faculty found excuses to turn a blind eye or even to assist Athletic Department manipulation of loopholes, soft spots, and bureaucratic trickery. Outspoken crit-ics were ignored or discredited. And the leadership hierarchies at each institution, busy waving pom-poms, waited always until the last possible minute before taking corrective action and disclosing problems that could no longer be ignored. (Michigan miraculously escaped ever having to acknowledge its problems. The Michigan precedent—victory through determined stonewalling and brazen doublespeak—should send shivers through the spine of every con-scientious educator.) Most disheartening of all is the simple fact that these universities cynically ignored their educational obliga-tions to the hardworking athletes who earn their schools fame and glory on the gridiron or the hard court.

It is time for big-time universities to end the charade and to honor their obligations to every student they admit.

Conclusion

Looking to the Future

In the summer of 2014, as this book went to press, the likelihood of imminent change in the world of college sport had never seemed greater. Congressmen Charlie Dent of Pennsylvania and Tony Cardenas of California had both developed major NCAA reform bills that were gathering support at the committee level. They and other congressional leaders were pressing officials of the NCAA to answer questions about its cartel-like practices. Faculty members associated with the Drake Group had drafted their own bill, the College Athlete Protection Act, and its authors were pushing for the creation of a presidential commission to address the contradictions at the heart of college sports. What distinguished all of these initiatives was their comprehensiveness. In different ways each of the new bills sought to improve the health and safety of athletes, the legal protections to which they have access, the academic standards that govern their lives as students, the terms of their scholarship agreements, the regulatory framework that is meant to ensure order and equity across the system, and the all-important revenue structure that has heretofore allocated "opportunity" only according to the logic of a fixed market. Since 2011 the general plight of college athletes—the many ways in which the system leaves them structurally disadvantaged—has caught the attention of people who wield real authority. With the interest of Congress suddenly aroused, the prospects for meaningful reform seemed brighter in the summer of 2014 than at any time since the 1980s.

The Chicago branch of the National Labor Relations Board, meanwhile, declared in the spring of 2014 that college football players at Northwestern University should be regarded as employees and afforded all the protections enjoyed by other university employees. Although the university has appealed the Chicago ruling to the NLRB's Washington office, the regional board's decision seems destined to enhance the bargaining power of athletes who, under the current system, effectively give up their rights on national signing day. In the wake of the Northwestern case, the myth of the student-athlete has never looked more mythical, and the attention that has been drawn to the prioritizing of athletic performance in the lives of college athletes makes it hard to imagine that the genie of amateurism will ever be stuffed back in the bottle.

Perhaps the greatest threat to the athletic status quo lies in the potential combined impact of the class-action lawsuits associated with former athletes Ed O'Bannon and Martin Jenkins. Already in August 2014 Judge Claudia Wilken sided with the O'Bannon plaintiffs in declaring the NCAA's defense of amateurism an insufficient rationale for denying financial compensation to college athletes for the use of their likenesses and images. (O'Bannon's testimony at trial put the lie to the NCAA's argument that athletes are compensated with educational opportunity. "I was an athlete masquerading as a student. I was there [at UCLA] strictly to play basketball . . . and I did basically the minimum to make sure I kept my eligibility academically so I could continue to play.")[1] The lawyer in the Jenkins case, Jeffrey Kessler, helped secure the free-agency rights of professional basketball and football players, and he now hopes to do the same for college athletes. It is time to "remove the shackles" that constrain the marketplace for athletic skills, he told Steve Eder of the New York Times. If Kessler prevails in the Jenkins trial, which is scheduled for the spring of 2015, he will deliver a "bazooka blast" to the NCAA's business model and force a major restructuring of the relationship between college athletes and the universities that recruit them.[2]

Athletes such as Ed O'Bannon, Martin Jenkins, Rashad McCants,

Northwestern quarterback Kain Colter, and others associated with the National College Players Association are at last speaking up to advance and protect their own interests. Thanks largely to their efforts, the country is increasingly alert to the inequities and structural defects that mar the enterprise of collegiate sport. The NLRB ruling, the pending resolution of class-action lawsuits (including one focused on concussions), and the newly skeptical tone of the national discourse in the wake of the Penn State scandal are all hopeful signs that change is coming. But hardened veterans of the reform movement would caution against complacency. The growing awareness surrounding the problems inherent in college athletics is of course essential to prospects for reform, but the powerful forces arrayed against the idea of change are poised for preemptive strikes and counterattacks. (In June 2014, for example, it was revealed that the NCAA had hired lobbyists who will work to protect its tax-free status.)[3] Awareness of inequities will not, by itself, be enough to overcome the resistance of the many who benefit so handsomely from the current system.

Proof of this maxim—that awareness often leads nowhere—appears in a remarkably prescient document drafted almost thirty-five years ago by Allen Sack, a former Notre Dame football player, a professor of sports management at the University of New Haven, and the founder of a now-defunct organization called the Center for Athletes' Rights and Education (CARE). In 1981 Sack and his associates compiled an Athletes' Bill of Rights that resonates loud and clear in the age of O'Bannon, player unionization efforts, concussion controversies, and the UNC academic-athletic scandal. Among other things, the bill of rights called for just compensation "for the revenues generated by the athlete"; guaranteed multiyear scholarships; legal assistance and due process for athletes facing disputes with athletic departments; the right to bargain collectively and even to unionize; access to "remedial courses, tutoring and counseling geared to a quality education, not athletic eligibility"; the right to be fully informed of health risks arising from athletic activities; and the right to complete one's undergraduate education, tuition free, at any time in the life of the scholarship athlete. In a laudatory article about the CARE bill of rights in the *New York*

ATHLETES' BILL of RIGHTS

College athletes are students *and* workers. Their time and sweat bring in millions of dollars to their universities from ticket sales, TV contracts and contributions. As students, they are entitled to an education similar in quality to other students. As workers they are entitled to safe working conditions and fair compensation for the money they generate. The CENTER for ATHLETES' RIGHTS and EDUCATION is committed to the development through Sport, of cooperation and individual excellence and advancing the rights of athletes in high schools and colleges across America. Among these Rights are:

1. The RIGHT to sports free from discrimination by race or sex.

2. The RIGHT to tuition-free courses (at any time)—if necessary to complete an athlete's undergraduate education.

3. The RIGHT to Legal assistance and due process in disputes with athletic departments and coaches.

4. The RIGHT to information about the benefits and dangers of diet, training methods, injury prevention & treatment.

5. The RIGHT to remedial courses, tutoring and counseling geared to a quality education, not athletic eligibility.

6. The RIGHT to an Athlete's Letter of Intent, signed by the coach, clearly outlining the school's educational and financial obligations to the athlete.

7. The RIGHT to a multi-year grant-in-aid which would allow athletes to complete their degrees, even if seriously injured.

8. The RIGHT of equal access to facilities, coaching and equipment for males *and* females.

9. The RIGHT to fair compensation for the revenues generated by the athlete.

AND 10. The RIGHT to form Unions and bargain collectively on all issues affecting financial aid and working conditions.

CARE
THE CENTER for ATHLETES' RIGHTS and EDUCATION
391 East 149th Street · Suite 319 · Bronx, NY 10455 · (212) 665-0602

a program of
SP Sports
People

Co-sponsored by
National Football League
Players Assoc.
and Nat'l Council of Black Lawyers

Fig. 4. Athletes' Bill of Rights

Times, columnist Dave Anderson signaled that the writing was on the wall. "Sooner or later, a college athlete is going to ask a court to declare him a 'professional' who deserves a piece of the pie." Observing that skeptics had once scoffed when professional baseball and football players had formed their own unions, Anderson relished the imminent comeuppance of "college sports administrators, who think it can't happen to them."[4]

What happened next? Nothing to change the lot of the athletes. Before the ink in Anderson's column had dried, the Universities of Oklahoma and Georgia decided to sue the NCAA for the right to negotiate their own television contracts. The Supreme Court in 1984 sided with the schools, calling the NCAA's attempt to control all television broadcasts an unlawful restraint of trade. In the wake of that landmark decision, more money flooded into the big-time athletic departments, creating new incentives to maintain a system that left players powerless and uncompensated. Together with ESPN, Nike, and Reebok, the case of *NCAA vs. Board of Regents of the University of Oklahoma* helped to reconfigure the sporting landscape in the 1980s. It ushered in the era of the million-dollar coach, the lavish skybox, the ever-expanding stadium, and the players whose silent acquiescence had been purchased through the shiny promise of professionalized "opportunity." The era before 1984 was no golden age—the existence of CARE's bill of rights in 1981 is proof positive that the inequities of the system were built in and not simply created by big money—but the pressure to sustain the status quo, and especially the financial investment in its protection, mounted steadily after the mid-1980s.

With all the money at stake, the increasingly addictive high-quality sport entertainment on offer, and the ever more deeply entrenched sporting interests crowding the seats of power at the big-time universities, the corruption in college athletics took on the character of an immovable object. The UNC experience would certainly seem to provide a case in point. In Chapel Hill the instinct to dig in and stonewall, to cut losses and "move on" so as to return to athletics business as usual as quickly as possible, was pervasive. Administrators misled the public and denied the deeper realities of which the individual wrongs of tutors, players, and professors were only symptoms. Students on campus remained apathetic and detached throughout the saga. Faculty leaders either ignored the institutional risks posed by the imperative to succeed athletically or celebrated small-bore reform measures that only underscored UNC's avoidance of bold action. With the exception of the *Raleigh News & Observer*, local media showed by their stubborn indifference to the scandal that they valued their continuing access to Athletic Department insiders more than they valued the public's right to know the truth. Resignation (or happy compromise) in the face of the athletic machine was the default setting in and around UNC–Chapel Hill between 2010 and 2014.

The most surprising evidence of institutional inertia came not from inside the UNC campus but from concerned outsiders who cheered the exposure of wrongdoing but chose to remain standing on the sidelines. In the weeks after Mary Willingham shared some of her experiences (and her assessment of athlete reading levels) with CNN in early January 2014, she received literally thousands of emails from around the country, virtually all of them supportive and many of them from people worried about the athletic programs at their own institutions. One associate athletic director wrote to say, "After having been through and experienced everything you're revealing and trying to correct, I truly respect and encourage [you]." He would not say anything about his own experience in public, he explained, because he needed to maintain his professional viability in the world of college sports. "If anyone doubts the veracity of your claims," wrote a professor in Tennessee, "they have not worked with 'student athletes' at American universities with ambitious . . . sports programs." Willingham was encouraged to "stay the course!" "There are many of us out here," wrote one correspondent from the state of Virginia, "who have worked with university athletes [and] who know what you are saying is true." Another writer from the West Coast expressed frustration at the "obstructionist positions" he had encountered during his own efforts to "look inside the black box that is college athletics." He encouraged Willingham to continue the slow work of "peeling back the various layers" that shield the system from scrutiny. Even a college president who presided over successful sports programs of his own expressed sympathy with Willingham's agenda. "Many of us are watching . . . your work from afar and greatly appreciate what you're doing." One tutor in South Carolina contacted Willingham and told her she would like to speak to the media to help corroborate the stories that the learning specialist had told CNN; after making an appointment with a high-profile news outlet, she backed out of her interview at the last minute.

What this small sampling of email exchanges demonstrates is that a great many people, including well-informed insiders, have known for a long time that the system of college sport is badly broken. Yet college campuses are not exactly teeming with whistle-blowers and crusaders for reform—and the reasons for the collective silence are perfectly understandable. The system seeks to crush those who would make waves, and every ounce of institutional leverage is mobilized to silence or punish the people who threaten the golden goose. Mary Willingham was ignored, shunned, demoted, harassed, publicly humiliated by the university's provost, viciously attacked in social media by UNC faculty and staff, and treated so badly in her new position that she ultimately felt forced to resign. Sadly, the Willingham example is all too familiar, as recent outspoken critics of the athletic machines at Georgia, Tennessee, Auburn, Minnesota, Florida State, and Marshall could all attest. Courageous insiders are destined to remain an endangered species. Absent a large and uncompromising coalition of tenured faculty, one that crosses institutional boundaries and encompasses all of the big-time schools, reform will never happen from the inside out. External forces—congressional action, court-mandated change, a presidential directive, new market regulations—will almost surely be required to set the system right.

If and when the seismic shock occurs—there are reasons to hope that the needed external agency may soon be arriving—and if educators and administrators find themselves putting the pieces of college sport back together, the rights and interests of the athletes themselves should finally take priority over all other concerns. Athletes should enjoy the same rights that every other college student, and every other citizen, takes for granted. As Taylor Branch has written, in a truly reformed college-sport environment, no freedom will be abridged "because of athletic status."[5] These basic freedoms, most of them enumerated decades ago by Allen Sack, include the right to pursue compensation, the right to due process, the right to legal representation, the right to bargain collectively, and the right to transfer from one school to another without penalty.

We see two paths forward. The most direct and uncomplicated solution to the problems that now beset college athletics is the one proposed by Jeffrey Kessler: "remove the shackles" that protect and structure the artificial market that now governs the life of college athletes in the profit sports. Make football and men's basketball autonomous commercial enterprises subject to all the rules of a free market, thus separating them operationally from university athletic departments. As part of their compensation packages, athletes could still be given access to university classrooms. They might still pursue a degree either during or after their playing careers if they choose to do so and if they have the requisite academic abilities; the likelihood that many would seize this educational opportunity would even maintain some meaningful connection between the schools' primary missions and the sports teams that would henceforth be only loosely affiliated with the institutions. But athletes' status as football and basketball players would have no connection to their performance as students. Their freedom to play, and their availability to their teams, would not depend on their compliance with arbitrary eligibility rules the purpose of which is to perpetuate the pretense that athletes are students first.

Under the new system, the university would continue to profit from the labors of the athletes they hire; they would lease their stadiums, continue to sell memorabilia, take a portion of ticket sales, and sell concessions. Some of the university's profits could be used to support the so-called Olympic sports, which draw few fans but whose mere mention brings a mist to the eyes of athletic administrators who work under the current system. If golf and diving and volleyball were to be imperiled by a business model predicated on a free market for football and basketball players, universities would simply have to find other ways to support the Olympic sports—assuming those sports are so valued by the university that they warrant the time, energy, and additional resources needed to keep them afloat. There would undoubtedly be winners and losers as a result of this restructuring—men's basketball players would collect decent salaries, AD's would see their salaries fall from the stratosphere, the parents of divers would possibly have to pay their sons' and daughters' tuition—but the new system would be free of hypocrisy and the market would be free to work its magic, allocating the greatest rewards to those who perform well in the most valued activities.

This sweeping fix for the hypocrisy and corruption of the current system, direct and appealing though it is, still seems a remote possibility. Jenkins and Kessler might lose their case. Congress might act preemptively to grant the NCAA an antitrust exemption. The NCAA and its defenders might succeed in their propaganda efforts to convince the public of the purity of their intentions. In the foreseeable future all college athletic activities seem likely to be housed within—rather than parallel to—the academic institutions that host them. But the recently reenergized movement for athletes' rights is not likely to be stopped. And if athletic operations continue to be housed under an academic umbrella, one right should take precedence over all others: the right to a quality education.

If athletes in the profit sports are to be treated as genuine students following a genuine course of study, their academic needs should take priority over the needs of their sport. Universities are in the business of educating, after all, and if the students-first rhetoric that administrators routinely spout is to be seen as anything other than a pious platitude, they need to begin attending to athletes' educational needs. The truth of that proposition seems so obvious that its statement would seem redundant. Ed O'Bannon, Kain Colter, Rashad McCants, and so many others have recently made clear, however, why universities need to be reminded of their most basic obligations.

The second path to reform that we envision involves a major restructuring of the academic-athletic relationship, with academics finally placed in a position of supremacy. Real reform can begin when we collectively acknowledge the primordial defect in the current system—the fact that many profit-sport athletes in big-time programs are not yet ready to perform college-level work (while others remain disinclined to do the work). If colleges continue to admit athletes with severe deficiencies in basic skills—and the failures of the nation's K–12 system as well as continuing competitive pressures in the collegiate sports arena suggest that this will surely be the case—they must commit themselves to realistic programs of remediation.[6] Every university that plans to lower its admissions standards in pursuit of athletic glory should be required to develop an intensive literacy program that will ensure college readiness by the player's second year in residence. New students whose board scores place them more than one standard deviation below the average admitted student at the university should be ineligible to compete in their first year; guaranteed scholarships of five or even six years (including summers) will ensure that the student has the opportunity to play for four years while also receiving appropriate remedial instruction and following a productive academic path that will ultimately lead to a meaningful degree. Coaches and other athletics personnel will need to bend their schedules and modify their demands to meet the academic needs of the students whose physical talents they are so eager to put to use.

An honest acknowledgment of the need for proper remediation is essential, but much more restructuring will be required. Practice time should be shortened, strictly monitored, and staggered semester to semester so that players have available to them what other students enjoy as a matter of routine—choices between all, or at least a great majority, of the university's courses and majors. To maximize athletes' experiences in all those courses and majors, conferences and universities will need to reduce travel time, shorten seasons (football players played ten games in the 1960s), and refrain from scheduling any games during final examination periods. Class attendance policies will have to be modified so that any absence from class for an athletic reason will come to be regarded by all university personnel as anomalous, extraordinary, lamentable, and corrosive to the academic enterprise.

All academic counseling and tutoring programs, including the delivery of remedial instruction, must be placed under the supervision of academic officers at the university and not within the Athletic Departments where they now generally reside. The single most powerful lesson to be drawn from the UNC scandal is that Academic Support Programs for athletes, if they are detached and insulated from the academic life of the rest of the university, become cauldrons of curricular flimflammery and incubators of corruption. The Nyang'oro course-fraud scheme could never have unfolded in the way it did if registration processes had been guided by faculty in their academic departments rather than by academic counselors in the conveniently distant athletic complex. If one purpose of reform is to integrate athletes more fully into the academic life of the university, it is imperative that athletes' academic advisers be integrated into the academic machinery of the central campus. Athletes will then interact on a regular basis with people inured to normal academic routines, focused solely on academic achievement, and unburdened by the pursuit of conflicting priorities.

One other reform is critical to the project of placing athletes' academic lives and experiences under the firm supervision and jurisdiction of faculty and academic officers. Universities must commit to the principle of transparency. The Family Educational Rights and Privacy Act of 1974, which was designed to ensure privacy and properly regulated access to student records, has become "the shield behind which higher education hides the academic corruption in college athletics."[7] Instead of protecting individuals, FERPA now protects institutions from having to endure the scrutiny their academic programs require. Officials invoke the needs of student privacy whenever they prefer not to divulge patterns of abuse they know would prove both embarrassing and revealing. At UNC, for example, officials refused to divulge information about football players' parking violations on the grounds that such records were "educational" in nature. The only reason the university refused release of those records was that they pointed to a long-term pattern of disregard for the rules among certain high-profile athletes (as well as their access to fancy rental cars supplied by anonymous boosters).

In any case, even the genuine educational records of athletes should be shared with the public so long as the disclosure does not violate a legitimate claim to privacy rights. The Buckley Amendment through which FERPA became law, which one Yale lawyer described as "a masterpiece of wretched draftsmanship," failed to make commonsense distinctions between public and private information. A grade earned in a particular course is clearly a private matter. Student attendance in a course is an open fact already available to a limited public (the public who sees the student go to class), and no one could seriously consider participation in a university course as sensitive information. Wide dissemination of the fact of a student's enrollment in a certain course therefore poses no real threat to privacy. To ensure meaningful institutional oversight, athletic programs must be required to reveal the course-selection triage process that unfolds "behind closed doors." As Matthew R. Salzwedel and Jon Ericson noted in a trenchant article more than a decade ago, "Colleges and universities need to disclose—that is, make available to the public—athletes' academic majors, academic advisers, courses listed by academic major, general education requirements, and electives (with the names of instructors and course grade point averages)." Only the regular display of course- and major-selection patterns, and aggregate data reflecting classroom performance, will enable faculty overseers to do their job of ensuring educational quality and protecting academic integrity.[8]

Admissions officers and athletic officials should also be prevented from using the obfuscating term *student-athlete* whenever they present to university faculty and the broader public evidence about athletes' classroom performance and their general academic lives. No one worries about the fencers, the volleyball players, the swimmers, or the field hockey players. The pressure to lower standards and bend rules comes from the high-profile sports where great profits are earned and the pressure to win is most relentless. Academic data should therefore always be presented in ways that construct meaningful cohorts and allow meaningful comparisons. Athletes should be sorted by team—no more exploiting of the fencers for the purpose of trumpeting "student-athlete" GPA—but they should also be sorted by scholarship status. The generally higher academic performance of the football team's walk-ons, for example, should not be used to dilute the data specific to the recruited athletes. The athletes whose academic interests are most likely to be overpowered and subsumed by the athletic demands placed upon them are precisely the most hotly recruited ones—the individuals coaches consider most vital to the success of the team. The performance of committee-case recruits must also be distinguished from the crowd—presented in aggregate form so as not to identify the individuals concerned. University faculty, and the public at large, can make critical judgments about the impact of lowered admission standards for athletes only if they can see the curricular itineraries and general performance data of the most at-risk students. *Transparency* must be the watchword of postreform collegiate athletics.

The UNC scandal provided opportunity. Officials in Chapel Hill were handed a golden opportunity to lead. All fans of college sport were given the opportunity to peer into the bowels of a corrupted academic-athletic relationship, one that stands as a useful microcosm for all that is wrong with the system of college sport today. Athletes were given the opportunity to reassess what their athletic careers had done for them academically, and some have begun to come forward to share their feelings of disappointment. Presidents, chancellors, and reform-minded faculty all around the country were given the opportunity to ponder what is required to bring university practices into alignment with institutional mission statements that emphasize education, the production of new knowledge, and service to the community.

In the 1940s University of Chicago president Robert Maynard Hutchins, most famous for his decision in 1939 to close down the school's high-profile football program, shared with faculty at Chicago his vision of the university's future. "The purpose of the university," he wrote, "is nothing less than to procure a moral, intellectual, and spiritual revolution throughout the world."[9] For four long years the authors hoped that UNC would be the place where Hutchins's moral, intellectual, and spiritual revolution might begin—with administrators and faculty leaders joining forces and resolving to say, "Enough already." That prospect now seems remote, to say the least. The great value of the UNC scandal was not its ability to galvanize faculty outrage but rather its demonstration of the sheer perversity of the current system. The flood of money, the pressure to win, the creation of a university brand that identified the institution with a tradition of athletic success, the customary disregard for the educational experiences of black athletes: all of these forces led sensible people to accept or overlook irrational behavior at UNC, to "normalize deviance," in the words of sociologist Diane Vaughan.[10]

In Chapel Hill a faculty chair threw integrity to the winds in order to modify an official report she feared might "raise further NCAA issues," a harried chancellor reacted to athletic scandal by proposing that athletic directors should henceforth handle all matters athletic, a long-respected faculty athletics representative worked with athletics officials to sell to a naive former governor a false story about faculty negligence, senior associate deans omitted from their AFRI/AFAM curriculum review incriminating evidence of athletic wrongdoing of which they were fully cognizant, and individual faculty and administrators who had known for decades about the subversion of a department's courses—and not just any department, but the department that had been created out of a desire to enhance the education of African American students—remained steadfastly quiet for four solid years, leaving a lone whistle-blower to twist in the wind. UNC proved itself to be an unlikely source for the moral transformation once envisioned by Robert Maynard Hutchins.

The revolution so desperately needed today could be generated by one group of "inside" actors at universities: the athletes themselves. If a big-time university's profit-sport athletes—the cheated—dig in and make a stand, administrators will suddenly learn who has the real power in the entertainment complex they have spent decades building. When athletes make up their minds to speak the truth and to demand what is owed them—coaches and administrators and the NCAA be damned—they are likely to find many faculty allies rushing to march under their banner. An alliance of students and faculty would have the power to reclaim the true educational purpose of the college experience and to reestablish the principles of honesty, equity, and fairness in America's institutions of higher learning. May the lessons of the UNC experience inspire athletes and faculty at other places finally to effect that transformation.

Epilogue

The day before Jay Smith and Mary Willingham submitted this book manuscript to Potomac Press, stunning news rolled out of Chapel Hill. According to the university's AD, Bubba Cunningham, UNC had received a "verbal notice of inquiry" from the NCAA, which had decided to launch a thorough investigation into campus "academic irregularities" it had previously determined to be a nonathletic problem. Earlier in the spring semester the university had hired former federal prosecutor Kenneth Wainstein to carry out an investigation designed finally to address the many unanswered questions about the origins and course of the academic fraud at UNC. Wainstein's decision to share some of his preliminary findings with NCAA personnel appears to have been the trigger that set in motion the new NCAA inquiry. It would seem, however, that the relentless questioning to which the NCAA had been subjected throughout much of the spring of 2014—the O'Bannon lawyers, Congressmen Tony Cardenas and Elijah Cummings, and an array of national journalists had been pushing the current NCAA president, Mark Emmert, for months to explain why no action had been taken on the massive course-fraud scandal at UNC—had also played a part in persuading the regulatory agency that it could no longer avoid getting to the bottom of the scandal.

Although no one can predict where exactly the new NCAA inquiry might lead, the announcement itself brought a form of closure to a four-year ordeal that had been stretched out needlessly by university leaders who had made the avoidance of athletic punishment their top priority. The news that the NCAA was coming back to town after all represented a resounding strategic defeat for all who had chosen to stonewall, deflect, and deny the realities of the corrupt athletic-academic partnership that had been nurtured in Chapel Hill. As Luke DeCock of the *Raleigh News & Observer* remarked, "The firewall North Carolina has so desperately built between athletics and academics with the explicit intention of keeping the NCAA from coming back onto campus has collapsed."[1]

Events in Chapel Hill will bear watching. But one salutary lesson has already emerged from the ruins of the Carolina Way myth. Relentless demands for accountability can still make a difference, even when the powers that be are not inclined to listen and react bitterly to the voices of their critics. When the truth lies concealed, those who value truth for its own sake should feel emboldened to keep pushing. Even when corruption runs deep and wide, persistence pays off.

We hope that this book, and our continued efforts to shine a light on the injustices and moral failures endemic to the current collegiate model of sport, will contribute to the creation of a more honest and healthy dialogue on the national stage. As of 2015 Jay Smith still teaches at UNC, and he has returned to his natural home in research that focuses on eighteenth-century France. But he remains and will forever be engaged with the athletic-reform issues first forced onto his radar in 2010. Mary Willingham left UNC in May 2014, but she submitted a declaration on behalf of the plaintiffs in the O'Bannon case, she became an officer and an active participant in the Drake Group, for months she has lobbied and informed legislators in Washington, and she is now in the process of launching a new literacy initiative oriented toward middle schoolers, high schoolers, and the coaches, teachers, and administrators who do so much to mold the young people in their charge.

Additional documents and data relevant to the story told in this book, as well as ongoing news about the activities of Mary Willingham and links to articles and websites of interest to those who follow the college athletic-reform movement, can be found at our website: http://www.paperclassinc.com.

Notes

.

Introduction

1. Writing from a hotel room in Miami, the star defensive lineman tweeted: "I live In club LIV so I get the tenant rate. bottles comin like its a giveaway." The reference to "bottles comin," as well as a series of other tweets suggesting a lifestyle inconsistent with that of the typical student-athlete, alerted NCAA officials to the possibility that a player or players from UNC had accepted "impermissible benefits" that would merit punishment. These suspicions led to the yearlong investigation that landed UNC's football program on probation. http://sports illustrated.cnn.com/multimedia/photo_gallery/1107/tweets-heard-round-the -world/content.16.html#ixzz2i1dZfalh.

2. Following Richard Southall, Mark Nagel, and others, the authors prefer the term *profit sports* to the more conventional *revenue sports*, because the terminology favored by the NCAA (*revenue sports, Olympic sports, student-athletes, collegiate model*) intentionally disguises the fundamental commercial realities of the big-time sport enterprise. Football and basketball teams in fact generate enormous profits for schools, coaches, administrators, and NCAA personnel; only the players—imprisoned by that other false label, *amateurism*—are denied any fruits of the profits. On the use of the terms *profit* and *loss sports* at the collegiate level, see Richard Southall and Ellen Staurowsky, "Cheering on the Collegiate Model: Creating, Disseminating, and Imbedding the NCAA's Redefinition of Amateurism," *Journal of Sport and Social Issues* 37 (2013): 403–29; and Richard Southall and Mark Nagel, "'How Did We Get Here?': Analysis of Legal and Ethical Issues Associated with the NCAA Collegiate Model of Intercollegiate Athletics, 2003–2014," Sport and Recreation Law Association conference, Orlando, 2014.

3. Taylor Branch, "The Shame of College Sports," *Atlantic*, October 2011, http://www .theatlantic.com/magazine/archive/2011/10/the-shame-of-college-sports/308643/.

For Nocera's message, see, for example, Joe Nocera, "The NCAA's Ethics Problem," *New York Times*, January 26, 2013. Jay Bilas's assault on NCAA amateurism rules is covered, for example, in Tony Manfred, "ESPN's Jay Bilas Destroys the NCAA in One Paragraph about the Johnny Manziel Scandal," August 5, 2013, http://www .businessinsider.com/jay-bilas-destroys-ncaa-johnny-manziel-scandal-2013-8. The Epix original documentary *Schooled: The Price of College Sports*, produced by Andrew Muscato and featuring Taylor Branch, was released in October 2013.

4. As noted in a summary of the president's views on the NCAA website. See http://www.ncaa.org/president.

5. There would be many iterations of this basic theme, but the most famous and controversial version of this claim appeared in the report prepared by former North Carolina governor Jim Martin in December 2012, discussed at length in chapter 6. See James G. Martin, "The University of North Carolina Academic Anomalies Review: Report of Findings," http://www.unc.edu/news/12/UNC -Governor-Martin-Final-Report-and-Addendum.pdf, ii.

6. The *N&O* reported in 2013 that the university had distributed more than a half-million dollars to public relations firms over a period of two years. One of the tasks for which the university sought help: refuting the whistle-blower claims of coauthor Mary Willingham. See Dan Kane, "UNC Spent More than $500K for PR Help in Academic Fraud Scandal," *N&O*, June 8, 2013, http://www.newsobserver .com/2013/06/08/2948376/unc-spent-more-than-500k-for-pr.html.

1. Paper-Class Central

1. Annual Reports, Curriculum in African and Afro-American Studies, 1983–84, 1986–87, 1988–89, Office of the Dean of the College of Arts and Sciences of the University of North Carolina at Chapel Hill, Series 40076, 2:2, University Archives, Wilson Library, UNC–Chapel Hill.

2. Gillian Cell to Paul Hardin, August 16, 1989, Office of the Dean, Series 40076, 2:2.

3. Sonja H. Stone to Cell, May 16, 1989, Office of the Dean, Series 40076, 2:2.

4. Sonja Stone, "Reappointment of Cell Shows Apathy of Administration," *Daily Tar Heel*, November 27, 1989.

5. Annual Report, Curriculum in African and Afro-American Studies, 1988–89, Office of the Dean, Series 40076, 2:2.

6. Annual Report, Curriculum in African and Afro-American Studies, 1989–90, Office of the Dean, Series 40076, 2:2.

7. Stone to Cell, May 16, 1989, Office of the Dean, Series 40076, 2:2.

8. William Rhoden, "At Chapel Hill, Athletes Suddenly Become Activists," *New York Times*, September 11, 1992.

9. Moelle Hutchins, "Stone Center Groundbreaking a Long Time Coming," *Daily Tar Heel*, April 26, 2001.

10. The records of the Dean of the College of Arts and Sciences contain no

documentation showing that an offer had ever been tendered to Nyang'oro, but deans evidently believed that they were now competing for Nyang'oro's services.

11. Annual Report, Curriculum in African and Afro-American Studies, 1988–89, Office of the Dean, Series 40076, 2:2.

12. The background to this decision can be gleaned from the University Archives. See Associate Dean Stephen Birdsall to Dean Gillian Cell, March 16, 1990, Office of the Dean, Series 40076, 2:2. As of March the university had had no plans to keep Nyang'oro, but on July 1 he was appointed to a tenure-track position.

13. A. Ann Ards, "Stop Belittling Students' Concerns," *Daily Tar Heel*, November 27, 1989.

14. Interview with Stephen Birdsall, August 22, 2013.

15. Annual Report, Curriculum in African and Afro-American Studies, 1994–95, Office of the Dean, Series 40076, 2:2.

16. Interview with Faculty Member A, June 26, 2013.

17. Interview with Michael West, May 15, 2014.

18. Interview with Faculty Member A, June 26, 2013.

19. Burgess McSwain died in 2004 after a long battle with cancer. A few months before McSwain died, Thad Williamson wrote a laudatory article conveying her prowess as a tutor. Only one faculty member was quoted in the story: Julius Nyang'oro. Introduced as one of "numerous UNC faculty members who regularly teach student-athletes," Nyang'oro praised McSwain because she refused to "baby-sit the athletes." Williamson, "Burgess McSwain '66, the Heart of Carolina Basketball," *Carolina Alumni Magazine*, July 2004, http://alumni.unc.edu/article.aspx?sid=886.

20. Letter from Julius Nyang'oro to Dean Stephen Birdsall, November 9, 1993, Office of the Dean, Series 40076, 2:2; Dan Kane, "Former UNC African Studies Chairman Had Close Ties to Athletic Counselors," *N&O*, June 8, 2013, http://www.newsobserver.com/2013/06/08/2948647/former-unc-african-studies-chairman.html.

21. Interviews with Adam Seipp, April 4, June 28, 2013.

22. Nyang'oro is identified as the instructor of this course in the 1988–89 Annual Report (Series 40076, 2:2) for the AFRI/AFAM curriculum.

23. History Department chair W. Fitzhugh Brundage offers typical testimony about his experience with independent studies. (He has supervised two independent study courses for a total of two students in his twelve years at the university.) "I am very, very hesitant to do them unless I am confident that the student is passionate about his/her topic. I don't want to be in the role of scold trying to get work out of a laggard." Email from Fitz Brundage to Jay Smith, January 8, 2014.

24. The independent studies void in curriculum records of the 1970s and 1980s is, in fact, one of the proofs of the identity of the instructor in the courses scheduled beginning in 1989. Beginning in 1990, hardly a summer went by over the next twenty years in which AFRI independent study courses were not offered. In the

pivotal summer of 1991, AFRI 65—one of Nyang'oro's bread-and-butter courses—was offered in addition to the two independent study courses. The AFRI 65, too, had a basketball player enrolled.

25. Interview with Seipp, June 28, 2013.

26. Annual Reports, Curriculum in African and Afro-American Studies, 1992–93, 1994–95, 1995–96, 1996–97, 1997–98, 1998–99, Office of the Dean, Series 40076, 2:2.

27. Letters of Julius Nyang'oro to the faculty and staff of the curriculum, June 29, 1992, and June 29, 1993. Office of the Dean, Series 40076, 2:2.

28. Andrew Zimbalist, *Unpaid Professionals: Commercialism and Conflict in Big-Time College Sports* (Princeton NJ: Princeton University Press, 1999), 30.

29. Faculty Council Minutes, February 21, 1986, General Faculty and Faculty Council of the University of North Carolina at Chapel Hill Records, 1799–2011, Series 40106, 1:4, vol. 1:42, University Archives, Wilson Library, UNC–Chapel Hill.

30. Interview with Seipp, June 28, 2013.

31. Martin, "University of North Carolina Academic Anomalies Review," addendum, 9, 12.

32. All calculations done on the basis of a review of official enrollment figures as reflected in UNC's Connect Carolina online registration system.

33. Readers of the *Raleigh News & Observer* caught a glimpse of this phenomenon when a series of emails between Crowder in AFRI/AFAM and academic advisers and academic counselors was published in June 2013. One adviser apologized to Crowder for a forthcoming request from one nonathlete: "I tried to discourage him when he brought up having heard about independent studies in AFAM. . . . I'm very sorry he showed up on your doorstep." See Kane, "African Studies Chairman Had Close Ties."

34. Emails from Don Mathews to Smith, January 24, 2014.

35. Computation based on the published partial transcript of Julius Peppers shared by the *Raleigh News & Observer* in August 2012. See http://media2.news observer.com/smedia/2012/08/13/12/32/1hk0p2.So.156.pdf#storylink=relast.

36. Martin, "University of North Carolina Academic Anomalies Review," 19.

37. Perhaps the semester that would best fit in the land of the absurd was the spring of 2004. That term Nyang'oro and Crowder offered one section of AFRI 190 for 11 students, but they also offered multiple sections of AFAM 190. Section 1 had 53 students, section 3 had 5 students, section 4 had 4 students, and section 2 had 95 students. With a total of 168 students in independent study that term, Nyang'oro—assuming he was the instructor for each section—would have been an extraordinarily busy man.

38. See Kane, "African Studies Chairman Had Close Ties." In fairness to Reynolds and other counselors, it should be acknowledged that most of them adapted to a system in place long before their arrival at UNC, and some sought to use paper classes and independent study courses to assist athletes who were

far behind on the learning curve. Systems can be corrupt without commanding the full and conscious complicity of those who perpetuate them.

2. A Fraud in Full

1. As noted on the UNC Athletic Department web page. See http://www.goheels .com/ViewArticle.dbml?DB_OEM_ID=3350&ATCLID=205497928.

2. David Loomis, "The Nike Contract with UNC–Chapel Hill: 'The Power of Money Here at Home,'" unpublished paper written for International Studies 92 in April 1998. See http://www.unc.edu/~andrewsr/ints092/loomis.html.

3. On the renegotiated contract of 2002, see the university press release of October 16, 2001: http://www.unc.edu/news/archives/oct01/nike101601.htm.

4. Carey was interviewed in 2003 by Tom Friend of ESPN: The Magazine. See http://a.espncdn.com/nfl/columns/misc/1511385.html.

5. Jonathan Hartlyn and William L. Andrews, "Review of Courses in the Department of African and Afro-American Studies, College of Arts and Sciences," May 2, 2012, http://www.unc.edu/news/050412/Review%20of%20courses.pdf.

6. Interview with Counselor A, July 5, 2013.

7. Williamson, "Burgess McSwain '66, the Heart of Carolina Basketball."

8. "No. 1 Alum Speaks Out: Jordan 'Disappointed' with UNC's Firing of Doherty," http://sportsillustrated.cnn.com/basketball/college/news/2003/04/03/jordan_doherty _ap/.

9. In one email from March 24, 2003, for example, McSwain forwarded to Crowder a list of rumors sent to her by a UNC fan who lived in Indianapolis and who evidently had some connection to the family of Sean May. Among the rumors: "Scott May met with [Chancellor] Moeser and told him that Sean was gone if Doherty stays." "Baddour has guaranteed his retirement after June or July of this year, so he could just keep his mouth shut and let Moeser handle things." "Prospects for the coaching job are Roy, Bill Self, and Larry Brown. . . . Dean apparently wants Larry Brown, who is then supposed to hire Phil Ford as an assistant, and hand the reigns [sic] to him after a few years."

10. When Roy Williams arrived in Chapel Hill in 2003, he brought with him Wayne Walden, who briefly shared basketball academic counseling duties with Burgess McSwain before taking over definitively in 2004. (McSwain lost her battle with cancer in July 2004.) Both Walden and McSwain provided academic guidance to the basketball team that won the championship in 2005.

11. See http://espn.go.com/espn/otl/story/_/id/11036924/former-north-carolina -basketball-star-rashad-mccants-says-took-sham-classes.

12. Dan Kane's reporting in the Raleigh News & Observer has provided an eye-opening glimpse at the process. In a March 2010 email, football academic counselor Jaimie Lee returned to some unfinished business in a conversation with Nyang'oro: "I failed to mention yesterday that Swahili 403 last summer was offered as a research paper course. I meant to ask, do you think this may happen

again in the future? If not the summer, maybe the fall?" Nyang'oro responded: "Driving a hard bargain, should have known . . . :)." See Kane, "African Studies Chairman Had Close Ties."

13. Interview with Adviser A, August 13, 2013.

14. Holladay made these remarks in an interview with Jones Angell of GoHeels.com. See http://www.goheels.com/mediaPortal/player.dbml?id=2580705&db_oem_id=3350.

3. The Making of a Cover-up

1. For a review of the tumult, see http://reesenewslab.org/2011/04/26/is-the -unc-honor-court-broken/15392/.

2. "Installation Oration by Allan Gurganus, October 12, 2008," http://www.unc.edu /chan/chancellors/thorp_holden/speeches/081012-installation-oration.php.

3. "Rationale for the Undergraduate Honor Court, Regular Hearing," case number 819-001-2010, UNC–Chapel Hill. The statement comes from the "Summary of the Facts" in the case of the AFRI 266 paper.

4. Caitlin McCabe, "The Cost of a Scandal: How Three Scandals in Three Years Left UNC–Chapel Hill with a $5 Million Bill," *Synapse.com*, November 13, 2013. Evrard and King cost the university more than $467,000.

5. Indeed, ASPSA knowledge about the paper-class system was so extensive that the directors of the program would later claim that they tried to express their own concerns about it to the Faculty Athletics Committee in both 2002 and 2006. The dispute over this claim spilled into the public forum and shaped the tenor of more than one Faculty Council meeting in early 2013.

6. Joe Schad, "UNC Investigating Academics," August 27, 2010, http://sports .espn.go.com/ncf/news/story?id=5501067.

7. Letter from Smith to Thorp, October 18, 2010.

8. John Blanchard's retirement was announced at the end of February 2013.

9. UNC–Chapel Hill Writing Center, "Ten Principles for Writing Consultants," October 3, 2013, http://www.unc.edu/depts/our/pdfs/supporting_surf _proposal_writers.pdf.

10. Blanchard described the basic training given to the tutoring staff: "The education of the tutors is a four hour process including an hour with the director of the writing center who goes over the do's and don't's, um, again, the um, Associate Dean from the Dean of Students' office spends time with the tutors on the Honor System and their view of plagiarism and other academic offenses and then we have time with our assistant athletic director for certification and eligibility in the Compliance Office who spends time with the tutors outlining" the NCAA perspective. The ASPSA staff also "go over an end of semester form about not participating [in] or witnessing any academic fraud and so they go over the process and some of the do's and don't's in working with student athletes." Tutors, Blanchard was making clear, had no excuse for not knowing the rules.

11. The strategy is explained well by former compliance officer B. David Rid-

path in *Tainted Glory: Marshall University, the NCAA, and One Man's Fight for Justice* (Bloomington IN: iUniverse, 2012), esp. chap. 15.

12. Joe Nocera, "The Academic Counseling Racket," *New York Times*, February 4, 2013. On May, who said of his choice of the AFAM major that its advantageous offerings of what he called "independent electives" made it possible for him to finish his degree in the summer, see Mark Alesia, "They Got Game, but Do NCAA Players Graduate?," *Indianapolis Star*, April 2, 2010.

13. We know this because the Honor Court, in the stated rationale for its not-guilty verdict in the case of the AFRI 266, noted that "Mr. McAdoo currently does not work with a tutor, for he applied for and was granted an independent study."

14. Dan Kane and J. Andrew Curliss, "UNC Players Needed Academic Help, Records Show," *N&O*, September 30, 2012, http://www.newsobserver.com/2012/09/30/2379206/unc-players-needed-academic-help.html.

4. Lost Opportunities

1. Branch, "Shame of College Sports."

2. Willingham was finally invited to address the Faculty Athletics Committee in December 2013, more than three years after her conversation with Broome and Keadey. She implored the committee to address honestly the academic needs of scholarship players in the sports of football and basketball. Most of the faculty around the table avoided making eye contact with Willingham, and at least one conspicuously read her email throughout the presentation. At the end of Willingham's twenty-minute pitch, which was cut off prematurely, she was impatiently told, "We're already moving in this direction."

3. Smith's request for these documents was denied by the university on August 14, 2013. The three individuals involved also turned down requests for interviews.

4. For the full report, see http://media2.newsobserver.com/smedia/2012/03/12/14/42/z3iSU.So.156.pdf.

5. Jonathan Hartlyn and William L. Andrews, "Review of Courses in the Department of African and Afro-American Studies, College of Arts and Sciences," May 2, 2012, http://www.unc.edu/news/050412/Review%20of%20courses.pdf.

6. "University of North Carolina, Chapel Hill: Public Infractions Report, 12 March 2012," http://chronicle.com/blogs/ticker/files/2012/03/UNC.pdf, 26.

7. Holden Thorp to Board of Trustees, June 7, 2012, http://media2.newsobserver.com/smedia/2012/06/08/21/02/uvpmH.So.156.pdf.

8. Jane Stancill, "UNC-CH Trustees Question How Academic Fraud Happened," *N&O*, May 25, 2012, http://www.newsobserver.com/2012/05/25/2087469/unc-ch-trustees-question-how-academic.html. See also Stancill, "Board of Governors Keeps Hands Off UNC Scandal," *N&O*, June 3, 2012, http://www.newsobserver.com/2012/06/03/2107976/board-of-governors-keeps-hands.html.

9. As reported by Dan Kane, "UNC Players Made Up 39 Percent of Suspect Classes," *N&O*, May 7, 2012, http://www.newsobserver.com/2012/05/07/2050241/unc-football-basketball-players.html.

10. Kane, "UNC Players Made Up 39 Percent of Suspect Classes."

11. Dan Kane, "Report Finds Academic Fraud Evidence in UNC Department," *N&O*, May 4, 2012, http://www.newsobserver.com/2012/05/04/2044178/report-finds -academic-fraud-evidence.html. Thorp would later say much the same with regard to a particularly embarrassing case of plagiarism involving a football player. The infraction was just "another sad part" of "the most difficult year in the lives of everybody involved." See Matt Brooks, "Report: UNC Receiver Erik Highsmith Plagiarized from 11-Year-Olds," WashingtonPost.com, October 12, 2012.

5. The University Doubles Down

1. This wording from the original draft of the report was made public only much later, in a 2013 story by Dan Kane. See "UNC Faculty Leader Pushed Rewrite of Key Report to Keep NCAA Away," *N&O*, July 20, 2013, http://www.newsobserver.com /2013/07/20/3044746/unc-faculty-leader-pushed-rewrite.html.

2. Boxill would later claim, in spite of documentary evidence that contradicts her, that the purpose of her July 26 email had been to ask Maffly-Kipp and the others to remove the word *booster* from the report because, as she would later say, "booster has a specific meaning for the NCAA[,] as somebody brought up in the [FEC] meeting—not me." The word *booster*, however, did not even appear in the text she was seeking to modify. Crowder was described as an "athletics sup-porter," not a booster. The discussion of the appropriateness of the word *booster* had evidently occurred earlier, perhaps at the FEC meeting when all FEC members had provided feedback to the authors of the report. (Boxill had written on July 26, of course, that the concerns she was now conveying had been communicated to her by individuals not present at the July 16 meeting. She thus made multiple irreconcilable statements about her actions and motives. If the concerns she took to the subcommittee on July 26 were "new"—having been expressed after the July 16 meeting—those concerns could not have been focused on the word *booster*, which was already removed from the report.) Boxill would repeat this faulty account of her July 26 email at a Faculty Council meeting in September 2013, and two members of the FEC, including Michael Gerhardt, vouched for the accuracy of that account; they had evidently grown confused over the relationship between two chronologically distinct instances of revision to the report. See Ran Northam, "Boxill: *N&O* Took 'Booster' Email Out of Context," August 29, 2013, http://chapelboro.com/news/unc/boxill-no-took-booster-email -out-of-context/; and minutes of the UNC Faculty Council meeting of Septem-ber 13, 2013, http://faccoun.unc.edu/faculty-council/meeting-materials-2013-2014 /september-13-2013/.

3. Email from Kevin Guskiewicz to Smith, July 10, 2012.

4. The Martin report's accusations against the FAC were decisively refuted by History Department chair Lloyd Kramer at a February 2013 meeting of Faculty Council. See http://faccoun.unc.edu/faculty-council/meeting-materials-past-years /meeting-materials-2012-13/february-8-2013/#heading-4, app. B.

5. Dan Kane, "Meeting Minutes Don't Confirm Martin Report in UNC Academic Fraud Scandal," *N&O*, December 29, 2012, http://www.newsobserver.com/2012/12/29/2572848/minutes-dont-confirm-martin-report.html.

6. John Drescher, "Baker Tilly Retracts Key Finding in UNC Report," *N&O*, February 1, 2013, http://www.newsobserver.com/2013/02/01/2649467/drescher-firm-retracts-key-finding.html.

7. Kane, "African Studies Chairman Had Close Ties."

8. Kane, "Meeting Minutes Don't Confirm Martin Report."

9. Andrew Carter, "UNC Releases Statement about NCAA Involvement in AFAM Scandal: NCAA Found No Violations," *N&O*, August 31, 2012, http://blogs.newsobserver.com/uncnow/unc-releases-statement-about-ncaa-involvement-in-afam-scandal-ncaa-found-no-violations.

6. On a Collision Course

1. Dan Kane and J. Andrew Curliss, "UNC's Kupec Worked to Establish Job Eventually Given to Tami Hansbrough," *N&O*, September 12, 2012, http://www.newsobserver.com/2012/09/12/2334880/uncs-kupec-worked-to-establish.html.

2. Kane and Curliss, "UNC Players Needed Academic Help."

3. Dan Kane, "More Plagiarism Questions Haunt UNC-CH," *N&O*, October 21, 2012, http://www.newsobserver.com/2012/10/21/2425386/more-plagiarism-questions-haunt.html.

4. A finding of "insufficient evidence" is impossible to imagine because the plagiarized passages were taken verbatim from a highly unusual source. Eleven-year-olds had written: "Poultry farming is raising chickens, turkeys, ducks and other fowl for meat or eggs. Poultry farms can be 1) Breeding farms where they raise poultry for meat, or 2) Layer farms where they produce eggs." Highsmith wrote: "Poultry farming is raising chickens, turkeys, ducks and other fowl for meat or eggs. Poultry farms can be breeding farms where they raise poultry for meat, or layer farms where they produce eggs."

5. Emeritus history professor Willis Brooks and coauthor Jay Smith pressed Thorp and Hunter in face-to-face meetings and in a series of letters and emails. Among the national news stories: Simon Samano, "Did Erik Highsmith Seriously Plagiarize 11-Year Olds?," *USA Today*, October 24, 2012; Brooks, "UNC Receiver Erik Highsmith Plagiarized 11-Year-Olds"; Christopher Young, "Why a College Football Player Would Plagiarize from a Little Kid," *New York Daily News*, October 24, 2012; Jack Moore, "College Football Player Busted for Plagiarizing 11-Year-Olds," buzzfeed.com, October 23, 2012.

6. Email from Thorp to Willis Brooks, November 5, 2012.

7. Through public records requests Dan Kane discovered that Vince Ille, the compliance director at UNC, had written to the NCAA in September 2013, seeking confirmation that "no additional investigation [of UNC] . . . is being contemplated." He soon received the confirmation he needed. Dan Kane, "NCAA Unlikely to Punish UNC for Academic Fraud, New Documents Show," *N&O*, November 8,

2013, http://www.newsobserver.com/2013/11/08/3352200/ncaa-unlikely-to-punish
-unc for.html.

8. Dan Kane, "UNC Tolerated Cheating, Says Insider Mary Willingham," N&O,
November 17, 2012, http://www.newsobserver.com/2012/11/17/2490476/insider-unc
-tolerated-cheating.html.

9. Joe Nocera, "The Academic Counseling Racket," *New York Times*, February
4, 2013, http://www.nytimes.com/2013/02/05/opinion/nocera-academic-counseling
-racket.html?_r=0.

10. Kane, "UNC Spent More than $500K for PR Help." Kirschner's letter had
contained such models of careful obfuscation as the following: "For example, the
story claimed that . . . Jennifer Townsend, who became the [basketball] team's
counselor in 2009, stopped enrolling players because she was appalled by those
[AFRI/AFAM] classes. Townsend did not make that statement about any classes
offered to student-athletes." Townsend "did not make that statement"? What statement? Here is what Kirschner should have written, had he been able to: "Townsend
had nothing to do with the changing enrollment patterns of the basketball team,
and our counselors never steer athletes to classes under any circumstances."

11. The one notable exception was Vince Ille, the associate athletic director
in charge of compliance. Ille wrote to Willingham to remind her that "compliance with NCAA, conference, and UNC rules is a shared responsibility" and that
"assertions you've made" in the press suggested that rules might have been broken. Willingham was invited to come tell Ille about that rule breaking. The suggestion that Willingham was the real rogue with contempt for the rules—which
disregarded both her long history of seeking redress during her time as a learning
specialist and her newly minted status as the only whistle-blower on the campus—
became more aggressive over time. In April, after Willingham had been in the
news again for winning the Drake Group's Robert Maynard Hutchins award as
an exemplar of academic integrity, Ille continued: "[It] is important that we rec-
oncile and document the contradictory statements you have made regarding
your knowledge of and involvement in violations of NCAA rules." Ille also asked
Willingham if she "chose to conceal" wrongdoing during her earlier interview
with Keadey and Broome. The Ille emails contributed to an increasingly hostile environment in which university interactions with Willingham modulated
between benign neglect and naked harassment. Emails from Ille to Willingham,
November 25, April 19, 2013.

12. Martin, "University of North Carolina Academic Anomalies Review," ii.

13. See chapter 5.

14. Relying on testimony from others, Martin falsely stated, for example, that
the sharp drop-off in AFRI/AFAM independent study enrollments in 2006–7 likely
resulted from the university renumbering project of 2006, since "the need for a
student to request an independent study to fulfill a degree requirement would
likely decrease" after the introduction of new courses with new numbers. Course
renumbering had no such impact on enrollments in the College of Arts and Sci-

ences, since few new courses were created during the renumbering process. In any case, it had always been college policy not to count independent study credits toward degree requirements outside one's major. Independent study enrollments in AFRI/AFAM dropped by two-thirds in one year, and the only plausible explanation for that phenomenon is that the warnings issued by Bobbi Owen, senior associate dean, had been taken to heart.

15. Nyang'oro and Jaimie Lee engaged in flirtatious yet innocuous banter on more than one occasion. When Lee asked Nyang'oro in March 2010 whether he might soon schedule a SWAH 403 "paper class," he responded: "Driving a hard bargain, should have known [with smiley-face emoticon]. Will have to think about this, but talk to me . . ." Later, after she had received an email from the AFRI chair, Lee responded, "So glad you emailed me. Time to harass you again! Should I come on Friday?? Monday?? What day is best for you??" Nyang'oro: "Either Wed or Th. Friday I am gone . . . Thought you didn't love me anymore [smiley-face emoticon]." See Kane, "African Studies Chairman Had Close Ties."

16. "We were granted unfettered access to University systems, records, and personnel," he announced to the BOT in his prefatory letter. See Martin, "University of North Carolina Academic Anomalies Review," ii.

17. Martin's oral remarks were reported in an alumni publication. See "Martin Says Fraud Isolated to African Studies Department," *Carolina Alumni Magazine*, December 2012, http://alumni.unc.edu/article.aspx?sid=9310.

18. Martin, "University of North Carolina Academic Anomalies Review," 7.

19. Martin reported in "The University of North Carolina Academic Anomalies Review: Report Addendum" of January 24, 2013, that athletes made up 16 percent of all AFRI/AFAM enrollments, but that figure included the inflated figures in the anomalous courses. With the anomalies removed from the sample, athlete enrollments fall to 12 percent of the total. Martin's only explanation for the serious discrepancies in his various public statements came in convoluted language seemingly designed to obfuscate: "Our prior statements that student-athlete enrollments were 'consistent' in a number of respects summarized our extensive analysis indicating that student-athlete enrollments related to anomalous courses and grade changes in the Department were reflective of patterns noted elsewhere in the Department and other departments." See Martin, "University of North Carolina Academic Anomalies Review: Report Addendum," 2, 5.

20. Martin, "University of North Carolina Academic Anomalies Review," 72.

21. Type I anomalies were courses that no instructor had admitted to having supervised, which seem to have been run from beginning to end without faculty involvement. Type II anomalies were courses for which the instructor of record was unknown, but likely had the approval of the department chair or his administrative assistant or both. For definitions of terms, see Martin, "University of North Carolina Academic Anomalies Review," 19.

22. Martin, "University of North Carolina Academic Anomalies Review," 60.

23. Martin, "University of North Carolina Academic Anomalies Review," 54.

24. Martin, "University of North Carolina Academic Anomalies Review," 19.

25. Department chairs were centrally involved in the curriculum changeover of 2005–6; chairs had to submit to the college through a password-protected software program all courses that were to be renumbered or reclassified in light of the new general education requirements to be implemented in the fall of 2006. Nyang'oro—alone among chairs in the College of Arts and Sciences—neglected to submit most of AFRI/AFAM's courses in a timely manner. With fewer courses meeting general education requirements, the department consequently saw a sudden 15 percent enrollment dip in the 2006–7 academic year. Enrollments would not fully recover until 2010. Insofar as Nyang'oro had a crass personal motive for offering so many fraudulent courses, it most likely would have been to gain valuable cover for his frequent international traveling; he was paid well to perform services at UNC that he often was not even present to perform.

26. Martin would assert that the retraction "in no way impacts the conclusions of our review," but there was no other evidence in his report that anyone other than ASPSA personnel had ever known about the fraudulent classes. This is why he cited the evidence about FAC's allegedly negligent oversight seven times in the course of the report. The retraction undermined the claim that the ASPSA had sought to put a stop to the academic windfall their athletes were enjoying. See Martin, "Clarification Regarding Faculty Athletic Committee References in Martin Report," February 5, 2013; and Dan Kane, "Baker-Tilly Removes Assertion That Athletics Officials Warned of Scandal," N&O, January 25, 2013, http://www.newsobserver.com/2013/01/25/2633448/baker-tilly-removes-assertion.html.

27. Faculty Council minutes, January 11, 2013, http://faccoun.unc.edu/faculty-council/meeting-materials-past-years/meeting-materials-2012-13/january-11-2013/.

28. Kane, "Meeting Minutes Don't Confirm Martin Report."

29. As quoted in Sarah Niss, "Findings of Martin Report Divide Faculty," *Daily Tar Heel*, January 15, 2013, http://www.dailytarheel.com/article/2013/01/faculty-dividedpoverpreport.

30. Kramer, speaking for eight of his committee colleagues, insisted that "the abuses that the [Martin] report rightly condemns were not condoned by the FAC, and the principle of academic freedom was not used to justify academic misconduct." The full letter can be accessed at http://faccoun.unc.edu/faculty-council/meeting-materials-past-years/meeting-materials-2012-13/february-8-2013/#heading-4.

31. Email from Tom Ross to Willingham, June 18, 2013.

32. Email from James Dean to Smith, October 5, 2013.

33. If one assumes two courses taught each semester over a period of eighteen years, with three semesters free of teaching because of research leaves (probably a low estimate), the average total would be sixty-six courses. That figure would be augmented, for some faculty, by the occasional summer teaching assignment.

7. *"No one ever asked me to write anything before"*

1. The attitudes of teachers of course reflect the assumptions of the culture at large. See Ann Arnett Ferguson, *Bad Boys: Public Schools in the Making of Black Masculinity* (Ann Arbor: University of Michigan Press, 2001); Billy Hawkins, *The New Plantation: Black Athletes, College Sports, and Predominantly White NCAA Institutions* (New York: Palgrave Macmillan, 2010); and Patrick Miller, "The Anatomy of Scientific Racism: Racialist Responses to Black Athletic Achievement," in *Sport and the Color Line: Black Athletes and Race Relations in Twentieth-Century America*, edited by P. B. Miller and David K. Wiggins (New York: Routledge, 2004), 327–44.

2. H. B. Ferguson, S. Bovaird, and M. P. Mueller, "The Impact of Poverty on Educational Outcomes for Children," *Pediatrics and Child Health* 12 (2007): 701–6. See also Greg J. Duncan, Jeanne Brooks-Gunn, and Pamela Kato Klebanov, "Economic Deprivation and Early Childhood Development," *Child Development* 65 (1994): 296–318.

3. As cited in Brandon E. Martin, Derrick L. Cragg, and Dennis A. Kramer II, "NCAA Academic Regulations: Impact on Participation Rates for African American Males," in *Racism in College Athletics*, edited by Dana Brooks and Ronald Althouse (Morgantown wv: Fitness Information Technology, 2013), 155–69, esp. 157. This same 2004 study, conducted at the Center for Study and Sport at Northeastern University, found that African American families are seven times more likely than white families to socialize their children through sports participation and to believe in the possibility that their children may follow a professional athletic career.

4. "Mack Brown Reveals Why He Resigned; Texas AD on What He Wants in a New Coach," *Dallas Morning News*, December 15, 2013.

5. The practice of using attractive female undergraduates as "hostesses" for athletic recruits is potentially abusive on so many levels that the continued existence of such recruiting programs should be regarded as a minor miracle. In America's litigious culture, it would seem only a matter of time before some university faces an expensive and highly embarrassing lawsuit for engaging in a practice that degrades and diminishes both current and prospective members of its own student body. The forces supporting these hostess programs remain powerful, however. An eye-opening exposé of the University of Tennessee program is provided in Armen Keteyian and Jeff Benedict, *The System* (New York: Knopf Doubleday, 2013), chap. 2.

6. Kirsten F. Benson, "Constructing Academic Inadequacy: African American Athletes' Stories of Schooling," *Journal of Higher Education* 71 (2000): 223–46, esp. 223, 229.

7. Benson, "Constructing Academic Inadequacy," 229–30.

8. Andy Katz interview with Roy Williams, January 15, 2014, http://espn.go.com/espnradio/play?id=10293968.

9. On the non-UNC stories in this paragraph, see John Canzano, "Memphis Basketball Teaches the Wrong Lesson," *Portland Oregonian*, June 5, 2009, http://www.oregonlive.com/sports/oregonian/john_canzano/index.ssf/2009/06/memphis_basketball_teaches_the.html.

10. Lawrence Taylor, LT: *Living on the Edge* (New York: Times Books, 1987), 79.

11. Interview with Teaching Assistant A, May 24, 2014.

12. Interview with Julia Wood, May 27, 2014.

13. Interview with Teaching Assistant B, April 23, 2013.

14. See the class profile for the fall of 2013, for example: http://admissions.unc.edu/apply/class-profile/.

15. Sandra Hughes-Hassell et al., "Building a Bridge to Literacy for African American Male Youth: A Call to Action for the Library Community," http://sils.unc.edu/sites/default/files/news/Building-a-Bridge-to-Literacy.pdf, 2.

16. Michael Holzman, *Minority Students and Public Education: A Resource Book* (New York: Chelmsford Press, 2013), 1:44. The bottom third of Holzman's literacy rankings is dominated by southern states, including Florida, South Carolina, Louisiana, Arkansas, Tennessee, Alabama, and Mississippi.

17. Educational Policy Committee, "Grading Patterns at UNC-CH, 1995–2008: Annual Report to the Faculty Council," April 22, 2009, http://faccoun.unc.edu/wp-content/uploads/2010/10/2009EPCFinalReportonGrading.pdf, 2.

18. Educational Policy Committee, "Grading Patterns at UNC-CH," 7, 15.

19. "Team Grade Reports, 1990," records of the Office of Academic Services, Office of the Dean, Series 40076, 2:2. Sixteen teams provided grade reports that year, but men's basketball was not one of them.

20. "Director's Report" of the Academic Athletic Support Program, 1992, Office of Academic Services, Office of the Dean, Series 40076, 2:2.

21. Steve Wieberg, "Study: College Athletes Are Full Time Workers," USA *Today*, January 13, 2008; Robert A. McCormick and Amy Christian McCormick, "A Trail of Tears: The Exploitation of the College Athlete," *Florida Coastal Law Review* 11 (2010): 639–65. For the NCAA survey, see http://usatoday30.usatoday.com/sports/college/2008-01-12-athletes-full-time-work-study_N.htm.

22. Jordan Weissman, "The NCAA's 'Student-Athlete' Charade Is Officially Crumbling," March 26, 2014, http://www.slate.com/blogs/moneybox/2014/03/26/northwestern_football_union_nlrb_says_players_can_unionize_because_they.html.

23. Email to Willingham, February 22, 2013.

24. Interview with Counselor A, July 5, 2013.

25. Robert McNeely, "Athletes Cluster across Departments," *Daily Tar Heel*, September 3, 2014. See also http://unc.blinkness.com/professor/unc-osborne-barbar.

26. These are figures reported by the popular student website http://www.blinkness.com.

27. Ben Smith, "UNC–Chapel Hill Students Knew Athletes Took Easy Classes," *College Fix*, January 21, 2014, http://www.thecollegefix.com/post/15985/.

28. UNC has implemented a set of reforms—for example, limiting the num-

ber of students supervised by any instructor and requiring formalized learning contracts for each independent study—that should prevent future abuse of these courses.

29. Stancill, "Trustees Question How Academic Fraud Happened."

30. Strongly expressed preferences were sometimes accommodated, to be sure. This helps to account for the small measure of variation one finds in profit-sport athlete course records. Upper-level political science, anthropology, or history courses virtually never appeared on course records for challenged athletes, and biology, chemistry, German, and classics constituted a true terra incognita. But athletes were permitted to take the occasional gamble—almost always in disciplines where the courses were thought to be "manageable."

31. For example, five of six business majors were walk-ons, as were two of three political science majors, one of two art majors, both biology majors, and each of the history and economics majors. See the UNC football roster: http://www .goheels.com/SportSelect.dbml?SPID=12962&SPSID=667866.

8. Tricks of the Trade

1. Sociologist Diane Vaughan developed the analytical framework of "normalized" deviance through her study of the National Aeronautics and Space Administration's Challenger disaster. In many large institutions, she hypothesizes, inertia allows unacceptable practices and standards to become acceptable over time. Diane Vaughan, *The Challenger Launch Decision: Risky Technology, Culture, and Deviance at NASA* (Chicago: University of Chicago Press, 1997). John Cummins and Kirsten Hextrum have applied the concept to their analysis of UC-Berkeley's athletic operation. See the white paper "The Management of Intercollegiate Athletics at UC-Berkeley: Turning Points and Consequences," http://cshe .berkeley.edu/sites/default/files/shared/publications/docs/ROPS.CSHE_.12.13 .Cummins%26hextrum.CalAthletics.1.6.2014.pdf.

2. Dan Kane and J. Andrew Curliss, "Requirements Questioned for Naval Class Taken by UNC Basketball Players," N&O, October 2, 2012, http://www.news observer.com/2012/10/02/2386415/naval-weapons-systems-class-at.html.

3. Interview with Administrator A, September 2014.

4. It is surely no coincidence that Tom Wolfe, in his novel *I Am Charlotte Simmons* (New York: Farrar, Straus, and Giroux, 2004), satirized the practice of scheduling athlete-friendly courses by recounting Simmons's accidental enrollment in a dumbed-down French-novel-in-translation course, one that happened to be packed with athletes. Wolfe conducted research for his novel by speaking with students and faculty at UNC–Chapel Hill, among other institutions.

5. Young female faculty are disproportionately victimized by uncivil male behavior in the classroom. See Rodney K. Goodyear, Pauline J. Reynolds, and Janee Both Gragg, "University Faculty Experiences of Classroom Incivility: A Critical Incident Study," NSF *Advance Workshop on Student Bias and Incivility Towards Female Faculty* (2010), http://www.portal.advance.vt.edu/Advance_2010_

pi_Mtg/StudentBiasandIncivility_Goodyear_2010PIMtg.pdf. A series of studies has also shown that male students, on end-of-course evaluations, are consistently more critical of faculty who are female; this is especially true in humanities disciplines such as English. See, for example, Susan A. Basow, "Student Ratings of Professors Are Not Gender Blind," *Association for Women in Mathematics Newsletter* 24 (1994), http://www.awm-math.org/newsletter/199409/basow.html.

6. In 2005, soon after Jay Smith assumed his role as associate dean for undergraduate curricula in the College of Arts and Sciences, he was offered what he considered at the time to be a "soft bribe." Robert Mercer, the director of the aspsa, offered to have him fly with the football team to Charlottesville for a Thursday-night game. He could walk the sidelines, talk to the players, and get to know "Coach." Smith, who was in charge of implementing a new general education curriculum about which Mercer and academic counselors had already expressed concerns, politely declined the invitation. He thought it interesting that no such offers had ever been extended to him in his previous fifteen years on the unc faculty; only when he assumed a position of influence in the dean's office did athletics officials suddenly become solicitous.

7. Interview with David Pizzo, January 22, 2014.

8. Rye Barcott, *It Happened on the Way to War: A Marine's Path to Peace* (New York: Bloomsbury usa, 2011), 24–25.

9. Kane and Curliss, "unc Players Needed Academic Help."

10. Kelly broke the mold in the Washington football program and studied in South Africa during one "off-season" semester. For his efforts, he saw his playing time cut and was thrust into a new role as team pariah. When three other players followed his example the following year, football coach Tyrone Willingham dropped all three to the bottom of the depth chart, complaining that "they have a responsibility" to football. Soon the study-abroad experiment ended, and Washington football players learned the important lesson that "student-athletes" must never let their "student" ambitions get in the way of their "athlete" duties. For Kelly's extraordinary story, and his assessment of his coaches' priorities, see Ken Armstrong and Nick Perry, *Scoreboard, Baby: A Story of College Football, Crime, and Complicity* (Lincoln: University of Nebraska Press, 2010), 260–71.

11. As noted in the transcript of *The Kojo Nnamdi Show* at American University, March 28, 2011, http://thekojonnamdishow.org/shows/2011-03-28/march-madness-politics-sports/transcript.

12. Michael Miner, "Trust Me, Academics Used to Be Important at Missouri," April 5, 2012, http://www.chicagoreader.com/Bleader/archives/2012/04/05/trust-me-academics-used-to-be-important-at-missouri.

13. Dan Kane, "Former unc Player Ties Counselors to No-Show Classes," *N&O*, January 15, 2014, http://www.newsobserver.com/2014/01/15/3535977/former-unc-player-ties-counselors.html.

14. McCormick and McCormick, "Trail of Tears," 639–65, esp. 649–50.

15. The sign is shown out of context in the film, with the university left uniden-

tified. The film's producer, Andrew Muscato, confirmed in a private conversation that the filming of that image had taken place at UNC–Chapel Hill.

16. Patricia A. Adler and Peter Adler, *Backboards and Blackboards: College Athletes and Role Engulfment* (New York: Columbia University Press, 1991), 189.

17. Angela Busch, "Seeking a Life after College Football," March 5, 2007, http://sportsillustrated.cnn.com/vault/article/magazine/MAG1105246/index.htm.

18. These UNC football players merely conformed to the pattern described in Adler and Adler's landmark study, *Backboards and Blackboards*. The athletes in their sample who had effectively "majored in eligibility," the authors noted, "abandoned the academic role entirely" at some point in their senior year (188–89). These basketball players simply capitulated to the gradual encroachment of their "athletic" role on the "academic" role that they had also been asked to play.

19. Interview with Faculty Member B, February 11, 2014.

20. Interview with West, May 15, 2014.

21. Black Student Movement, 1968, Office of the Dean, Series 40076, 1:7.

22. Interview with Steele staff member, June 16, 2014.

23. Conversation of March 23, 2014.

24. Interview with Adviser A, August 15, 2013. Owen's sentiment—if no one complains, who am I to question existing practice?—sounded an eerie echo in May 2012. When Dean Karen Gil was asked at a board of trustees meeting how it was possible that so many instructorless courses had flown under the radar for so many years, she responded: "There were no student complaints about these courses." Stancill, "Trustees Question How Academic Fraud Happened."

25. Interview with Cookie Newsom, July 15, 2013.

9. Echoes across the Land

1. This recap of the Auburn scandal follows Pete Thamel, "Top Grades and No Class Time for Auburn Players," *New York Times*, July 14, 2006, http://www.nytimes.com/2006/07/14/sports/ncaafootball/14auburn.html?pagewanted=all.

2. Ray Glier and Pete Thamel, "Auburn Ousts 2, but Doesn't Fault Athletics," August 10, 2006, http://www.onlinemontgomery.com/news-mainmenu-2/102-sports/653-auburn-ousts-2-but-doesnt-fault-athletics.

3. Armstrong and Perry, *Scoreboard, Baby*, 301.

4. Armstrong and Perry, *Scoreboard, Baby*, 191.

5. Armstrong and Perry, *Scoreboard, Baby*, 280.

6. Armstrong and Perry, *Scoreboard, Baby*, 99.

7. The following account of practices at the University of Michigan is based mainly on a remarkable series of articles: "Academics and Athletics: A Four-Day Ann Arbor News Series on the University of Michigan," March 16–19, 2008, http://www.mlive.com/wolverines/academics/.

8. This account of the vice provost's quashing of an April 2008 faculty investigation follows closely a June 2008 *Ann Arbor News* article. See Dave Gershman, "University of Michigan Officials Balk at Academic and Athletics Probe," June

15, 2008, http://www.mlive.com/wolverines/academics/stories/index.ssf/2008/06/
university of michigan_officia.html.

9. Jim Knight, "University of Michigan Buries Scrutiny of Athletes' Academics," *Ann Arbor News*, June 15, 2008, http://www.mlive.com/wolverines/academics
/stories/index.ssf/2008/06/um_buries_scrutiny_of_athletes.html.

10. George Dohrmann, "U Basketball Program Accused of Academic Fraud,"
St. Paul Pioneer Press, March 10, 1999, http://www.pulitzer.org/archives/6281.

11. Pat Doyle et al., "Gangelhoff, Archambault Appear at News Conference,"
Minneapolis Star Tribune, March 23, 1999, http://www.startribune.com/sports/
gophers/11663291.html?page=1&c=y.

12. Dohrmann, "U Basketball Program Accused of Academic Fraud."

13. "More Trouble for Haskins? Third Tutor Steps Forward in Minnesota
Cheating Scandal," March 24, 1999, http://sportsillustrated.cnn.com/basketball/
college/news/1999/03/23/gopher_scandal/.

14. Paul McEnroe and Chris Ison, "Memos Claim Favors to U Players," *Minneapolis Star Tribune*, March 13, 1999, http://www.startribune.com/sports/
gophers/11662861.html?page=1&c=y.

15. McEnroe and Ison, "Memos Claim Favors to U Players."

16. "More Trouble for Haskins?"

17. Doyle et al., "Gangelhoff, Archambault Appear at News Conference."

18. Mary Willingham was similarly challenged by UNC compliance director
Vince Ille after she first went public with her allegations about ASPSA knowledge
of the paper-class fraud. He noted in multiple emails that "recent public state-
ments made by Ms. Willingham appear to contradict information she provided
[UNC investigators] Mr. Keadey and Ms. Broome in September 2010." Email from
Ille to Smith, May 7, 2013.

19. Geneva Overholser, "Minnesota Basketball Cheating Case," in *Thinking
Clearly: Cases in Journalistic Decision-Making*, edited by Tom Rosenstiel and
Amy S. Mitchell (New York: Columbia University Press, 2003), 82–109, esp. 91.

20. For summaries of most of these cases, see Paul Barrett, "Bad Sports:
The Fake Classes Scandal at Chapel Hill and the $16 Billion Business of Col-
lege Athletics," *Bloomberg Businessweek*, March 3, 2014. On the UC-Berkeley
case, involving the awarding of grades to athletes in a class they never took,
see Rebecca Trounson and Kenneth R. Weiss, "UC Outreach Chief Quits in
Scandal," *Los Angeles Times*, April 25, 2001. On Notre Dame, see Stewart Man-
del, "In Wake of Academic Scandal, Notre Dame's Haughty Image Falls Flat,"
Fox Sports, August 15, 2014, http://www.foxsports.com/college-football/story/
notre-dame-fighting-irish-academic-scandal-four-players-081514.

Conclusion

1. Lee Romney and David Wharton, "Ex-UCLA Star Ed O'Bannon Takes Stand in
Antitrust Suit against NCAA," *Los Angeles Times*, June 9, 2014, http://www.latimes
.com/local/la-me-obannon-trial-20140610-story.html#page=1.

2. Steve Eder, "A Legal Titan of Sports Labor Disputes Set His Sights on the NCAA: Jeffrey Kessler Envisions Open Market for College Athletes," *New York Times*, August 27, 2014, http://www.nytimes.com/2014/08/28/sports/jeffrey-kessler -envisions-open-market-for-ncaa-college-athletes.html?_r=0.

3. Megan R. Wilson, "NCAA Hires Lobbyists as Athletes Battle for Pay," *Hill*, June 18, 2014, http://thehill.com/business-a-lobbying/lobbying-hires/209767 -ncaa-hires-lobbyists-for-the-first-time-as-athletes-battle#.U6Ni0ieNL3Y.twitter.

4. Dave Anderson, "Sports of the Times; James Madison Writes Again," *New York Times*, October 1, 1981, http://www.nytimes.com/1981/10/01/sports/sports -of-the-times-james-madison-writes-again.html.

5. See Branch's three-point reform agenda at http://taylorbranch. com/2012/06/14/a-three-point-reform-agenda-for-sports-in-higher-education/.

6. The founders of UNC created in 1795 an "academy" to serve students who needed remediation before beginning their university course work—most of the remediation then coming in Latin and Greek. Unfortunately, the academy existed for only about a decade, and its example has been forgotten. The precedent has been set at UNC, however, and other universities might wish to emulate it. Similar kinds of programs could be established for the purpose of addressing the deficiencies in basic academic skills that afflict some of our most gifted athletes—the ones usually most responsible for entertaining the masses on game day and providing funding for all of the other sports on campus. On the precedent of the UNC academy, see William D. Snider, *Light on the Hill: A History of the University of North Carolina at Chapel Hill* (Chapel Hill: University of North Carolina Press, 2004), 28–30.

7. Matthew R. Salzwedel and Jon Ericson, "Cleaning Up Buckley: How the Family Educational Rights and Privacy Act Shields Academic Corruption in College Athletics," *Wisconsin Law Review* 6 (2003): 1053–113, esp. 1061. On the "wretched draftsmanship," see 1066.

8. Salzwedel and Ericson, "Cleaning Up Buckley," 1061–62.

9. See the university's biography for the legendary leader: "Robert Maynard Hutchins, 1929–1951," https://president.uchicago.edu/directory/robert-maynard -hutchins.

10. Vaughan, *Challenger Launch Decision*.

Epilogue

1. Luke Decock, "UNC Athletic, Academic Case Not over Yet, nor Is It Anywhere Close," *N&O*, June 30, 2014, http://www.newsobserver.com/2014/06/30/3976713/ decock-unc-athletic-academic-case.html#storylink=cpy.

Index

academic progress forms, 179–80
Academic Progress Rate, 181, 196
Academic Support Program for Student Athletes (ASPSA), 61, 105, 121, 165–66, 244; African and Afro-American studies partnership with, 44, 46, 171, 255n10, 255–56n12; as "black box" of course-fraud scandal, xviii–xix, 98; dispute over paper-class knowledge of, 58, 256n5; FEC subcommittee report and, 95, 106–8; governing culture of, 68, 70, 133, 178, 203; and Highsmith plagiarism case, 122–24; intimidation tactics of, 187–89, 193, 230; Martin protection of, 133, 134–36, 142, 143; and McAdoo case, 70–71, 74–75; Nyang'oro relationship with, 9–10, 17, 255–56n12. *See also* counselors, ASPSA
Acho, Shari, 222, 223
admissions process, 147–48, 150–51, 159–60, 166
African American students: assumptions and stereotypes about, xii, 23, 152, 198, 200–202, 215, 230; reading skills of, 164–65; sports seen as road to success for, 156–57, 263n3
African and Afro-American studies (AFRI/AFAM): Academic Support Program partnership with, 44, 46, 171, 255n10, 255–56n12; administration view of, 198–201; athletes' disproportionate participation in, 7–9, 32–33, 44, 49; audit of, 32; and Black Cultural Center, 5; double curriculum of, 18–19, 149–50; emergence of Nyang'oro leadership in, 6–7; enrollment statistics, 2–3, 20, 140–41, 262n26; establishment of, 2, 201; faculty in, 2, 3–4, 18–19; grade changes as practice in, 29, 38, 47, 145, 196; Hartlyn-Andrews report on, 86; independent study courses in, 8, 11–15, 23, 24–28, 29–30, 128, 254n33; lack of review of, 20–21, 199–200; majoring in, 14–15, 39, 70, 175, 181, 257n12; national reputation of, 4; paper classes in, 11–19, 41, 46, 96, 98, 108–9, 121, 149, 153, 173, 186; university inquiries into, 80, 83. *See also* Nyang'oro, Julius
amateurism, 84, 236
Anderson, Dave, 237–38
Andrews, William, 83. *See also* Hartlyn-Andrews report
Ann Arbor News, 217, 218, 220, 221–22, 224, 225, 226–27
Archambault, Russ, 228, 233
Armstrong, Ken, 211, 213

109–10, 143; scandal management by, 83, 85
Evrard, Rick, 57
Exercise and Sport Science Department, 47, 172, 173, 175, 184
external reviews, 199–200

faculty: administration officials and, 58, 75, 92, 117; in African and Afro-American studies, 2, 3–4, 18–19; Athletic Reform Group of, 91–92; ignoring of academic fraud by, 159, 202–3, 239; and independent study courses, 10–11, 253n23; teaching load of, 90, 146, 262–63n33
Faculty Athletics Committee (FAC), 62, 79; slanders against, 105–15, 135, 142, 143, 262n30; Willingham address to, 257n2
Faculty Council, 22, 53–54, 117, 142, 144
Faculty Executive Committee (FEC), 92, 103–4, 119
Faculty Executive Committee subcommittee, 92–94, 96–105; findings of, 95, 105, 106–8; revision and contamination of report by, 95–96, 100–105, 112–13
Family Educational Rights and Privacy Act (FERPA), 138, 214, 245
Fardig, Danny, 218
Farmer, Steven, 126
football, as profit sport, 157, 251n2
football team: and course-fraud scheme, 27–28, 40, 113, 175, 177, 190; performance of, 22, 27, 31, 42, 84; recruitment efforts by, 157–58; time demands on, 170–71; at University of Washington, 211–13; walkons, 157–58, 175, 246, 265n31
Forte, Joseph, 40
Friday, Bill, 32, 78; and Willingham, 126–27
Friedman, Richard, 224–26
Friends of the Library, 78

Gallman, Robert, 4, 7
Gangelhoff, Jan: criticisms on, 233; disclosure of wrongdoing by, 227–29, 231, 232–33
Geography Department, 173
Gerhardt, Michael, 93, 96, 100, 101–2, 103, 258n2

gifts, 47, 59, 117–18, 187–88, 216, 266n6
Gil, Karen, 83, 88–89, 267n24; Smith meeting with, 80–81
Goulding, Alexandra, 231
grade changes, 29, 38, 47, 145, 196
grades and GPAs, 38–39, 44, 149, 150, 162, 186, 196; in Auburn scandal, 208, 209; of Austin, 51–52, 120, 185–86; Nyang'oro issuance of, 12, 14, 17–18, 37, 38, 39, 45, 179; in Peppers transcripts, 34–37; statistics on, 139, 140, 165–66; temporary, 38, 47; in University of Washington scandal, 215–16
graduation rates, 196, 201, 202, 208
graduation requirements, 22, 71, 187, 190
Gundlach, James, 208, 209, 210
Gurganus, Allan, 54
Guskiewicz, Kevin, 105–6
Guthridge, Bill, 42

Hagen, John, 217–21, 223
Hamm, Mia, 22
Hanlon, Phil, 224–25, 226
Hansbrough, Tami, 115, 117–18
Hansbrough, Tyler, 115, 117
Hardin, Paul, 5
Harris, Trudier, 3, 5, 6
Hartlyn, Jonathan, 83, 84–87, 114
Hartlyn-Andrews report, 84–91, 113; critical response to, 89–90, 91; issuance of, 88–89; omissions from, 87–88
Haskins, Clem, 228, 229–30, 231–32
Hasselmo, Nils, 232
Haywood, Brendan, 40
Herman, Amy, 66
Highsmith, Erik, 122–25, 259nn4–5
Hobert, Billy Joe, 215
Holladay, Joe, 48
Holzman, Michael, 164
Honor Court system, 53, 58; about, 55–56, 124; and Highsmith plagiarism case, 122, 123, 259n4; and McAdoo case, 51, 52, 56–57, 65–76
Hunter, Erik, 124
Hutchins, Robert Maynard, 247, 248

I Am Charlotte Simmons (Wolfe), 265n4